THE LEGACY OF
THE WISECRACK

THE LEGACY OF THE WISECRACK
STAND-UP COMEDY AS THE GREAT AMERICAN LITERARY FORM

EDDIE TAFOYA

BrownWalker Press
Boca Raton

The Legacy of the Wisecrack:
Stand-up Comedy as the Great American Literary Form

BrownWalker Press
Boca Raton, Florida • USA
2009

ISBN-10: 1-59942-495-9 *(paper)*
ISBN-13: 978-1-59942-495-8 *(paper)*

ISBN-10: 1-59942-496-7 *(ebook)*
ISBN-13: 978-1-59942-496-5 *(ebook)*

www.brownwalker.com

Cover design by Fernando Julio Barraza
Author photo by Jonah Tafoya

Library of Congress Cataloging-in-Publication Data

Tafoya, Eddie.
   The legacy of the wisecrack : stand-up comedy as the great American literary form / Eddie Tafoya.
       p. cm.
   Includes bibliographical references.
   ISBN-13: 978-1-59942-495-8 (pbk. : alk. paper)
   ISBN-10: 1-59942-495-9 (pbk. : alk. paper)
   1. Stand-up comedy--United States. 2. Comedy--History and criticism. I. Title.

PN1969.C65T34 2009
792.7'6--dc22

2009000296

To Richard Pryor, Steven Wright, Whoopi Goldberg,
Woody Allen, Bill Cosby, George Carlin,
Jackie Mason and Paula Poundstone,
because they rank among history's greatest stand-ups;
and to Chico, Harpo and Groucho—
because they were just so damned funny.

ACKNOWLEDGMENTS

First and foremost I would like to thank Charles Hansen Pike and Robyn Rose for their patience, wisdom, expertise, energy and input. I would also like to thank those who read the manuscript in its various forms: Heather Winterer, Shawn Woodyard, Beth Devore and Nancy Tucker. Also, Helen Tafoya, Jeffery Candelaria, Colleen Jiron and Maria Jerenic were enormously helpful with the individual chapters, while Melanie LaBorwit's help with research was indispensable. I would also like to the thank the New Mexico Highlands University Faculty Research Committee, Ms. Prescilla Salazar, and the students in my American Humor, Stand-up Comedy as Literature and American Fool classes. And thanks to the many comedians I have worked with over the years including Russ Rivas, Tony Vicich, Chris Fonseca, James R. Zingleman, Marc Shuter, Jeff Wozer, Curt Fletcher, Rick Semones, John "Hippieman" Novosad, Margaret Smith, Chris Clobber, Gabriel Rutledge, Freddy Charles, Jay Benedict Brown, Patrick Candelaria, George McKelvey, Charlie Moreno and Oscar Solis; furthermore, this book would not have been possible without the help and support of Don, Mary Kay, Vilmos, Dani, Denise and Dione at Wits End Comedy Club in Westminster, Colorado, and Tammy, Terri, Erika and the rest of the folks at Laffs in Albuquerque, my home club.

CONTENTS

INTRODUCTION

The Mayfair Theater in Santa Monica is filled to capacity and completely dark when an offstage announcer calls out: "Will you please stand for the singing of our national anthem?" Presently, the song begins: "O-ho say can you motherfuckin' see, by the dawn's early motherfuckin' light?" By the time the singer gets to "whose broad motherfuckin' stripes," light is spilling from a hole in the middle of the stage and the singer is rising out of the hole onto stage level. It is Whoopi Goldberg in the persona of her most celebrated alter ego, Fontaine. The song ends when Fontaine pauses, takes a few steps to the right, clears his throat and belts out, "and the home of the motherfuckin' brave." Thus begins Goldberg's forty-six-minute HBO special from 1988, *Fontaine . . . Why Am I Straight?* Soon it is revealed that Fontaine is a homeless, Black, disaffiliated and androgynous (at one point he refers to himself as "she") reformed junkie with a Ph.D. from Columbia. What ensues is a running commentary on the scandals that characterized America during the Reagan years, matters such as the Iran-Contra affair, the fall of Jim and Tammy Faye Bakker's multi-million-dollar Christian televangelist empire, the firing of Jimmy "The Greek" Synder for making an apparently racist comment, and a sequence about Rock Hudson's contracting AIDS. As the show's title suggests, the performance implicitly asks why anyone would take seriously Nancy Reagan's exhortation to "say no to drugs" when being perpetually intoxicated seems to have a better payoff than having to deal with a world that is being ruined by the so-called "straight" people.

In many ways, the symbolism of the profanity-riddled version of "The Star-Spangled Banner" is ingeniously revealing, especially about the nature of the literary form that is stand-up comedy. Coming out of the blackness into the light and appearing out of the depths suggests that the marginalized Fontaine is both a personification of the fears, attitudes and wisdom that dwell deep within the collective American subconscious and a character who gives voice to anger that can no longer be ignored. What has bubbled up to the surface is a long-denied genius, an angry, questioning social commentator, the Jungian shadow that demands its moment at center stage.

It is no coincidence that this unique entrée came when it did, right at the height of an epoch that stand-up comedians would come to refer to as "The Boom," a period characterized by a sudden and dramatic explosion of interest in stand-up comedy. The art form, after all, tends to flourish in times of heightened social tension, to wit, the early years of the Cold War, when middle-class Americans were streaming to nightclubs; the height of the Vietnam conflict in the late 1960s and early 1970s, when George Carlin seemed to be jumping from one variety show to another; and, of course, during the 1980s, when President Ronald Reagan's supposed war-mongering was widely believed to be bringing the world closer to nuclear devastation. While other literary forms such as the novel, the short story, the poem and the play so often are directed toward revealing a nation's loftier intellectual and aesthetic ideals, stand-up comedy tends to point itself in the other direction. More often than not, the art form leans toward revealing that which is unpleasant and even visceral, angry and profane (in various senses of the word), turning the floor over to observations and commentaries that grow out of negativity, disgust and carnal appetites. Perhaps this is why, although it has been a mainstay of American entertainment since early in the twentieth century, stand-up comedy has received precious little scholarly attention. While books such as John Limon's *Stand-Up Comedy in Theory or Abjection in America*, Larry Wilde's *Great Comedians Talk About Comedy* and Robert Stebbins' *The Laugh-Makers: Stand-up Comedy as Art, Business and Life-style* have proven indispensable to anyone seriously concerned with understanding stand-up's deep play, precious little study has been devoted to analyzing the stand-up as a literary form.

Consequently, with the present volume I seek to accomplish three things. First of all, I hope to provide a framework by which to examine the art of stand-up comedy—an art form that is undoubtedly a sophisticated kind of language play that cannot help but reveal a culture's fears, values, hopes and, most profoundly, our sins—in distinctly literary terms. Secondly, I would like to look at the way in which comedians' jokes grow out of the conversation between two different competing regions of the subconscious, that which is concerned with social decorum and complies with the social contract and that which is dedicated to instant gratification, more or less the two regions Sigmund Freud identified as the super-ego and the id. Finally, I seek to provide a study of how stand-up comedians exploit this interplay in ways that the novel, short story, poem and play cannot.

The study is divided into three sections. The first, which comprises the first three chapters, establishes a framework first by looking at the nature of literature, then by dissecting the American ethos and finally by reviewing theories of humor and presenting a theory for stand-up itself. To do this, I have chosen what I believe to be the most logical starting point, a question that tends to be overlooked (at least in my experience) in literature classes: "What is literature?" I ask the question knowing full well that it almost begs for responses that can quickly become mired in semantics. Nevertheless, this entry point easily opens up to discussion on what literary critic Terry Eagleton has to say on the subject. Presently, I reform the question, suggesting that it would be more fruitful to abandon that inquiry in favor of one that examines what literature does. The functions I examine are the ways that literature codifies experience, defamiliarizes the world, informs and reveals the zeitgeist, plays with language, engenders wonder and invites the reader to find multiple layers of interpretation.

To examine the American ethos I employ an analogy particularly befitting a book on stand-up comedy: a large stage is encircled by five spotlights, each of which is aimed at a center spot and each of which has its own color and quality. One way to begin understanding that center pool of light, then, is to examine each beam individually. Among those I have identified are the frontier, whether it is that explored by Christopher Columbus, Lewis and Clark or *Star Trek*'s Captain James Kirk, and the Puritan foundation, the vestiges of which, even in the twenty-first century, are alive and well in right-wing American politics, Christian Pentecostalism, American hegemony and the American attitudes of privilege. Next is the landscape which, characterized by the lushness of the eastern seaboard and the high mountains, low deserts and vast plains west of the Mississippi, has left Americans with the feeling that we are larger than life, that we roam among the gods. The last beam to be examined is the sanctity of the individual which, with its concomitant liberties such as a free-market economy and freedom of speech, is an innovation which (although it was inspired by European thinkers) has over the centuries become distinctly American.

The third chapter explores a more psychological and philosophical terrain. I begin by reviewing the three theories of humor that have received the most attention over the centuries: Relief Theory, Superiority Theory and Incongruity Theory, each of which has been favored by one acclaimed thinker or another, philosophers such as Freud, Henri

Bergson, Thomas Hobbes and Arthur Schopenhauer, and each of which can explain many laughter events even though none can explain all completely. In fact, laughter, joking and humor are such mysterious phenomena that even all three theories when taken together cannot tell the whole story. Most stand-up comedians are well aware that every performance comes with more than a few surprises. At times the best jokes can fall flat while the mediocre material can elicit explosions of laughter. Even at a time when scientists are on the brink of producing a single theory that explains everything in nature from sub-subatomic particles to an endless string of universes, laughter remains mysterious.

From there I move on to explicate my own theory of humor, how the majority of jokes tend to grow out of a conversation, if not a heated argument, between bodily appetites and the demands of social propriety or, in other words, the id and the super-ego. Consequently, I situate the beginning of humor with the phenomenon of apes throwing feces, acts that, like good jokes, are simultaneously hostile and intimate as they tell an aggressor to stay away (who would want to go near that?) yet parallel an infant's "gifting" his feces to a parent, something that is recalled in a more sanitized form each time a comic movie involves a pie in the face. Also, I argue that just as humor begins with feces-throwing, the prototypical joke is human flatulence since, like a vocalization, the passing of intestinal gas comes from an opening in the digestive tract that involves mucous membranes and emits sounds and smells. We need go no farther than the local playground to find linguistic evidence for the connection: a person whose words have little value is often referred to as "an asshole," while someone causing trouble is or talking nonsense is "talking shit," or "talking shit out his ass" or, in more polite company, is referred to as being "full of hot air." Likewise, it is not uncommon for a person making inappropriate or irreverent remarks to be called a "smart ass" and his utterances to be inadvertently compared to short bursts of intestinal gas, or "cracks." The very term "wise crack," consequently, is a rich conceptual metaphor in that it linguistically links the higher and lower faculties, the onomatopoeic "crack" from the rectum and the supposed wisdom of the mind. This section argues, in other words, that the wisecrack has a long and distinguished legacy, that eons before it was employed by the likes of Groucho Marx and David Letterman it was useful in diffusing tension between both intratribal and intertribal enemies.

The chapter concludes with the explication of an insight that came to me after my twelfth reading of Scott Fitzgerald's masterpiece, *Tender*

Is the Night. That is that one of the great engines propelling world literature is the complex of neuroses surrounding paternal abandonment
and the quest to heal that rift. To make the argument, I take cursory
glances at some of the world's most influential masterpieces—works
such as *Oedipus Rex*, the story of Cronos, the New and Old Testa-
ments, the *Tao Te Ching*, *Hamlet*, *The Scarlet Letter*, *Great Expectations*, *The
Adventures of Huckleberry Finn*, *The Sound and the Fury*, *Absalom, Absalom!*
and *Death of a Salesman* to name but a few—the great majority of which,
to one degree or another, have the quest for unification with an abandoning parent, usually a father, be it actual or surrogate, as a central
concern.

With this foundation in place, I make the argument that the stand-
up comedian, who must remain emotionally available and accessible in
order to have a successful show, is able to address and perhaps even
heal this rift immediately although temporarily. With each successful
performance, audience members subconsciously revert to childhood as
they stand before a father figure who, because of a sound system and
an elevated stage, is in the position of the prototypical father in that he
has a booming voice and elevated stature. Like their actual fathers, fathers of myth or the parish priest (who by no accident is called Father),
the comedian—even a female comedian—is in a fatherly role as he (or
she) is the locus of both power and attention and is ready to admonish
those less powerful when they get unruly or speak out of turn. Because
a comedian must remain emotionally connected, he is in a position to
provide an anodyne to the paternal trauma. By doing this, he is in fact
ready, willing and obligated to make fun of larger authorities such as
the president, the government, movie stars and social mores. To put
the matter another way, we can say that the comedian is an authority
figure whose job it is to undermine authority.

In the second section of the book I seek to provide a historical
context for the art form. Chapter Four summarizes the pre-history of
stand-up comedy beginning with the previously mentioned simian feces-throwing and the effect audible flatulence undoubtedly had on hostile hunter-gatherers. From there, I examine several high points in the
evolution of comedy such as trickster tales, the remnants of which we
see today most obviously in cartoons featuring the likes of Bugs Bunny
or Bart Simpson. Then there are the court jesters, who not only have a
documented presence throughout the history of civilization, but share
close metaphorical connections to flatulence and bodily appetites. Also
included in the discussion is the Commedia dell'arte of Renaissance

Italy, a comedy troupe that essentially invented the improv sketch. Then there is the clown who in one guise or another also has had a presence in virtually every society in recorded history, and the minstrel show, which not only featured the comedic Tambo and Bones characters, but often concluded with a stump speech, which has been considered a primitive form of stand-up. Another key development came by way of the Chautauqua, an entertainment phenomenon that popularized the direct-address performance, speeches that were often designed with the specific intention of eliciting laughter from the audience. Finally, no discussion of the history of stand-up could be complete without some mention of that fateful day in January 1856 when a twenty-year-old Samuel Clemens, while attending a convention of printers celebrating Benjamin Franklin's one-hundred-and-fiftieth birthday, gave an after-dinner speech that introduced the world to a new level of direct-address comedy.

The succeeding chapter examines the age of stand-up proper, beginning with a look at Charley Case, an African-American vaudevillian who worked in blackface and is arguably history's first stand-up comedian. From there, I examine various high points in stand-up history, including vaudeville and its more ethnic parallels, the Borscht Belt of Sullivan County, New York, which was designed to cater to Jewish audiences, and the Chitlin' Circuit, which catered to Black audiences; *The Ed Sullivan Show* and other variety shows; the "New Wave" of stand-up that involved the likes of Mort Sahl and Lenny Bruce compromising their laughs-per-minute ratios in order to address more heady and topical issues; the rise of the nightclub and the "Boom" of the 1980s.

The third and final section is made up of more specific examinations. Chapter Six provides a closer look at the New Wave comedians and their legacy, mainly Bruce, Sahl and Dick Gregory, whose incisive parodies and social commentaries complemented the Civil Rights protests of the 1950s and 1960s. The chapter concludes with a look at the work of those who have picked up the mantle, comedians such as George Carlin, who in the 1960s and 1970s became the hippies' comedic spokesman; Bill Hicks, whose monologues consistently called the Reagan administration to task; Chris Rock, whose shows provide a running commentary on a misguided world in post-Civil Rights and politically correct times; and of course, Whoopi Goldberg, whose one-woman theatrical pieces have the look and feel of stand-up as they closely examine the nation's ills. In short, I compare these comedians to the American Puritans of colonial times and argue that they, like

Cotton Mather and Jonathan Edwards, provide a running critique on how their nation as a whole is failing to live up to its contractual promises. While for Mather and Edwards the contract was between the Puritans and the God of Abraham, for Bruce, Carlin and Rock it was between America and the God of Reason, He who inspired the Declaration of Independence and the Bill of Rights.

The penultimate chapter looks at how comedian Steven Wright's three decades of work jell into a single story that draws on the power of one of the most ancient of all comedians, the fool archetype, makes him the protagonist in an ongoing picaresque story, and uses the character as a means of exploring post-modern anxieties, not the least of which is the threat of nuclear annihilation. Resembling a walking, breathing, joke-telling corpse, Wright simultaneously reveals and assuages modern humans' (and especially modern Americans') deepest fears by simultaneously manipulating us into entering a universe where conventional logic no longer applies and then assuaging these fears by convincing us that he, not us, is the one residing in this most horrifying of realms.

The final chapter looks at what more than likely is the most talked-about of stand-up comedy performances: *Richard Pryor Live on the Sunset Strip*. Recorded just a year and half after his famous suicide attempt that left him near death with third-degree burns over half his body, this 1982 performance film functions for late twentieth-century America much as Dante Alighieri's epic poem *Inferno* did for Renaissance Europe in that it chronicles descent into an underworld, climaxes with a confrontation with a demon and, by the end, provides a horrific assessment of its society's sins and shortcomings as well as a calling out for change.

In sum, this book is an argument that, as a literary form that has been enabled and nourished by America's most cherished innovations, stand-up comedy remains a wildly popular and deeply provocative worldwide phenomenon because it can accomplish what its literary cousins cannot. Its performances can be molded, remolded and reremolded in the course of a single evening. A performer can exploit the art form's plasticity to fit each venue, each audience and even individual audience members. While other literary forms can address the paternal cleavage mentioned above, they can do so only obliquely. The poem, short story and novel must be transmitted through the written or spoken word, in situations where bright lines persist between the author and narrator and the real and imagined audience. With stand-up comedy, however, the metaphorical father usually talks in his real voice, wears clothes that can hardly be called "a costume" and addresses his audience directly and immediately. He can interrupt his own performance, change directions, return to an earlier sequence, add a comment here and subtract or condense a joke there. Such adjustments would be much harder to make in a performance of *Hamlet* and are virtually impossible with a novel or a poem.

Even beyond that, stand-up comedy is unique in the way that its products tend to take on lives of their own. While it would be odd for coworkers to linger around the office coffee urn exchanging haiku, it is not at all uncommon for those in similar situations to exchange jokes they heard at a comedy club the week before. In fact, it is likely that intraoffice banter includes jokes that were first heard on a comedy club stage months or even years before and managed to be passed from person to person, office to office, and even state to state, spreading out in a network that even the most sophisticated sociologist would be hard-pressed to track.

While my primary objective is to study stand-up comedy rather than to classify it, I nevertheless hope that one day soon editions of *The Norton Anthology of American Literature* will not be seen as complete unless they come packaged with DVDs demonstrating the power and artistry of performers such as Pryor, Wright, Carlin and Goldberg. In the twenty-first century, literary audiences are changing rapidly, becoming less concerned with the written and more concerned with the spoken and performative. The time is ripe for stand-up comedy to stop being the Rodney Dangerfield of the literary world and to get some of the respect it deserves.

CHAPTER ONE

"I WANT A *REAL* LITERATURE CLASS"

Not long ago, an honor student at New Mexico Highlands University, a small teaching college in Northern New Mexico, scooped up a legal pad, a highlighter and a ballpoint pen, shoved them into her backpack and stormed out of her junior-level American literature class, never to return. Minutes before, her professor was deep into a lecture about the 1982 performance film *Richard Pryor Live on the Sunset Strip*, pontificating about how it was nothing less than stand-up comedy's answer to Dante Alighieri's fourteenth-century epic poem *Inferno*. His contention was that the comedian who was as famous for his self-destructive behavior as he was for his jokes had constructed an epic tale, a one-man show that was every bit as harrowing and complex as anything penned by the canonized masters.

"He just stands up there and cusses," said the nineteen-year-old lover of American literature, a devoted scholarship student who planned to write her dissertation on Flannery O'Connor. "And look how he treats women."

This was enough to set the professor off again, ranting about how when layers of the performance were peeled away, some of the most nefarious American sins lay exposed, sins like slavery, hegemony, the proliferation of drug addiction and the reduction of people to commodities. He went on about how the show incorporates personifications of each of the Seven Deadly Sins and a conversation with a demon, about how it was literature at its most personal, horrifying and intimate.

"The show begins with a rebirth," the professor said, "and it climaxes with a dual baptism. One by water and one by fire. Look at the structure. This is the stuff of classical mythology."

The student pushed up her glasses, folded her arms and glanced out the window before saying, "Dante didn't yell the word 'motherfucker' in every other sentence."

She shook her head, zipped her backpack and slipped the strap on her shoulder. "The second day of this class you wouldn't shut up about shit and farts. Now this. I want a *real* literature class."

And she walked out.

That professor was me. This scene took place years ago, when I was still starry-eyed about my pursuit of stand-up comedy as literature. The student's reaction was hardly unique. Since I began this study I have received more than a few derisive scoffs, more than a few eye-rolls from students and colleagues alike, people who sneered at me as if to echo the student's sentiment that I should direct my efforts toward *real* literature. One professor admitted that even though he believed the art form to be worthy of study, it was more befitting American studies or cultural studies. Despite a softening of my position over the years, the core of my argument remains intact: stand-up comedy is nothing less than the great American literary form, and *Richard Pryor Live on the Sunset Strip* remains an American masterpiece, a work of art that reveals, at the very least, as much about the American ethos as do minor masterpieces such as Bernard Malamud's *The Natural*, John Steinbeck's *Tortilla Flat* and Alice Walker's *The Color Purple* and that it is certainly more worthy of attention than some works that often show up on American literature reading lists. If great literature, as William Faulkner said in his 1950 Nobel Prize acceptance speech, grows out of "the human heart in conflict with itself," then *Live on the Sunset Strip* fits the bill in two ways. First of all, it is the story of a man so incapacitated by drug addiction that he can ask for help only by setting himself on fire and, secondly, it is a portrait of a nation that, more than a century after the signing of the Emancipation Proclamation and a generation after the Civil Rights marches, still cannot come to terms fully with the promises of the Declaration of Independence.

I have continued to argue that just as Faulkner, in his masterpiece, *The Sound and the Fury*, takes us into the suicidal world of Quentin Compson and his pathological devotion to family honor, just as Shakespeare takes us deep into the chaotic mind of the deposed King Lear and just as Dante takes us on a guided tour of Hell, Pryor also takes us deep into the pit of madness, a madness fueled by cocaine addiction. In his one-person show, Pryor draws us into the junkie's home, then into his secret room and finally into his private torture chamber and the most mortifying of nightmares, one replete with horror scenes that rival the best work of Nathaniel Hawthorne, Edgar Allan Poe and Ernest Hemingway.

All this is not to say, however, that my student's concerns were not without merit. Her unwillingness to accept what I believed to be a well-founded and well-thought-out argument raises important questions, the most important of which I have never heard discussed in a college class-room, despite some twenty-five years devoted to literary study. That is, "What, exactly, is literature?" A secondary question is, "If stand-up comedy is not literature, then what is it?"

If we consult the Oxford English Dictionary, the waters may become less muddied, but not in any immediate or significant way. It defines "lite-rature" as "written works, especially those regarded as having artistic me-rit." An etymological definition of "literature" (which actually works against my argument) also offers little help. According to the *Arcade Dictionary of Word Origins*, the word "literature" comes from the Latin word *littera*, meaning "letter," and thus formed the basis of the "further deriva-tive *litterātūra*, which denoted 'writing formed with letters.'" While it might be argued that *Live on the Sunset Strip* or certain of George Carlin's routines have superior or lasting merit, whether stand-up routines qualify as "writ-ten works" may be a matter of dispute, since not all stand-ups commit their jokes to the legal pad or Word for Windows file. Furthermore, even those comedians who do keep meticulous records of their jokes will, in the midst of a performance, add, subtract, embellish or edit a joke or a routine. In the strictest sense, then, stand-up comedy cannot be literature.

If a work's being committed to paper is the chief requirement, how-ever, other problems arise. Where, for instance, does this leave works like *The Iliad, The Odyssey* or sections of the New Testament, for that mat-ter, works whose authors never considered print or publication? What about the stories of those peoples for whom written language was either unimportant or never considered? Are Winnebago trickster tales not literature? What about Norse myths or the *corridos* from the Spanish-speaking regions of North America? What about the fairy tales that cir-culated around Europe before the Brothers Grimm collected them? Are such stories, poems and songs not literature? Are they something other than literature? Is the term "oral literature" an oxymoron?

Even to someone as respected as British literary theorist Terry Eag-leton the answers do not come easily. In the initial chapter of his seminal book *Literary Theory: An Introduction*, Eagleton examines the matter, ar-guing that

> Perhaps literature is definable not according to whether it is fictional or
> "imaginative," but because it uses language in peculiar ways. On this

theory, literature is a kind of writing which, in the words of Russian critic Roman Jakobson, represents an "organized violence committed on ordinary speech." If you approach me at a bus stop and murmur, "Thou still unravished bride of quietness," then I am instantly aware that I am in the presence of the literary. I know this because the texture, rhythm and resonance of your words are in excess of their abstractable meaning—or, as the linguists might more technically put it, there is a disproportion between the signifiers and the signifieds. Your language draws attention to itself, flaunts its material being, as statements like, "Don't you know the drivers are on strike?" do not.[1]

Eagleton then goes on to suggest that the defining feature of literature may be its amorphousness, arguing that it is "non-pragmatic language" in that it differs from textbooks and grocery lists because literature "serves no immediate practical purpose"[2] or that the very word "literature" functions much like the word "weed" since "weeds are not particular kinds of plant, but just any kind of plant which for some reason or another a gardener doesn't want around. Perhaps 'literature' means something like the opposite: any kind of writing which for some reason or another somebody values highly."[3] The upshot, however, seems to be that even for one of the world's leading authorities on the subject, there are no hard, fast or easy answers.

Perhaps then the core of the problem is not the lack of answers but the inadequacy of the question, and therefore some reframing is in order. Rather than looking at what literature *is*, perhaps it would be more fruitful to examine what literature *does*. Although this approach has been a matter of public debate since, at the very least, the days of Aristotle and does not offer any quick and easy answers, it allows for certain parameters to be set in place and, consequently, enables us to begin an inquiry that is not mired in the muck of semantics. Without delving into heavy-duty literary theory or aesthetic philosophy, we can explore at least a few of the primary functions of literature that have been identified throughout the ages.

Literature Codifies Experience

Perhaps this dynamic, which echoes Leo Tolstoy's argument that the purpose of literature is to promote a brotherhood of man,[4] is best explained by Robert Pirsig who wrote in his landmark autobiography/novel *Zen and the Art of Motorcycle Maintenance* about how the mythos, that body of myths and stories that shape human consciousness, "unites our minds as cells are united in the body of a man." Pirsig explains, "each child is born as ignorant as any caveman. What keeps the world from reverting to the Neanderthal with each generation is the continuing, ongoing mythos. . . . To feel that one is not so united, that one can accept or discard this mythos as one pleases, is not to understand what the mythos is."[5]

In other words, Pirsig is arguing that any normal person's understanding of the world is shaped in no small way by the countless stories, legends and anecdotes, whether real or fantastical, that a person reads, hears or sees. A child living in a Kansas village, for instance, knows about monkeys, whales, oceans and spaceships even though he or she may have never ventured more than a few miles from home and may never have experienced any of these entities first-hand. Much the way Leonardo da Vinci and the Wright Brothers were able to conceive of human flight because of stories like that of Icarus and Daedalus, literature allows this child to imagine life on another planet, life in a gulag or what it might be like to be raised by wolves. This is because each normal human being draws from a common literary pool in order to begin making sense of an otherwise chaotic world. This pool contains, in addition to a vast mosaic of images, stories and characters, the words, expressions and idioms that shape and define human consciousness. We know how, for instance, American expatriates in 1920s Europe might have talked, what they valued and what they feared because of Hemingway's *The Sun Also Rises* and Scott Fitzgerald's *Tender Is the Night*. College students in future centuries, meanwhile, will be better able to understand the words, deeds, attitudes and conflicts of the early twenty-first century because of the work of Toni Morrison, Cormac McCarthy and rapper Eminem.

A different take on the same idea can also be found in Sigmund Freud's landmark study from 1899, *The Interpretation of Dreams*. Here, the premier psychoanalyst discusses how Sophocles' drama *Oedipus Rex* resonates within all people whether they are aware of it or not, because it is simultaneously a story that is universal and yet deeply personal. Writes Freud,

> If the *Oedipus Rex* is capable of moving a modern reader or playgoer no less powerfully than it moved the contemporary Greeks, the only possible explanation is that the effect of the Greek tragedy does not depend upon the conflict between fate and human will, but upon the peculiar nature of the material by which this conflict is revealed. There must be a voice within us which is prepared to acknowledge the compelling power of fate in the *Oedipus*. . . . His fate moves us only because it might have

been our own, because the oracle laid upon us before our birth is the very curse which rested upon him. It may be that we were all destined to direct our first sexual impulses toward our mothers, and our first impulses of hatred and violence toward our fathers; our dreams convince us that we were. King Oedipus, who slew his father Laius and wedded his mother Jocasta, is nothing more or less than a wish-fulfillment—the fulfillment of the wish our childhood.[6]

We see this same dynamic coming into play even in the first decades of the twenty-first century as the perennial Creationism-versus-Evolution debate continues to loom large in American classrooms, churches and courtrooms. This is because the creation story found in those early chapters of Genesis is also simultaneously universal and deeply personal. Although it is undoubtedly mythical and has no scientific evidence to support its facts, the story touches the very core of human experience. The story begins with the divine pronouncement, "Let there be light," proceeds to a discussion on the separation of water from the dry land and then to the formation of Adam and his naming of the plants and animals of Eden. From there it moves on to the discovery of free will and sexuality before climaxing with the expulsion from paradise. This is nothing less than a metaphor for the story of every normal human being who, upon being born, experiences the power of light, separation from amniotic fluid, the separation of the subject and the object or the "I" and the "not-I," the awakening of sexuality and the subsequent expulsion from the paradise of childhood.

Much the way every child is, at least to some degree, Oedipus, every person is, to some degree, Adam or Eve. If, as the Existentialists have argued, the quest to transcend the confines of the solitary experience is the central human motivation, then literature in this way is one of the most useful, efficient, time-tested and indispensable tools to aid us in such a quest. Perhaps this was put most succinctly by the student who, in William Nicholson's play *Shadowlands*, declares to writer C.S. Lewis that "we read to know we are not alone."

Literature Provides an Emotional Catharsis

The Greek philosopher Aristotle notes in his treatise *Poetics* that the appeal of a tragic drama is the way in which a spectator experiences an emotional purging after having been taken through the ups, downs and tumults of a story. In addition to being given opportunities to laugh, cry, grieve, tremble and identify with the protagonist, says Aristotle, the audience member is also treated to situations and dialogue that arouse his fear and pity and leave him feeling as though he or she has suffered through the death of a loved one, romantic betrayal or a horrific tragedy and yet, by the end of it all, gets to walk away unscathed, although not unchanged. Philosopher Hans-Georg Gadamer builds upon Aristotle's theories, arguing that what is experienced when one reads a book or views a play is that the

> spectator recognizes himself [or herself] and his [or her] finiteness in the face of the power of fate. What happens to the great ones of the earth has exemplary significance. . . . To see that "this is how it is" is a kind of self-knowledge for the spectator, who emerges with new insight from the illusions in which he [or she], like everyone else, lives.[7]

In other words, the fear of dominance, fear of being crippled or fear being killed is brought out into the open when someone watches or reads an effective story about dominance, violence or murder. While the protagonist of a drama may suffer financial ruin, loss of love or even may die a horrible death, the spectator is provided the opportunity to project himself onto the characters and suffer with them while never compromising his security.

While Aristotle applied his analysis primarily to tragedies, one can easily see that the dynamic works well with other genres, perhaps most obviously horror films. A great many of these, movies such as *Halloween, Saw II* and *Nightmare on Elm Street*, for example, are appealing not because they are cinematic masterpieces (it is no secret that a great many of the most popular are not) but because they are the modern cinema's answer to the roller coaster ride as they take the viewer through a series of theatrical ascents, plunges, spins and lurches.

A rather offbeat take on this same dynamic comes from horror story guru Stephen King, who writes in his essay "Why We Crave Horror Movies":

> The mythic horror movie, like the sick joke, has a dirty job to do. It deliberately appeals to all that is worst in us. It is morbidity unchained, our most base instincts let free, our nastiest fantasies realized . . . and it all happens, fittingly enough, in the dark. For those reasons, good liberals often shy away from horror films. For myself, I like to see the most aggressive of them—*Dawn of the Dead*, for instance—as lifting a trapdoor in

the civilized forebrain and throwing a basket of raw meat to the hungry
alligators swimming around in that subterranean river beneath.

Why bother? Because it keeps them from getting out, man, it keeps
them down there and me up here.[8]

Consequently, the most outlandish and grotesque horror stories
serve the human spirit in various ways. First of all, they satisfy the
innate longing for aggression much the way a good football game
might. Secondly, they ask us to contemplate the extremes of human
experience. Finally, they allow us to experience what Rudolph Otto
called the *mysterium et fascinosum*, that which is so horrible we dare not
turn away from it.

Literature Entertains Us

Whether we are discussing the work of ancient raconteurs or that of
Steven Spielberg, there can be little doubt that stories are spun so
that audiences stay interested. The storyteller's job is take readers into
realms where they vacillate between the familiar and the strange,
where ordinary, mundane objects take on strange and even magical
qualities: where apple trees pluck off their own fruit and fling them at
unassuming wanderers, where a salty old sea captain becomes so ob-
sessed with killing a white whale that he is willing to risk his own life
and that of his crew in the pursuit, where the Mississippi River becomes a divine mother and where a common, henpecked husband
can sleep for twenty years. In most cases, the job of the writer, then,
is to construct for the reader solid comfortable contexts or founda-
tions to which surprises are summarily introduced. When the foundation is not strong enough, when the imaginary world isn't founded
firmly enough upon the real, even the most credible acts and words
become lackluster, ineffective and unbelievable. When the foundation
is strong enough, the most discerning spectator can believe, at least
temporarily, the most outrageous things—even that a wily coyote
can, with the help of the ACME mail order company, go to insane
lengths in his attempts to catch a roadrunner or that the teenaged
sleuth Nancy Drew can solve murder after murder when the police
cannot.

The obvious truth is that if readers do not keep turning pages,
then the books go out of print. When the books go out of print the
stories they contain are more than likely cast into oblivion.

Literature Defamiliarizes the Ordinary

In the early years of the twentieth century, a group of Russian intellectuals turned the worlds of art, literature and criticism on their heads by explaining and identifying the ways in which art takes the familiar and makes it strange, a dynamic they called "defamiliarization." American and European artists quickly embraced the notion as a way of creating and understanding art, and among the most enthusiastic were those who associated with Dada, a movement that rejected prevailing standards, attitudes and values. One of the most notable figures was artist and intellectual Marcel Duchamp, who was known for his painting *Nude Descending a Staircase*, which depicted a stylized nude at virtually every step on a staircase, thereby suggesting movement and adding a temporal dimension to a two-dimensional medium. Duchamp was also famous for the works he called "ready-mades" and "assisted ready-mades" which were ordinary objects that he simply designated as art. Some of the most famous of these included were a print of Leonardo's *Mona Lisa* with a goatee and mustache penciled on her face, a bicycle wheel mounted onto a barstool and an inverted urinal that he signed and entered in a New York art competition. These works and others like them subsequently became a tacit argument that what made something art was not a matter of the artist's skill or philosophical stance but rather a matter of how the artist chose to recontextualize the ordinary.

Today, there is little doubt that defamiliarization is a function of literature. Novels such as Joseph Heller's *Catch-22* or Don DeLillo's *White Noise*, for example, have been known to have readers laughing out loud as they read about characters who must confront death, oblivion or any number of horrific realities. Similarly, some of Flannery O'Connor's most memorable stories such as "A Good Man Is Hard to Find," "Good Country People" and "Everything that Rises Must Converge" draw their power from the ways in which they construct worlds in which so-called—and self-proclaimed—"righteous" protagonists are revealed, via defamiliarization, to be contemptible while the brutal and violent are revealed to be heroic.

For still another example, we can look at a scene from Ken Kesey's 1964 novel *Sometimes a Great Notion*. In this scene, the narrator imbues an echo with otherworldly and even sentient qualities, reframing it as an allegory for choice and consequences:

> Up river from the Stamper house and south, back into the sudden thrust of mountains, up the deep granite canyon of the South Fork of the Wa-

konda Auga, I know a place where you can sometimes sing along with yourself if you take a notion. You stand on a wooded slope overlooking the crooked little deep-green river far below, and sing into a lofty amphitheater of naked rock scooped from the steep mountain across the way: "Row, row, row your boat, gently down the stream . . ."—and just as you start on the merrily-merrilies, the echo comes in, "Row, row, row . . ." right on cue. So you sing with the echo. But you must be careful in choosing your key or your tempo; there is no changing of the pitch if you start too high, no slowing down the tempo if you start too fast . . . because an echo is an inflexible and pitiless taskmaster: you sing the echo's way because it is damned sure not going to sing yours. And even after you leave this mossy acoustical phenomenon to go on with your hiking of fishing, you cannot help but feeling, for a long time after, that any jig you whistle, hymn you hum, or song you sing is somehow immutably tuned to an echo yet unheard, or relentlessly echoing a tune long forgotten . . . .[9]

Indeed, it is a work's ability to defamiliarize, an ability that is so often fueled by the writer's talent to notice what others cannot or dare not, to show us the familiar in the unreal or to infuse the mundanities of daily live with new meaning, that so often keeps us turning pages.

Literature Reveals the Culture

Perhaps one of the best illustrations of the ways in which art reveals the culture, its values, hopes and fears, comes not from the world of classical art or literature, but from the world of rock 'n roll. On a Monday morning in August 1969, on a farm outside White Lake, New York, guitarist Jimi Hendrix launched into his rendition of "The Star-Spangled Banner" at the Woodstock Music and Art Fair. With just his guitar and a little help from drummer Mitch Mitchell, Hendrix introduced to the melody sirens, screams, the sounds of battle, psychedelia and thunderous peals that characterized an epoch shaken by the war in Vietnam, hallucinogenic drugs, shifting cultural attitudes and failing trust in Cold War values. In that one interpretation, which lasted just under four minutes, we can hear and see what amounts to the shifting of tectonic plates in the American consciousness presented more completely and concisely than any commentary by a Harvard historian.

Literature also does this and in a variety of ways. One of the most poignant examples comes from the quintessential American novel, *The Adventures of Huckleberry Finn*. In the following scene, the protagonist has an epiphany as he surreptitiously watches his buddy, Jim, a runaway slave, crying for his family:

When I waked up just at daybreak he was sitting there with his head down betwixt his knees, moaning and mourning to himself. I didn't take notice nor let on. I knowed what it was about. He was thinking about his wife and his children, away up yonder, and he was low and homesick; because he hadn't ever been away from home before in his life; and I do believe he cared just as much for his people as white folks does for their'n. It don't seem natural, but I reckon it's so. He was often moaning and mourning that way nights, when he judged I was asleep, and saying, "Po' little 'Lizabeth! po' little Johnny! it's mighty hard; I spec' I ain't ever gwyne to see you no mo', no mo'!" He was a mighty good nigger, Jim was.[10]

Even the most unseasoned literary critic can appreciate the symbolism: Huck is not merely an adolescent inadvertently discovering the depths of his empathy, but he is also a personification of an adolescent America emerging from the trauma of the Civil War much the way Jim is the personification of a people who have survived centuries of slavery. Just as Huck is waking up to the reality of Jim's humanity, America is beginning to come to terms with four centuries of its most heinous sins. As scenes like this demonstrate, literature is an indispensable tool for dissecting and understanding a given ethos. This is why literary texts, including novels, collections of poetry and narrative films, are utilized in history, anthropology and sociology classes much more often than literature classes utilize history, anthropology or sociology texts.

Literature Invites Multiple Levels of Interpretation

On its surface, Ernest Hemingway's novella *The Old Man and the Sea* is a rather simple story: a lonely old laughingstock of a fisherman named Santiago, after months of bad luck, hooks a gargantuan marlin that he must fight for two days and two nights as it pulls him farther and farther out into the open sea. The angler eventually defeats the great fish, lashes him to the side of the boat and heads back to his home on the island of Cuba, only to have sharks tear chunks out of the great fish. By the time the Santiago returns all that is left are the head and naked bones, scraps of a fish that his protégé, a boy named Manolin, is told would have been "eighteen feet from nose to tail."[11] The story, which earned Hemingway the Pulitzer Prize in fiction for 1952 and, according to Hemingway biographer Carlos Baker, "was instrumental in winning him the Nobel Prize two years later,"[12] grew, like so many of Hemingway's stories, out of actual events the author had read about some years earlier. The kernel of this particular story was an article from 1936 that told of how

> An old man fishing alone in a skiff out of Cabanas hooked a great marlin that, on the heavy sashcord handline, pulled the skiff far out to sea. Two days later the old man was picked up by fishermen 60 miles to the eastward, the head and the forward part of the marlin lashed alongside. What was left of the fish, less than half, weighed 800 pounds. The old man had stayed with him a day, a night, a day and another night while the fish swam deep and pulled the boat . . . [once the marlin was lashed] alongside [the skiff] the sharks had hit him and the old man had fought them out alone . . . clubbing them, stabbing at them, lunging at them with an oar. . . . He was crying in the boat when the fisherman picked him up, half crazy from his loss.[13]

Despite the frequent claim of made-for-television movies that a story is "based on actual events," the fact of the matter is that no story, not even a science fiction or horror tale, can be based on anything else—every story must, to one degree or another, be based on something that really happened and something the artist experienced, either first-hand or vicariously. Nevertheless, as if relying on his journalistic training, Hemingway is telling us a story, more or less, as it happened and is using credible accounts as the foundation. Much of the story's power, however, comes from the way in which Hemingway layers Christian symbolism on the empirical facts: the very name "Santiago," which translates as "Saint James," recalls two of Christ's apostles, James the son of Alpheus, who is also called "The Lord's Brother," and James the son of Zebedee, who was a fisherman. Furthermore, we see that Santiago becomes a Christ figure as he suffers a "cut over his eye and on his forehead,"[14] which recalls Jesus' crowning with thorns, is scourged by his own fishing line,[15] suffers cramped hands[16] and imitates Jesus' walk to Mount Calvary as he shoulders his mast, starts for home and falls repeatedly. Furthermore, while he is fighting the marlin we hear him utter the word "ay," about which Hemingway says, "There is no translation for this word and perhaps it is just a noise such as a man might make, involuntarily, feeling the nail go through his hands and into the wood."[17]

Yet another reading of the story reveals that the relationship between Santiago and Manolin is the stuff of myth. What we see here is the mentor-apprentice relationship, one that is common throughout world literature. We see it in the relationship between Merlin and Arthur, John the Baptist and Jesus, the prophet Nathan and King David, the Zen master and his novitiate, *Star Wars'* Obi-Wan Kenobi and Luke Skywalker and *The Godfather's* don Vito Corleone and his son Michael. In short, Santiago serves as the wise old man who brings the child Manolin into adulthood, to demonstrate through his actions how a man should and should not act in the face of tribulation. Just as the stories of Jesus, Arthur and the others involve some sort of rebirth, Manolin, by the end of *The Old Man and the Sea*, is reborn as he rejects his parents and devotes himself fully to Santiago's tutelage.

We can, of course, examine countless other aspects of *The Old Man and the Sea*. Key symbols such as the water and the journey itself, for instance, teem with meaning, virtually demanding to be decoded. Certainly, the marlin itself resonates with symbolism, as the fish, throughout the ages, has symbolized sacrifice, the need to kill to survive, being caught in the "stream of life" and, in Christian mythology, Jesus Himself. An even more complex reading of the story might argue that it is an allegory for the numinous experience, what the Gnostics might term as the experience of *gnosis* or what the Buddhists call "enlightenment."[18] Such a reading would argue that Santiago's external journey from the Cuban coast out to the open sea parallels an internal journey from the mundane experience to that bead of holiness that lives deep within the human consciousness, that which Carl Jung would call the Christ-Self. Along the way, the old fisherman only catches glimpses of the fish, which Hemingway describes in unabashedly magnanimous terms, such as when "the surface of the ocean bulged and the fish came out. He came out unendingly and water poured from his sides . . . he rose full length from the water and then re-entered it, smoothly, like a diver,"[19] a vision that leaves the old man awestruck as he says to himself, "Christ, I didn't know he was so big."[20]

Consequently, once he is back safely on the island, Santiago is left with only scraps that Hemingway describes as "the white naked line of his backbone and the dark mass of the head with the projecting bill and all the nakedness between."[21] It seems that the full experience of the fish is not something that can be transmitted to ordinary life, just as the fullness of the numinous experience cannot be transmitted to words, prayers, recollections or ceremonies.

In this way, works of literature function for a people much the way dreams, which were the first stories, function for the individual: they reverberate with endless layers of meaning, each revealing new dimensions of our potentials, wishes and fears.

Literature Is Language Play

Much of the joy—and frustration—of high school and college literature classes is that novelists, poets and playwrights take great delight in
saying things obliquely, so as to communicate nuances of experience in
ways that are simultaneously familiar and strange. Consider, for example, this poem by e.e. cummings:

l(a

le

af

fa

ll

s)

one

l

iness[22]

While the unsuspecting reader might find this poem unintelligible,
multiple readings will more than likely reveal that it is about detachment, solitude and even melancholia. Not only are these themes underscored by the parsing of the word "loneliness" into divisions that
include repeated instances of the character "l," which can be the lower-
case letter L or the number "one" (in fact, the numeral one was typed
on old typewriters with a lower case L) and which suggests two separate individuals—two "I"s rather than one "we." The themes of separation and alienation are consequently emphasized with the other two
segments, namely "one," which symbolizes a person who is alone, and
"iness," which can be read as "I-ness," as opposed to "we-ness." Furthermore, the phrase "a leaf falls" is set off with parentheses to un-
derscore the alienation theme and is spread out over six succeeding
lines so as to suggest the leaf's downward motion. An even deeper
reading might suggest that this is the experience of a person sitting
alone, staring out a window, the frame of which is suggested by the
parentheses, and that this person is actually watching this leaf fall. That
leaf, its detachment and descent also provide for an allegory, a glimpse
into the mind of the speaker who is also detached, alienated and descending into a depression as a result of loneliness.

In much the way cummings was wont to play with words, letters
and syllables, American novelist William Faulkner was prone to playing
with points-of-view, as he did in this, the opening scene from his 1930

novel *As I Lay Dying*, the story of the poor Bundren family that embarks on a multi-day journey in the middle of July to deliver the rotting corpse of its matriarch to her family burial ground:

> Jewel and I come up from the field, following the path in single file, although I am fifteen feet ahead of him, anyone watching us from the cottonhouse can see Jewel's frayed and broken straw hat a full head above my own. . . . When we reach [the cottonhouse] I turn and follow the path which circles the house. Jewel, fifteen feet behind me, looking straight ahead, steps in a single stride through the window. Still staring straight ahead; his pale eyes like wood set into his wooden face, he crosses the floor in four strides with the rigid gravity of a cigar store Indian dressed in patched overalls and endued with life from the hips down.[23]

While this scene, at least on the initial reading, might grab the reader because of its vivid renderings of the characters' movements, subsequent readings reveal that something quite remarkable is going on: the narrator, Darl Bundren, either via skillful reasoning, a rich imagination or extra-sensory perception, is able not only to adapt the point-of-view of someone watching him and his brother from far away, but also to narrate events that are going on behind him with so much perspicacity that he can count the number of steps required of his brother to cross the interior of the cottonhouse.

Similarly, Colombian novelist Gabriel García Márquez manipulates words so as to capture various layers of time in this famous opening line from his masterpiece, *One Hundred Years of Solitude*: "Many years later, as he faced the firing squad, Colonel Aureliano Buendía was to remember that distant afternoon when his father took him to discover ice."[24] In this sentence that grammarians respond to as mathematicians might respond to an elegant proof, we find ourselves considering and reconsidering the narrative stance. As we read the phrase "Many years later," we find ourselves wondering about some mysterious temporal reference point as we ask, "Many years later from when?" The phrase "was to remember" suggests that Buendía is, sometime in the future, going to remember something that happened in the distant past. With its temporal zigzagging, the scene allows the reader to transcend the ordinary temporal experience.

If playing with words, savoring their rhythms, meanings, nuances and sounds were not quite so entrancing and so magical, then literature and storytelling would offer very little joy.

Literature Engenders Wonder

One of the great pleasures of studying literature is the way in which it connects us to other worlds and entertains us by revealing worlds of infinite possibilities. Not only does the stuff of science fiction oftentimes find its way into the so-called real world, such as the way the communicators from the early *Star Trek* shows served as the prototypes for clamshell cell phones in the early twenty-first century, but the whole of human experience is allowed to expand through the world of literature. In stories, poems and plays, humans are allowed to entertain scenarios in which new realms of potential open up to us. In his novel *One Flew Over the Cuckoo's Nest*, for instance, Kesey allows us to see the world through the eyes of the paranoid schizophrenic Chief Bromden, just as William Faulkner, in Book One of his classic novel *The Sound and the Fury*, allows us to adopt the mindset of a thirty-three-year-old man who is severely mentally handicapped.

Literature does not merely accomplish this by discussing fantastical or numinous events, but also by finding the miraculous and the numinous in the ordinary. Consider, for instance, the other-worldly quality of a simple kiss as described by Fitzgerald in *The Great Gatsby*:

> Out of the corner of his eye Gatsby saw that the blocks of the sidewalk really formed a ladder and mounted to a secret place above the trees—he could climb to it, if he climbed alone, and once there he could suck on the pap of life, gulp down the incomparable milk of wonder.
>
> His heart beat faster and faster as Daisy's white face came up to his own. He knew that when he kissed this girl, and forever wed his unutterable visions to her perishable breath, his mind would never romp again like the mind of God. So he waited, listening for a moment longer to the tuning fork that had been struck upon a star. Then he kissed her. At his lips' touch she blossomed for him like a flower and the incarnation was complete.[25]

Much of the genius of this passage, beyond the multi-layered assemblage of images and the poetry of the sentences, is the way in which Fitzgerald melds the real with the ideal. On the surface is a pivotal moment in a simple love story, how a modest soldier and the Southern belle he is deeply in love with stroll along a street, face each other and kiss. And yet, the author, not content to leave it at that, constructs an allegory, a marriage between the divine and eternal, represented by Gatsby, and the mundane and ephemeral, represented by Daisy. With the final line—"and the incarnation was complete"—

we encounter the most poetic of moments as Gatsby chooses to sacrifice his divinity for the sake of love.

Another instance in which the ordinary becomes wedded to the real comes in Margaret Atwood's masterpiece, *Cat's Eye*, the story of a Toronto girl who is mentally abused by one of her peers. In this scene, one in which the protagonist has walked onto a frozen river and fallen through the ice, Atwood provides for the reader this numinous moment:

> I know I should get up and walk home, but it seems easier to stay here, in the snow, with the little pellets of snow caressing my face . . .
>
> I hear someone talking to me. It's like a voice calling, only very soft, as if muffled. I'm not sure I've heard it at all. I open my eyes with an effort. The person who was standing on the bridge is moving through the railing, or melting into it. It's a woman, I can see the long skirt now, or is it a long cloak? She isn't falling, she's coming down toward me as if walking, but there's nothing for her to walk on. I don't have the energy to be frightened. I lie in the snow, watching her with lethargy, and with a sluggish curiosity. I would like to be able to walk on air like that.
>
> Now she's quite close. I can see the white glimmer of her face, the dark scarf or hood around her head, or is it hair? She holds out her arms to me and I feel a surge of happiness. Inside her half-open cloak there's a glimpse of red. It's her heart, I think. It must be her heart, on the outside of her body, glowing like neon, like a coal.
>
> Then I can't see her any more. But I feel her around me, not like arms but like a small wind of warmer air. She's telling me something.
>
> *You can go home now*, she says. *It will be all right. Go home.*
>
> I don't hear the words out loud, but that is what she says.[26]

While strict empiricists might argue that such moments are the products of imagination or happen only in the world of fiction, others might respond to these passages and recognize how such moments transpired in their own lives, how they too once felt as though they were being guided by invisible hands or how certain salvific opportunities became startlingly clear, if only for a nanosecond. By capturing and validating such sublime experiences, literature, like all art, can connect us to wondrous realms in a world where empiricism and traditional religions too often fail us.

Stand-up Comedy and Literature

Any person with moderate exposure to the world of stand-up comedy can easily identify a few ways in which the comic performance fulfills functions like those described above. Among Bill Cosby's most impressive gifts, for instance, is his talent for bringing universal experiences onto the stage—in the way he allows us to see ourselves, our friends and our families in his stories of family life. Such uncanny illustrations indeed codify experiences as they connect people from various backgrounds—perhaps even different countries—and present the subtle and tacit message that we are all of one community. Similarly, much of Bob Newhart's act is built upon defamiliarization. Whether it is a phone call from Sir Walter Raleigh to the head of the West Indies Company in which he describes how you can take tobacco, shred it, "put it on a piece of paper, roll it up, stick it between your lips . . . set fire to it . . . [and] inhale the smoke"[27] or the conversation between Abraham Lincoln and his press agent, Newhart takes grade school history lessons and makes them oddly amusing if not downright hilarious. In much the same way, a great deal of Jerry Seinfeld's act revolves around the way he takes the most unremarkable objects and experiences, such as a trip to the supermarket, taking a shower or encountering a traffic sign that says, "left turn okay" and defamiliarizing the mundane so as to expose the dormant absurdities.

While stand-up comedy's ability to entertain may be too obvious to warrant much comment—it is, after all, a large part of the entertainment industry—perhaps it would be prudent to comment on stand-up's effectiveness in revealing cultural subtleties. In her article "The Stand-up Comedian as Anthropologist: Intentional Cultural Critic," which concerns precisely this subject, Stephanie Koziski argues,

> Documenting areas of tacit knowledge and bringing them to the conscious awareness of their particular audiences are important functions performed by the anthropologist and the stand-up comedian in their respective roles. The social and cultural function of popular culture materials along with the anthropologist's and standup comedian's perspectives as social critics fused for me, as I considered the role of the standup comedian in American culture through an examination and analysis of selected recorded comedy routines.[28]

Koziski then goes on to comment on how both the comedian and the anthropologist "pattern their . . . material close to everyday reality, making obvious behavioral patterns, explicit and tacit operating knowledge and other insights about American society objects of conscious reflection."[29] Since the days of Mark Twain and Charley Case, the direct-address comedy performance has concerned itself with the stuff of everyday life. Whether it is Jackie Vernon or Red Skelton discussing car vacations, a phenomenon that is primarily a product of post-World War II America, Carlin discussing America's obsession with both legal and illegal drugs, Paul Reiser riffing on the difficulties of communicating with his wife or Brian Regan talking about the perils of reading food labels, stand-up comedy provides glimpses into what Americans collectively fear and value, how we live, what we struggle with and how we fail to communicate with each other.

Yet another obvious point might be the cathartic benefits of a visit to the comedy club or the viewing of a stand-up DVD. As Sigmund Freud and Arthur Schopenhauer, among others, have argued, one of the main functions and benefits of laughter is the way in which it works as a safety valve by allowing the release of "nervous energy built up before the person entered the laughter situation."[30] Just as watching a stellar performance of *Hamlet* or *The Diary of Anne Frank* might move a person to tears, and therefore result in an Aristotelian catharsis, there is little doubt that witnessing a great comedic performance, whether it is live or recorded, can bring about a burst of vitality, lift one's spirits and thereby provide an "emotional cleansing" that is so powerful it has measurable physiological benefits. A famous case illustrating this point involves *Saturday Review* editor Norman Cousins who, as Morreall tells us, after returning from a trip to the Soviet Union in 1964,

> fell sick with a serious collagen disease—the connective tissue in his spine and joints was disintegrating. The pain was intense . . . he was given only a 1-in-500 chance of recovering. . . . Cousins checked . . . into a hotel, where he began his own form of therapy. He surrounded himself with humor books, and from his friend Allen Funt, producer of the television program *Candid Camera*, he got some of that show's funniest segments. Within a short time he found that hearty laughter had an analgesic effect—ten minutes of it would allow him to sleep without pain for a few hours . . . as the weeks went by, his condition improved further; his doctors found that the connective tissue in his joints was regenerating. A short time later he was able to go back to work full time, and though it took years for his condition to fully reverse itself, he knew that, thanks to humor therapy, he was recovering.[31]

And of course, there is no doubt that stand-up is language play. In fact, one of the distinguishing characteristics of the art form, and one of the reasons it could have been born only in the United States when the country was becoming the most affluent and literate country in history, is that it is primarily a verbal art. One of the great masters of stand-up as word play is Carlin, whose 1973 album *Occupation: Foole* contains a bit in which he discusses racial labels, saying, "I never really liked Caucasian, you know," and illustrates how the word sounds like something other than a racial designation. He says it "sounds like a shoe style," saying in the voice of a hipster, "Let me get a hold of a Caucasian in a nine-D." He goes on to suggest that the word sounds like it could be "an order of monks somewhere," a medical operation or a mountain range, illustrating the latter point by saying in the voice of an elderly middle-class woman, "We're going to the Caucasians again this week."

Less noticeable, however, is the way in which stand-up comedy invites multiple levels of interpretation. Consider, for instance, how when Flip Wilson adopts the persona of his alter ego, an angry Black woman named Geraldine, the result is a social commentary that is much larger than a bunch of jokes strung together. The feisty wife of a preacher, Geraldine becomes the voice of those who are newly bourgeois but nevertheless still marginalized while the Devil who haunts her—perhaps even stalks her—is the personification of American consumerism. With a voice and attitude that are cool, reasonable and even charming, the Devil consistently goads and manipulates Geraldine into doing things like forging her husband's name on a check in order to pay for a new dress. He is a personification of the demon who nudges Americans to consume at all costs, even when this consumption causes us to compromise the relationships of those we love most.

Finally, stand-up comedy consistently engenders wonder. This much we see in the fundamental set-up/punchline format. Take, for instance, the most pedestrian of jokes, such as the old Henny Youngman line that has been around so long it is now considered stock material: "My best friend ran away with my wife, let me tell you, I miss him."[32] The set-up creates a scenario in the mind of the audience, which in this case more than likely involves images such as the comedian glumly looking at a good-bye note or eating dinner alone. When Youngman comes through with the punchline, what emerges is a portrait of a man who cherished his drinking buddy more than his wife. Like an electric spark leaping off one electrode through empty space to another post, the spark of a joke leaps from a world governed by an understandable and logical set of rules, through empty space, to a world in which a completely different set of rules apply. The audience, meanwhile, when suspended between the two poles, cannot help but be trapped in wonder. Wonder is indeed at the heart of every joke. This is why second-guessing a punchline, even the punchline of a child's joke, is so often difficult.

It is hardly surprising that the comedian is very much in the position of a preacher or priest. Not only is he the only person in the room facing the back, but his stage functions as an altar and often he presides over "unholy communion," that is, the sharing of food and libations. And just as the priest or shaman serves as the go-between who unites the mundane world with the realm of the sacred and mysterious, the comedian serves as the go-between as he links the realms of the painfully ordinary and the mysteriously entertaining.

Is it any wonder, then, that so many ancient tribes saw their clowns, jesters and fools as sacred?

Consequently, the question "Is stand-up comedy literature?" is one that perhaps will be answered in the years to come and, with any luck, it will force us to look at previously ignored artistic subtleties. Until then, it appears that even if the art form is not literature, it still has the power to do everything literature is supposed to.

CHAPTER TWO
DISSECTING AMERICANNESS

Labels that classify groups of people—terms such as "Christian," "Hispanic," "people of color" or "homosexual"—tend to be rather unruly beasts. Just as it would be short-sighted to deny that differences may exist between, say, Mexican and Icelandic sensibilities, it would be utterly absurd to assume that all African-Americans have all the same concerns, needs, attitudes and vote for the same candidates for precisely the same reasons. In much the same way, the label "American" is troubling because of its amorphousness. When the term is used to describe works of literature, the picture may become a bit clearer, but not in any immediately recognizable way. While certainly works such as Nathaniel Hawthorne's *The Scarlet Letter*, Mark Twain's *The Adventures of Huckleberry Finn* and Walt Whitman's *Leaves of Grass* tend to be considered quintessential examples of American literature, the inclusion of a great many other works into the category leaves more than a little room for argument. Even though the American-born poet T. S. Eliot moved to England at age twenty-five, became a British subject and spent most of his life in England, his poems have always had a comfortable home in American literature courses, while the work of Native American writers such as Leslie Marmon Silko and Sherman Alexie have not. While a convincing argument can be made that the American intellectual foundation is much more Puritan than it is Roman Catholic, ignoring certain Spanish contributions to American letters is nevertheless difficult to justify. Certainly, Bartolomé de las Casas, who wrote of the massacre of American natives a century before William Bradford's arrival on the Eastern seaboard, and poet Gaspar Pérez de Villagrá, a Mexican-born Spaniard whose epic poem "*La historia de nuevo mexico*" precedes John Winthrop's famous sermon "A Model of Christian Charity" by decades, provide indispensable insights on the American experience. Even in the days of political correctness, other problems persist. While it is not uncommon to find the work of Canadian novelists and poets such as Alice Munro, Margaret Atwood, Malcolm Lowry or Robertson Davies on American literature reading lists, it is indeed rare to find investigations of the American imagination that incorporate stories and poems from Mexicans such as Sor Juana Inez de la Cruz, Octavio Paz or Juan Rulfo, even though their works are classified as "*Literatura americana*" in Mexican bookstores.

Perhaps, then, an examination of the American character or those elements that shape the American ethos is in order. To do this, I propose an analogy befitting a book on stand-up comedy: let's imagine we have a large stage, the perimeter of which includes various spotlights, each of which is made from a different manufacturer, is operated by different technicians, has a different quality, brightness and gel and all of which are aimed at the same center spot that we can call "Americanness." By analyzing the circuitry, light bulbs, candle power, filters and orientation of the individual beams, we can at least begin to get a deeper understanding of that center pool of light.

What follows is a description of the most important of these elements.

The Edenic Myth

Ever since Christopher Columbus' arrival in the Bahamas, the myth of America as the land of opportunity has lived in the world's imagination. The earliest projections built up America as nothing less than a fifteenth-century answer to the biblical Eden, a place of limitless fertility, opportunity and prosperity. As Howard Mumford Jones mentions in his study *O Strange New World: American Culture, the Formative Years*, the earliest European imaginings of the New World were that it was where the "Earthly Paradise, Arcadia, or the Golden Age . . . could actually be found."[1] Columbus himself upon first sighting the new land was quick to describe it in similar terms, declaring it to be "a marvel," a place of endless resources including "marvelous pine groves . . . birds of a thousand kinds" singing "in the month of November," trees that "never lose their foliage" and "seem to touch the sky."[2] Two centuries later this was echoed by Winthrop who wrote from aboard the *Arabella* "that wee shall be as a Citty upon a Hill, the eies of all people are upon us."[3]

Even though in the centuries since then America has been revealed as something much less than a paradise, the initial vision continues to live in the American imagination. We see this much in the novel *The*

Scarlet Letter, where Hawthorne presents the protagonist, Hester Prynne, as the personification of the New World and its potential, first by suggesting that Hester is, like the land, uncontrollably fertile—the premise of the story, after all, is that she conceives a child, easily, willingly and readily out of wedlock despite living in a sexually repressive society—and then by suggesting that she, like the continent itself, is alluring, indomitable and teeming with potential. Just as North America is seen as an Arcadia, Hester is seen as "lady-like" and a figure of "perfect elegance."[4] Furthermore, her "broad shoulders and well-developed busts, and round and ruddy cheeks" suggest that she is among the breed of humans identified by eighteenth-century French-American writer J. Hector St. John de Crèvecoeur as someone who possesses a deep confidence and personal power and who is ready to follow Ralph Waldo Emerson's advice to "absolve you to yourself" so that she might have "the suffrage of the world."[5] All of this is underscored by Hester's self-possession, tenacity and "boldness and rotundity of speech."[6]

Consequently, it is not surprising that Hester, like so many American protagonists, is closely associated with a garden, which in this case involves the immediate surroundings of the "small thatched cottage" in which she lives, one that is built on "converted forest land" and "stood on the shore, looking across a basin of the sea at the forest-covered hill toward the west."[7] While the gardens, forests and woods certainly play a large part in fairy tales and folktales across the globe, for American authors the metaphor is all but indispensable. Whether it is Puritans embarking on their "errand into the wilderness" so as to construct the New Eden on the Eastern seaboard, Captain Ahab's Pip looking upon an underwater garden in *Moby-Dick*, Huckleberry Finn and the runaway slave Jim being nourished and protected by the Mississippi River, Janie Crawford appreciating the sublime interaction between a bee and a pear blossom in Zora Neal Hurston's *Their Eyes Were Watching God*, *Gone with the Wind*'s Scarlett O'Hara representing the American Lilith as she rules over her piece of paradise, the plantation called Tara, or Ernest Hemingway's Nick Adams escaping the horrors of war by hiking deep into the Michigan woods, visions of the American Paradise—and that which threatens to ruin it—are fixtures in the American imagination.

While most times the linkage is veiled, such as when George and Lenny of John Steinbeck's novel *Of Mice and Men* chase their slice of Heaven or when Henry David Thoreau moves out to Walden Pond to recreate himself as the Transcendentalist's answer to Adam, at other times the connection is rather obvious. Consider, for example, Caddy, the central character of William Faulkner's *The Sound and the Fury*, a novel widely regarded as one of America's greatest masterpieces. In this story laced with biblical metaphors, the reader is repeatedly nudged toward connecting Caddy, who is disowned by her family for bearing a bastard child, with the biblical Eve. Each woman is expelled from her home and each is associated with a fruit tree, a connection Caddy's retardate brother makes for us by repeatedly declaring that "Caddy smelled like trees." In one scene, a scene which Faulkner himself indicated was the initial vision and inspiration for the novel,[8] Caddy's brothers watch from below as she climbs a pear tree hoping to peek into an upstairs window to see the body of her dead grandmother. Dilsey, the family's servant, discovers what the children are up to and scolds Caddy:

> "Shhhhhhh." Caddy said in the tree. Dilsey said,
> "You come on in here." She came around the corner of the house.
> "Whyn't you all go on up stairs, like your paw said, stead of slipping out behind my back. Where's Caddy and Quentin."
> "I told her not to climb up that tree." Jason said. "I'm going to tell on her."
> "Who in what tree." Dilsey said. She came and looked up into the tree. "Caddy." Dilsey said. The branches began to shake again.
> "You, Satan." Dilsey said. "Come down from there."
> "Hush." Caddy said. "Don't you know Father said to be quiet." Her legs came in sight and Dilsey reached up and lifted her out of the tree.[9]

With the satanic association and the references to the mysteries of death, the pear tree becomes very much the Compsons', and by implication America's, Tree of Life and Tree of Knowledge. It is the axis mundi, the place where Paradise is both found and spoiled, a central point that connects us to the woman who must be expelled for breaking the rules.

Associating America with the biblical Eden even comes into play when the country as a whole confronts the most horrific of nightmares, nuclear devastation. Consider, for example, how just after the Japanese city of Hiroshima was obliterated by an atomic bomb on August 6, 1945, America's collective consciousness tried to believe the paradisic age was finally at hand. The August 7 edition of the *New*

York Herald Tribune proclaimed the discovery of atomic power to be "a blessing that will make it possible for the human race to create a close approach to an earthy paradise," while a few days later the *Dallas Morning News* forecast a "cancer-curing isotope"[10] and twenty-one months later *Collier's* magazine featured an article on "the medical benefits of radioactive isotopes . . . illustrated with two photographs superimposed to create a single image: that of a pajama-clad man, obviously a recently recovered invalid, standing erect and smiling in the midst of a mushroom-shaped cloud, his empty wheelchair in the background."[11] In many ways, then, nuclear power has been cast as the new Jesus, a power that lords over the age and is believed to have the ability to heal the lame and cure the sick.

Whether it is the New Eden, the New Jerusalem, the New Promised Land, the Land of Opportunity or the Land of the Free, the myth not only lives on but its influence leaches out into every corner of the American imagination. Amorphous though it may be, the very idea of America, since its inception, has been the place where people from across the globe go to reclaim what was lost the day that Adam and Eve discovered they were naked.

The Puritan Foundation

Popular conceptions notwithstanding, the Puritans did not venture across the Atlantic aboard the *Arabella* seeking religious freedom, but rather because they saw themselves among the elect, that is, as God's chosen people, and were on an "errand into the wilderness" so as to impose a Christian presence on a profane landscape. While the influence of those early settlers is sometimes very much on the surface of the texts—as in *Moby-Dick*, with both Father Mapple's famous sermon and Melville's use of a prose style that recalls the rhythms and imagery of the King James Bible, and the character of the Widow Douglas who, in *The Adventures of Huckleberry Finn*, is essentially a Southern Puritan—at other times it is detectable in the unquestioned attitudes of characters and speakers, such as with the haughty elitism and *noblesse oblige* of Willa Cather's Archbishop Latour in the 1927 novel *Death Comes for the Archbishop*, the damning society that ruins the life of the protagonist Wing Biddlebaum in Sherwood Anderson's "Hands," from the *Winesburg, Ohio* collection or the pious but hypocritical protagonists of Flannery O'Connor's short stories, characters who, despite their professed devotion to Christianity, are revealed to be short-sighted, hypocritical, elitist and racist.

Some of the most vibrant and influential works in American literature, however, are powerful because of the passion they bring in their
reaction against Puritanism, the prototypical example being Ralph
Waldo Emerson's "Divinity School Address," an essay/speech in
which the most celebrated nineteenth-century American lecturer advises future Christian ministers to rely on intuition rather than Christian
doctrine. A more modern example comes from Joseph Heller's celebrated anti-war novel, *Catch-22*, particularly in the scene in which the
protagonist, Yossarian, argues with his girlfriend, Lt. Scheisskopf's
wife, and ends up calling the God of the Puritans to task for all the evil
in the world:

> "And don't tell me God works in mysterious ways," Yossarian con-
> tinued, hurtling over her objection. "There's nothing so mysterious about
> it. He's not working at all. He's playing. Or else He's forgotten about us.
> That's the kind of God you people talk about—a country bumpkin, a
> clumsy bungling, brainless, conceited, uncouth hayseed. Good God, how
> much reverence can you have for a Supreme Being who finds it necessary
> to include such phenomena as phlegm and tooth decay in His divine sys-
> tem of creation? What in the world was running through that warped,
> evil, scatological mind of His when He robbed old people of the power
> to control their bowel movements? Why in the world did He ever create
> pain? . . . we musn't let Him get away scot-free for all the sorrow He's
> caused us. Someday I'm going to make Him pay. I know when. On
> Judgment Day. . ."
>
> "Stop it! Stop it!" Lieutenant Scheisskopf's wife screamed suddenly,
> and began beating him ineffectually about the head with both fists. . .
>
> "What the hell are you getting so upset about?" he asked her bewil-
> deredly in a tone of contrite amusement. "I thought you didn't believe in
> God."
>
> "I don't," she sobbed, bursting violently into tears. "But the God I
> don't believe in is a good God, a just God, a merciful God."[12]

Perhaps one of the most interesting and entertaining products of
American's Puritan intellectual foundation is found in Tom Wolfe's
classic piece of New Journalism from 1968, *The Electric Kool-Aid Acid
Test*, the chronicle of a group of hippies who dub themselves the Merry
Pranksters, led by *One Flew Over the Cuckoo's Nest* author Ken Kesey.
The book tells of how the Pranksters, through their experimentations
with the hallucinogenic drug LSD, become in essence post-modern
Puritans: while Edwards and the Mathers preach the good news of
Christian salvation, the Pranksters preach the good news of LSD. The

centerpiece of the Puritan religious ritual is the Communion bread and wine, just as the centerpiece of the Pranksters's ritual is LSD. The Puritans believe that one is either saved by divine grace or is not, just as the Pranksters believe that "either you are on the bus or you are off the bus," that is, either you are transformed by the hallucinogenic experience or you are not—in either case there is no middle ground.

The Puritan influence also reaches out, of course, beyond the world of literature and can easily be spotted in the world of politics. According to *Newsweek* magazine, for example, twenty-two percent of those who voted in the 2004 presidential election said they were more concerned with gay marriage than they were with the war in Iraq, and seventy-nine percent of those voted in favor of George W. Bush, a longtime and vociferous opponent of gay marriage.[13] Even into the twenty-first century, a romantic union of two people of the same sex—which violates nobody's rights—is largely considered to be more morally repugnant than a war that kills and threatens hundreds of thousands of innocents and is waged for reasons that are, at best, questionable.

In sum, the Puritans' great gift to the people of the United States is the rich set of metaphors they brought with them—not to mention the unshakable faith in the privilege, promise and duty that comes with being an American.

The Sanctity of the Individual

When being interviewed by PBS's Bill Moyers for a PBS program in the mid-1980s, comparative mythologist Joseph Campbell discussed how, while reading *The Quest for the Holy Grail*, he was struck with an insight. That thirteenth-century text, Campbell said, "epitomizes an especially Western spiritual aim and idea, which is, of living the life that is potential in you and was never in anyone else a possibility." He then goes on to say, "this, I believe, is the great Western truth: that each of us is a completely unique creature and that, if we are ever to give any gift to the world, it will have to come out of our own potentialities, not someone else's."[14]

If the word "West" in Campbell's utterance were replaced with the word "America" or the phrase "the United States," the statement's meaning would hardly change. Even though the countries of Western Europe are certainly part of the West, the United States remains in many ways the pinnacle of the Western world, or more precisely, the place where the ideals of European individualism can be brought to fruition. This much is brought to light earlier in the interview, when Moyers and Campbell discuss the significance of the Great Seal of the United States, something Campbell describes as, more or less, an image that is to the followers of the God of Reason what the crucifix is to Christians. Campbell says,

> We need myths that will identify the individual not with his local group but with his planet. A model for that is the United States. Here were thir- teen different little colony nations that decided to act in the mutual inter- est, without disregarding the individual interest of any of them. . . . That's what the Great Seal is all about. I carry a copy of the Great Seal in my pocket in the form of a dollar bill. Here is the statement of the ideals that brought about the formation of the United States. Look at this dollar bill. Now here is the Great Seal of the United States. Look at the pyramid on the left. A pyramid has four sides. There are the four points of the com- pass. . . . When you're down on the lower levels of the pyramid, you will be either on one side or the other. But when you get up to the top, the points all come together, and there the eye of God opens. . . . Over here we read, "In God We Trust." But that is not the god of the Bible. [The Founding Fathers] did not believe in a Fall. They did not think the mind of man was cut off from God. The mind of man, cleansed of secondary and merely temporal concerns, beholds with the radiance of a cleansed mirror a reflection of the rational mind of God. Reason puts you in touch with God. Consequently, for these men, there is no special revela- tion anywhere, and none is needed. . . . All men are capable of reason. That is the fundamental principle of democracy.[15]

The matter is discussed in even greater depth in the essay "Indivi- dualism in a Trans-National Context" by Richard O. Curry and Law- rence B. Goodheart. Here, the two historians point out how "indivi- dualism (or more precisely, that what has been called individualism) has had a more pervasive influence and, indeed, a more positive con- notation in the United States than elsewhere in Western culture."[16] To Curry and Goodheart the concept of individualism, while challenging and complex, is not amorphous, but is, rather, "a chameleonlike con- cept—one that encompasses or affects diverse aspects of American life in fundamentally different ways."[17] They then go on to list the numer- ous components of individualism that pervade the American ethos. Among the most important of these are:

> 1. A supreme and intrinsic value of the human being; the right, if not the obligation, of self-development and self-cultivation; the idea of self- direction or autonomy;

2. The right to "a private existence within a public world";

3. Economic individualism, which emphasizes the idea of economic liberty and its concomitants, namely, the sanctity of private property and a free and competitive market; and

4. The right to religious individualism, which "rejects the idea that individuals need intermediaries to communicate with God," and promotes the idea that each individual has the right, if not the duty, to establish their own personal relationships with God.[18]

To be sure, all such statements are merely extrapolations on what virtually every American already knows: that the foundational philosophy of the country is the belief that it is a self-evident truth that each person is created equal, at least in the eyes of the Creator, and, at least in theory, in the eyes of the law. Each person has the God-given right to freedom of speech and expression, freedom of religion, freedom to assemble and freedom to petition the government for redress of grievances; the right to be free from unreasonable search and seizure and self-incrimination, the right to trial by jury, the right to property and, of course, the right to fail.

In American literature we see this expressed boldly and unequivocally in some of the most celebrated masterpieces. Perhaps the most obvious examples are the essays and lectures of Emerson and his colleague, Henry David Thoreau. Emerson, for instance, announces in his essay, entitled appropriately enough "Self-Reliance," that "nothing is at last sacred but the integrity of one's own mind," a sentiment that is a recasting of his comment from a few years previous that the "the highest revelation" a person can receive is "that God is in every man."[19] Thoreau, meanwhile, takes the matter further by isolating himself in the woods near Walden Pond outside Concord, Massachusetts, for two years, two months and two days in an experiment in which he seeks to live simply and independently and unlike "the mass of men" whom he believes "lead lives of quiet desperation."[20] Thoreau tells us in the chapter entitled "What I Lived For,"

I went to the woods because I wished to live deliberately, to front only the essential facts of life, and see if I could not learn what it had to teach, and not, when I came to die, discover that I had not lived. I did not wish to live what was not life, living is so dear; nor did I wish to practise resignation, unless it was quite necessary. I wanted to live deep and suck out all the marrow of life, to live so sturdily and Spartan-like as to put to rout all that was not life, to cut a broad swath and shave close, to drive life into a corner, and reduce it to its lowest terms, and, if it proved to be mean, why then to get the whole and genuine meanness of it, and publish its meanness to the world; or if it were sublime, to know it by experience, and be able to give a true account of it in my next excursion. For most men, it appears to me, are in a strange uncertainty about it, whether it is of the devil or of God, and have *somewhat hastily* concluded that it is the chief end of man here to "glorify God and enjoy him forever."[21]

In later texts, this spirit of self-reliance the two Transcendentalists speak of becomes personified in the lone cowboy or frontiersman, characters like the nameless protagonist of Clint Eastwood's 1973 Western film *High Plains Drifter*, the story of a mysterious loner who appears in a small Arizona town in the days of the Wild West. In a more contemporary setting we see much of the same attitude and values in Ken Kesey's 1963 masterpiece, *Sometimes a Great Notion*, a novel about the Stamper logging family living along the Oregon coastal range. The ideals of individualism are very much at the center of the book, which pits the Stampers, and especially their leader, Hank, against the local union, the very conception of which opposes individualism. The novel, in fact, begins with a powerful statement regarding the matter. A day after he had agreed to scale back his operation so as to allow the striking loggers to return to work, Stamper changes his mind and decides to make one final delivery to the local saw mill, a move that infuriates the town and especially the union officials. To indicate his change of heart to the townspeople camped across the river from his house, Stamper makes a tacit and gruesome announcement. Kesey tells us how

> A pack of hounds pads back and forth, whimpering with cold and brute frustration, whimpering and barking at an object that dangles out of their reach, over the water, twisting and untwisting, swaying stiffly at the end of a line tied to the tip of a large fir pole . . . jutting out of a top-story window.
>   Twisting and stopping and slowly untwisting in the gusting rain, eight or ten feet above the flood's current, a human arm, tied at the wrist, (just the arm, look) disappearing downward at the frayed shoulder where an invisible dancer performs twisting pirouettes for an enthralled audience (just the arm, turning there, above the water).[22]

A few pages later, the horrific image and its message becomes even clearer when the omniscient narrator tells us that

Whoever hanged the arm from its pole had made certain that it was as much a gesture of grim and humorous defiance as the old house; where whoever had taken the trouble to swing the arm out into the sight of the road had also taken the trouble to tie down all the fingers but the middle one, leaving that rigid and universal sentiment lifted with unmistakable scorn to all who came past.[23]

While the there is no mistaking the surface meaning of The Finger, the image also reverberates on other levels as it suggest that Stamper, who like the arm is "cut off" from the other loggers and townspeople, is standing tall and standing alone, that he is number one and that he is, as the saying goes, "looking out for number one." This sentiment is not lost on commentator Gilbert Porter who comments that while in *"Cuckoo's Nest* Kesey examined what the hero owes to others . . . in *Sometimes a Great Notion* he examines what the hero owes to himself— and paradoxically, how being true to the self ultimately serves the community."[24]

The emphasis on the individual over the group also informs other dimensions of the American experience, not the least of which is that which is so often referred to as the American Dream—the idea that spiritual and economic salvation can be attained through honest hard work. According to political economist Max Weber, it is precisely this cross-pollination of Protestantism and capitalism that has fueled the American economy since the arrival of the Puritans and certainly provided the nation with a willing workforce during the Industrial Revolution.

Such rights necessarily involve the right to fail—in America, each person lives or dies, falls or flies, due to his own choices. In the face of failure, sanctity for the individual also provides a path toward salvation through the opportunity for self-reinvention. Both of these dynamics come together poetically in *The Great Gatsby*, the story of a poor World War I soldier named James Gatz who reinvents himself as the prosperous socialite Jay Gatsby, a character whom narrator Nick Carraway tells us "sprang from his Platonic conception of himself."[25] As with the hero of the Horatio Alger rags-to-riches dime novel of a century earlier, this capacity for reinvention allows Gatsby to go from poverty and longing to affluence and romance. Ironically enough, the two vehicles Gatsby employs for his reinvention are two other conventions quite often associated with the American experience: capitalism and drugs. Gatsby makes his fortune by teaming up with a bootlegger, Meyer

Wolfshiem, a gangster who understands that prohibition laws take a relatively inexpensive product and make it quite profitable.

Finally, sanctity of the individual means the freedom to express oneself freely. While the United States has banned more than its share of books—classics such as Walt Whitman's *Leaves of Grass*, Ray Bradbury's *Fahrenheit 451*, J.D. Salinger's *The Catcher in the Rye* and Charles Darwin's *The Origin of the Species*, to name but a few—one of the founding principles of the country, one closely associated with the idea that all people are created equal, is that all citizens have the right to express themselves as they see fit, to criticize the government and critique the culture. Certainly, the American literary tradition is rife with examples of literature which challenge cultural values and apathy, masterpieces like Thoreau's *Civil Disobedience* and Martin Luther King's speech from April 4, 1967, "Beyond Vietnam: A Time to Break the Silence," in which he calls the administration of President Lyndon Johnson to task for its involvement in the war in Vietnam, and Toni Morrison's novel *The Bluest Eye*, which indicts the country for the values it imposes on children.

Perhaps one the most stunning examples of this comes by way of Flannery O'Connor's short story "A Good Man Is Hard To Find" which, in many ways, is one of the most offensive and anti-American stories in all of American literature. The story concerns a nameless but obviously middle-class grandmother who considers herself "a lady" and a Christian despite obvious racist and elitist attitudes, who has gone on vacation with her son, Bailey, his wife and their two children. As they drive, the grandmother tells her grandchildren of a "nigger boy" who stole a suitor's watermelon and then reacts to the sight of an indigent child who wears no pants by declaring, "Oh look at the cute little pickaninny! . . . Wouldn't that make a picture now?"[26] The scene is revealing as it shows that the grandmother is blind to the child's plight and can only reduce him to an object, to a picture she might use to spruce up her house. The family then stops at a restaurant called The Tower and visits with its owner, Red Sammy, who dominates his wife to the point of silencing her speech and who lounges around while his wife brings the orders, "carrying the five plates all at once without a tray, two in each hand and one balanced on her arm."[27] Shortly thereafter, the family is lost on a dirt road, one thing leads to another and the car crashes. Soon, they are approached by three men, one of whom is The Misfit, who has just escaped from prison. As The Misfit's henchmen drag the other family members into the woods to execute them,

the grandmother and The Misfit, who is described as having "red an-
kles" and "silver-rimmed spectacles that give him a scholarly look,"[28]
discuss Jesus Christ as well as The Misfit's history. The Misfit provides
her with what amounts to a proletarian résumé, saying,

> I was a gospel singer for a while. . . . I been most everything. Been in the
> arm service, both land and sea, at home and abroad, been twict married,
> been an undertaker, been with the railroads, plowed Mother Earth, been
> in a tornado, seen a man burnt alive oncet. . . . I even seen a woman
> flogged . . . but somewheres along the line I done something wrong and
> got sent to the penitentiary. I was buried alive.[29]

The story climaxes when, after The Misfit and his crew have murdered the grandmother's family in cold blood, the grandmother for the
first time in her life follows Jesus' command that we love our enemies.
She extends maternal love to the convict, saying, "Why you're one of
my babies. You're one of my own children!" At this, "The Misfit
sprang back as if a snake had bitten him and shot her three times
through the chest. Then he put his gun down on the ground and took
off his glasses and began to clean them."[30] The story's denouement is
one of the most notable in American literature as The Misfit comments, "She would of been a good woman . . . if it had been somebody
there to shoot her every minute of her life."[31]

While often regarded as an Existentialist masterpiece, the story also
serves as a Communist allegory. The members of the murdered family
are clearly bourgeois—they, after all, own a car, have the luxury of leisure time and can afford to go on vacation. From his rhetoric, meanwhile, we learn that The Misfit is uneducated, that he has had only one
job that could have been middle-class, as an undertaker, and that that
stint apparently did not last very long. His "scholarly look" designates
him as the intellectual, in this case an autodidact whose job it is, according to Karl Marx, to keep the working class in check and who, in
this case, has united with the common man. Such a Marxist analysis
tells us that, because of their racism, elitism and the ways in which
women are exploited in the story, the grandmother and her family
would not be acceptable in the Communist state and cannot and
should not be saved. Consequently, the shots fired in this story are the
beginning of the working man's revolution, and The Misfit and his
crew are therefore acting heroically and for the good of mankind. We
do not notice this at first because, indeed, a good man is hard to find.

Though inarguably one of the greatest American short stories, "A Good Man Is Hard to Find" illustrates distinctly un-American values. First of all, it attacks the shallowness and hypocrisy of American Christianity by revealing the grandmother—who advises her attacker to "ask Jesus for help" and to "pray, pray"[32]—as a racist and an elitist who tells The Misfit that she can tell that he's got "good blood" as opposed to "common blood"[33]—a statement that completely ignores the dictum that "all men are created equal." Secondly, the picture it paints of the common American is one that is hardly flattering. The children in this story are spoiled and disrespectful while the quaint old grandmother, a recasting of Huckleberry Finn's Widow Douglas, is despicable, someone who is hardly capable of thinking of Black people as human beings. Thirdly, it depicts the American middle class as numbed to the exploitation and oppression that faces it everywhere. Finally, published during the height of the Red Scare of the 1950s, the story promotes an ideology that, if carried out, could easily have led to the downfall of capitalism and the United States itself.

It is indeed ironic that one of America's great innovations is the way (as "A Good Man Is Hard to Find" demonstrates) that it allows for self-criticism, for the free exchange of ideas that could one day lead to its undoing. Nevertheless, it could be argued that much of the power of this story comes from its power to criticize America, from the cherished right—if not the duty—of the individual American to criticize the country when it has been deemed necessary. Certainly this lives at America's ideological core, a value that to this day is incomprehensible to many of the world's denizens. The notion that "all are equal before the law" would seem nonsensical to many Bengalis or Mumbaikars, to whom a caste system might be considered normal, just as it might be to natives of countries where a royal family is an essential part of the culture, such as England or Japan. So radical is the concept, in fact, that, like the nameless grandmother, America as a whole, a country that still struggles with racial profiling, gay marriage and a "glass ceiling" that often prevents women from rising to the topmost corporate ranks, still cannot fully embrace the idea that all humans are created equal.

Pluralism

In a 1998 installment of the radio documentary show *This American Life*, Jonathan Gold, a columnist for the *L.A. Weekly*, discusses the pastrami burrito, sold by Oki-Dog, a Los Angeles hot dog stand. The first food critic to win the Pulitzer Prize, Gold tells how the burrito typifies a trend in Los Angeles, a city that has become known for its "multi-cultural concoctions of things." The creation, he says, is a "truly fearsome creation capable of feeding four people for four days." It is made up of "fried pastrami, fried cabbage, fried peppers, a glob of chili, pickles and onions, if you want 'em, and wrapped inside a burrito, which is to say, food with influences of Chinese food, Jewish food and the Los Angeles chili tradition, wrapped in a burrito, which is Mexican-style, cooked by Japanese guys for an almost exclusively African-American clientele."[34] Surely, the framers of the U.S. Constitution could not have foreseen this kind of cultural overlapping when hammering out the foundation for their new country. In fact, one of their well-respected colleagues, Crèvecoeur, in his 1782 collection *Letters from an American Farmer*, envisions an America that is far more homogenous:

> What then, is the American, this new man? He is either an European, or the descendant of an European, hence that strange mixture of blood, which you can find in no other country. I could point out to you a family whose grandfather was an Englishman, whose wife was Dutch, whose son married a French woman, and whose present four sons have now four wives of different nations. *He* is an American, who leaving behind him all his ancient prejudices and manners, receives new ones from the new mode of life he has embraced, the new government he obeys, and the new rank he holds. He becomes an American by being received in the broad lap of our great *Alma Mater*. Here individuals of all nations are melted into a new race of men, whose labours and prosperity will one day cause great changes in the world.[35]

In the first decades of the twenty-first century, it appears that the typical American has much more in common with the pastrami burrito than the "New Man" the transplanted French intellectual describes since Crèvecoeur's vision only involves descendants of Western Europe while the greasebomb draws from several continents.

Yet while the American version of pluralism, when the magnitude of the country is considered, sets a new standard in cultural and ethnic mixing, it has undoubtedly brought with it a great many challenges, the most obvious of which is racism. While racism and prejudice certainly exist in virtually every other country, in the United States, where the ideological foundation virtually invites the intermingling of people with different values and mores, the problem is dramatically more pronounced.

For illustration we can certainly, once again, turn to Mark Twain and *The Adventures of Huckleberry Finn*, the first major American novel to look the problem square in the face, or else we can look at another American masterpiece, one that is often listed alongside *Moby-Dick* and *The Sound and the Fury* as one of the greatest achievements by an American novelist: William Faulkner's *Absalom, Absalom!* The story concerns Thomas Sutpen who, like many great American characters, rises from abject poverty to a position of power and wealth. With a title that directly recalls the biblical story of King David who, at the death of his favorite son, Absalom, cries out, "Oh my son Absalom, my son, my son Absalom! Would I had died instead of you, O Absalom, my son, my son,"[36] the novel from the beginning bids the reader to compare the two stories of transformation. David slays the giant Goliath—and does so on his own terms—while Sutpen slays the monster of poverty, also on his own terms, before falling into ruin. But just as the America that bred him remains haunted by its most heinous crimes, slavery and the eradication of the native peoples, Sutpen also can never be free from his past, though he tries. After dismissing his Haitian wife and their son upon learning she has traces of African blood, Sutpen moves to rural Mississippi, to Faulkner's famed Yoknapatawpha County, to build his empire. Decades later, Sutpen learns that that child he abandoned, Charles Bon, has not only befriended his son, Henry, but is set to marry his daughter, Judith, and this is enough to destroy both Sutpen and his empire. According to the first-person narrators, Quentin Compson and Shreve McCannon, two college boys who get so wrapped up in the drama and logic of Sutpen's story that they reconstruct secretive meetings and lost conversations, "it's the miscegenation, not the incest,"[37] which topples the Sutpen dynasty.

Even though Faulkner would, some twelve years later, confront the matter of American racism more directly with *Intruder in the Dust*, a novel that has essentially the same premise as Harper Lee's 1960 classic *To Kill a Mockingbird*, a powerful social commentary emerges from *Absalom, Absalom!* As yet another personification of America, as an amplified Horatio Alger hero and as the America's answer to King David, Sutpen represents an America that is well-advised to celebrate the gifts of pluralism rather than collapse with the weight of racism.

Ironically, a different but more progressive take on this same issue comes some four decades earlier from none other than Mark Twain, this time in the 1894 novel *The Tragedy of Pudd'nhead Wilson*, a story that concerns a nursemaid named Roxana who is one-sixteenth Black (and "that sixteenth did not show"[38]) and who switches her infant child, Chambers, with the child she cares for, Tom Driscoll, so that her son might grow up privileged. Although the maneuver ends up ruining both boys' lives, the novel forecasts something that anthropologists and geneticists would come to learn a century later: that so-called "racial" differences are merely facile categorizations that the human mind tries to impose on its world and that, genetically speaking, all humans resemble each other more closely than, say, wolf cubs from the same litter. The story's premise suggests one of the great American principles: with each human mind and body so ready to accept and adapt to other cultures, gene pools, *Weltanschauungen* and languages, people of different clans cannot help but influence, change and transform each other.

Another take on this same subject—and certainly one more pertinent to America in the twenty-first century—comes from Pulitzer Prize winner Jhumpa Lahiri and her 2003 novel, *The Namesake*. A *bildungsroman* in which border-crossing trains become the central motif, Lahiri's first novel follows the life of Gogol Ganguli, an American of Bengali parentage. The story begins with an explanation of how, because of certain bureaucratic mishaps in the days following his birth, the protagonist ends up being named after his father's favorite writer, the nineteenth-century Russian playwright and pioneer of the short story, Nikolai Gogol, a decision that haunts the family for three decades. From the time he enters kindergarten through the early years of his career as a New York architect, this son of an MIT engineering professor is slowly seduced away from his East Indian traditions and therefore his family, something that is allowed, in no small measure, because of his odd name. As a high schooler, Gogol is very much like the great majority of Americans his age as he enjoys the same things and fights the same demons: marijuana, pop music, teenage angst, philosophical dabblings and the perils of romance.

Gogol's romantic education, however, comes through the various women in his life. The first is his mother, Ashima, whose name means "she who is limitless, without borders"[39] and who, by the end of the book, becomes in many ways the spirit of American pluralism. Next is Ruth, whom Gogol meets when he is in college, a woman who is eventually, like Gogol, seduced away from her culture and traditions. This happens when her initial twelve-week visit to Oxford University becomes an eight-month stay, something their relationship cannot endure. Gogol's second love interest, and in many ways the most significant, is Maxine, or Max, the daughter of a well-to-do Manhattan couple. It is her world of privilege that causes Gogol to separate himself from his parents more than ever. Through the course of their courtship, as Gogol becomes increasingly more deeply settled in Max's world, a world in which it is expected that he will spend the night with Max in her bedroom in her parents' house, he finds that he is "conscious of the fact that his immersion in Maxine's family is a betrayal of his own."[40] Indeed Max and her parents, who "are people who do not go out of their way to accommodate others, assured . . . that their life will appeal to him,"[41] typify an attitude widely associated with white-bread, bourgeois America: because their lifestyle is so obviously one of comfort, privilege and minimal restrictions, it is assumed that it is one which the rest of the world covets, and while there may be room for argument on this point, there is little need for it. And just as Max—whose name and lifestyle hint at bourgeois extremism—has a "habit . . . of not shutting the door when she goes to the bathroom,"[42] affluent America is a place of obscured moral, cultural and personal boundaries.

Yet it is when the seduction is most powerful, when his relationship with Max is creating its own trajectory, that Gogol's toughest challenge begins to take shape. One night during the Christmas season when Gogol is chatting with a group of New York intellectuals at "a book party for one of Maxine's writer friends,"[43] Gogol's father, who is teaching for a year at a "small university outside Cleveland,"[44] dies of a massive heart attack. The next day, the young architect is in his father's last residence where, after collecting his father's belongings in garbage bags and tying up loose ends, he calls Maxine who instructs him, "For God's sake, get out of there. Check yourself into a hotel."[45]

Even though Gogol, who "is accustomed to obeying her, to taking her advice," initially consents, the power of his need to reconcile with all that he has spent years rejecting proves to be too strong. He calls a hotel and

> asks if there are any rooms available for the night, but while he is on hold he hangs up. He doesn't want to inhabit an anonymous room. As long as he is there, he doesn't want to leave his father's apartment empty. He lies on the couch in the dark, in his clothes, his body covered by his jacket, preferring that to the stripped mattress in the bedroom. For hours he lies in the dark, falling in and out of sleep. He thinks of his father, in the apartment just yesterday morning, what had he been doing when he'd begun to feel so badly? Was he at the stove making tea? Sitting on the so-

fa, where Gogol sits now? Gogol imagines his father by the door, bend-
ing over to tie his shoelaces for the last time. Putting on his coat and
scarf and driving to the hospital. Stopping at the traffic light, listening to
the weather report on the radio, the thought of death absent from his
mind. Eventually Gogol is aware of the bluish light creeping into the
room. He feels strangely vigilant, is if, were he to pay close enough attention, some sign of his father might manifest itself, putting a stop to the
events of the day.[46]

As he "watches the sky whiten"[47] Gogol finds himself ready to assume a fatherly role, first by literally occupying his father's final residence and by returning his father's rental car, and secondly by metaphorically stepping into his father's shoes by taking a leadership role in
a family crisis.

After grieving for ten days in private, according to Indian custom,
Gogol's family invites their friends to their home for a ceremony to
mark the end of the mourning period. Once again the voice of American prosperity, represented by Maxine, tries to lure him away from his
home. Maxine, who feels "useless" and "a bit excluded in this house
full of Bengalis," suggests to Gogol that they "try to go on up to New
Hampshire" for New Year's Eve, but Gogol declines. To this, Maxine
says, "It might do you good. . . . To get away from all this," the implicit
message being that American luxury can be a worthy substitute for ancient ceremony. Gogol, however, counters by saying, "I don't want to
get away."[48] Whether he is conscious of it or not, Gogol has heeded his
father's message and allowed himself to become the new head of the
family.

The final stage of Gogol's growth is marked by his marriage to
Moushumi, another Bengali-American whom Gogol has known since
childhood. A doctoral student in French literature at New York University, Moushumi is very much the bride Gogol's parents have
dreamed of. Gogol and Moushumi's wedding resembles theirs, Moushumi understands their customs and their families are not strangers.

Yet, this relationship also fails after Moushumi begins an affair
with a German literature specialist named Dimitri Desjardins, an old
flame who is described as "wiry, slight, with small, downward-sloping
eyes and an intellectual, ravaged-looking face that she found sexy
though not handsome."[49] This, combined with a first name that recalls
Demeter, the Greek fertility deity, and a last name that translates literally as "of the gardens," suggests that Dimitri is a man of great potential and reproductive powers who is in danger of getting walked on.

Gogol learns of the affair one day, also during the Christmas season, when, while on a train to visit his mother, Moushumi tries to convince him that they should spend the summer in Siena, Italy:

> Gogol was resisting, when she said, "Dimitri says Siena is something out of a fairy tale." Immediately a hand had gone to her mouth, accompanied by a small intake of breath. And then, silence. "Who's Dimitri?" he'd asked. And then: "Are you having an affair?" The question had sprung out of him, something he had not consciously put together in his mind until that moment. . . . His first impulse had been to get out at the next station, to be as physically far from her as possible.[50]

This leads inevitably to a divorce and the story concludes a year later when Gogol, while at his mother's Christmas party, goes upstairs to get a camera and runs across a copy of Nikolai Gogol's short stories that his father had given him on his fifteenth birthday. We are told how Gogol

> turns to the first story, "The Overcoat." In a few minutes his mother will come upstairs to find him. "Gogol," she will say, opening the door without knocking, "where is the camera? What's taking so long? This is no time for books," she will scold, hastily noting the volume open against the covers, unaware, as her son has been all these years, that her husband dwells discreetly, silently, patiently within its pages. "There is a party downstairs, people to talk to and food to be taken out of the oven . . . come see the children under the tree" . . . But for now his mother is distracted, laughing at a story a friend is telling her, unaware of her son's absence. For now, he starts to read.[51]

The simple final gesture brings the story to a tidy close as it signifies that Gogol has made peace not only with his father and childhood, but also with the nineteenth-century Russian influence on his identity, just as Ashima has made peace with her husband's passing and American cultural rituals.

Ultimately, it is Ashima, she who is without borders, who becomes *The Namesake*'s attendant spirit and perhaps even the spirit of American literature's future. With each passing year, as America's cultural influence expands, as the rule becomes less homogenization and more hybridization, the tired comparison of America to a melting pot becomes increasingly inadequate, since various colors of wax blended together eventually even out to brown or gray. Instead, despite the ostensible comedy in creations like the pastrami burrito, the green chile bagel, Stauffer's Lean Cuisine Greek Style French Bread Pizza, the Our Lady of Guadalupe origami statue or the hip-hop song composed specifically for a Jews for Jesus revival, the United States throughout the course of the twentieth century has become an increasingly dynamic cultural mosaic, created from various traditions, languages, customs, *Weltanschaungen* and ethoi that are constantly being refined, introduced, discovered, rediscovered, shared, forgotten, blended, resurrected and watered down so as to make the country and its populace richer in terms of its art, culture, language and genetic makeup.

In this way, America is becoming very much like Ashima as it draws from the ultra ancient and ultra modern and is also limitless and without borders.

The Landscape

Finally, one element that cannot be overlooked in a study of the American sensibility is the land itself. Consisting of more than three million square miles and six distinct geographic regions, the terrain between the Atlantic seaboard and the Pacific slope continues to nourish the American soul in two distinct ways. The first concerns the frontier, the quest undertaken by the likes of Columbus and *Star Trek*'s Captain James T. Kirk who hope "to explore strange new worlds, to seek out new life and civilizations and to boldly go where no man has gone before"—never mind that in these cases these "strange new worlds" were already inhabited. Even though the land itself has been explored, the urge to venture into the unknown has continued to inform the American ethos into the twenty-first century. The second way concerns the continent's exaggerated features, features that to this day suggest that Americans, for good or bad, roam among the gods.

Among the first to address the role the frontier played in shaping the American consciousness was Henry Nash Smith, whose 1950 book *The Virgin Land: West as Symbol and Myth* argues that since America's beginning, the frontier has served both pragmatically and mythically as the centerpiece of the American ethos, a source of spiritual and economic revitalization. We could argue, in other words, that the American consciousness began when Columbus pointed the *Santa Maria* west for the first time and set off to explore and conquer a land he didn't even know existed.

We see this spirit manifest in novels like Owen Wister's *The Virginian*, from 1904, a love story set in the Wild West, and Thomas Berger's 1964 classic *Little Big Man*, both of which tell stories of what is commonly thought of as the frontier, while other works such as William Gibson's 1984 science fiction novel *Neuromancer* take us into the frontier world of cyberspace. For other authors, the unexplored territory is more conceptual than spatial. For instance, Kesey's *One Flew Over the Cuckoo's Nest*, Robert Pirsig's *Zen and the Art of Motorcycle Maintenance* and even *Catch-22*, in which the protagonist suffers a nervous breakdown on the streets of Rome, explore realms of madness, regions preeminent American literary critic Leslie Fiedler has argued constitute the true last frontier.[52]

Indeed, the frontier spirit has informed virtually every American story in one way or another and thus it is no coincidence that the novel Ernest Hemingway once praised as that from which all "modern American literature comes,"[53] *The Adventures of Huckleberry Finn*, ends with the protagonist choosing to "light out for the territory ahead of the rest," lest he be "sivilized."[54] As the prototypical American living on the cusp of the ancient and modern worlds, Finn cannot help but be drawn into the frontier.

Not only is the continent expansive, but as one moves from East to West the natural features became harsher, more dramatically beautiful and certainly more exaggerated. For the earliest pioneers, the central lowlands of what is now Minnesota and North Dakota introduced harsh and bitter winters while the Rocky Mountains dwarfed the Appalachians in height, width and length. The Great Plains were indeed great as were the lakes of the northern Midwest, just as the high desert of the Southwest was brutal in both winter and summer. According to Pierce Lewis, professor emeritus at Penn State University, "America's encounter with their land was abrupt and often violent, consuming much of the nation's energies and powerfully gripping its collective imagination. It has been said that America is a nation with an abundance of geography and a shortage of history."[55] Indeed, to subdue such a monster in a scant three centuries, as did the Americans, required confidence, if not outright hubris, as well as a gargantuan pioneering spirit.

The expansiveness and the exaggerated features of the landscape can undoubtedly be seen in the characters who inhabit America's tall tales, one of the most obvious examples of which is Paul Bunyan. A titan of a logger who was said to be "sixty-three axe handles high"[56] and so big he combed his beard with a pine tree,[57] Bunyan represents the indomitable American pioneering spirit that is capable of surviving on and conquering such an awesome terrain. Just as the image of the

American doughboy who, with his exemplary integrity and legendary strength, fought for "truth, justice and the American way" eventually morphed into the image of Superman, Bunyan is nothing less than the American landscape personified. Said to be born in either Wisconsin or Minnesota, that is, where the Great Lakes region opens up to the Great Plains, Bunyan with his great size, strength, stamina, industriousness and horse sense, possesses all the superhuman qualities necessary for those who dared to venture past the Mississippi River.

Even though Bunyan may have been an environmentalist's nightmare who will not stop his chopping "until the last tree is down,"[58] and is the reason that today "there are no traces of pine forests" in the state of North Dakota,[59] his presence nevertheless echoes throughout American literature. He is the man's man who cannot be subdued by anything as trivial as the violence of nature. We see reflections of him in characters such as Lenny, the unwitting murderous retardate in *Of Mice and Men*, in *The Old Man and the Sea*'s Santiago who summons super-human power in his days-long battle with a great marlin, and in Kesey as presented in *The Electric Kool-Aid Acid Test*. Here, Kesey is described in larger-than-life terms as Wolfe tells us that he "looks taller than he really is, maybe because of his neck. He has a big neck with a pair of sternocleido-mastoid muscles that rise up out of his prison workshirt like a couple of dock ropes" and whose "jaw and chin are massive."[60]

Perhaps the most direct heir, however, comes from Kesey himself in *Sometimes a Great Notion*. Descriptions of the book's protagonist, Hank Stamper, virtually demand comparisons with tall-tale heroes. In a moment befitting an anecdote out of the chronicles of Mike Fink or Davy Crockett, for instance, Hank, as a ten-year-old, burrows three times through a berry thicket that is said to be "a wall of thorns that appears totally impenetrable" in order to steal bobcat kittens from their nest, each time crawling back to the clearing with the kitten scruff clenched between his teeth.[61] Later on Stamper describes himself as "one of the Ten Toughest Hombres this side of the Rockies,"[62] and is referred to as a lumberjack who "can hold a double-edged ax straight out arm's length for eight minutes and thirty-six seconds," more than doubling the previous record of "four-ten."[63] Sturdy, unyielding, rugged, larger than life, alluring, seductive, proud, dangerous and independent, Stamper, like Paul Bunyan, is a direct outgrowth of the American landscape.

All this does not mean, however, that the landscape can speak only in harsh terms. Sometimes, in fact, the voice is quite gentle, as when it speaks in *On the Road*, Jack Kerouac's celebrated *roman á clef* from 1951.[64] The story of a young man whose name, Sal (apparently short for Salvatore) Paradise, suggests that he considers himself the "savior of the American paradise," this novel is essentially a Whitmanesque paean to the beauty of the continent. In this scene, with its unmistakable nod to the passage in Walt Whitman's "Song of Myself" in which the poet sounds his "barbaric yawp over the roofs of the world," Paradise, true to his name and the Emersonian tradition, cannot help but commune with nature as he wanders outside while visiting a small Colorado town:

> I wondered what the Spirit of the Mountain was thinking, and looked up and saw jackpines in the moon, and saw ghosts of old miners, and wondered about it. In the whole eastern dark wall of the Divide this night there was silence and the whisper of the wind, except in the ravine where we roared; and on the other side of the Divide was the great Western Slope, and the big plateau that went to Steamboat Springs, and dropped. . . . We were on the roof of America and all we could do was yell, I guess. [65]

For Kerouac, the spirits of the land at other times appear in more subtle, but no less powerful ways, such as in this scene in which he encounters a "rawhide oldtimer Nebraska farmer" whose laugh, reminiscent of Bunyan's, could be heard "clear across the plains, across the whole gray world." Paradise cannot help but be moved by this character, a man who personifies the West in much the same way that Bunyan personifies the continent. Says Paradise, "He didn't have a care in the world and the hugest regard for everybody. I said to myself, Wham, listen to that man laugh. That's the West."[66]

Thus it seems that the land itself speaks through such characters. Even though Judeo-Christian tradition tells us unequivocally that God created "humankind in Our own image, according to our likeness; and let them have dominion over the fish of the sea, and over the birds of the air, and over the cattle, and over all the wild animals of the earth, and over every creeping thing that creeps upon the earth,"[67] passages like Kerouac's suggest that the North American landscape has throughout the centuries continued to infect, shape and inform American consciousness.

For students of the Puritans and those who hold hard and fast to Enlightenment values, all this may sound counterintuitive. The opening pages of Genesis, after all, tell us that Adam, Eve and their progeny were created to have domain over the Earth, not the other way around. Yet, as stories like those mentioned above indicate, the landscape indeed speaks out and does so in myriad voices. So profound is its impact, in fact, that the argument can be made that with each passing year the American, shaped by the landscape, is becoming increasingly more like those native peoples who tended to see themselves as part of the earth rather than above it. Consider, for instance, that while the earliest European settlers looked askance at Native practices such as serial monogamy, daily bathing, a gentle hand in the rearing of children and treating women as equals,[68] at the beginning of the twenty-first century we see that such native sensibilities are becoming the norm: the divorce rate continues to hover around fifty percent and it is not uncommon for divorced Americans to have two or three marriages—so serial monogamy is becoming the rule rather than the exception. Similarly, most Americans regard a shower as part of a daily routine and increasingly frown upon sexism and the beating of children. Furthermore, organic foods are becoming more popular, the environmentalist movement is becoming stronger and one's gender is regarded as more a matter of spirit than of genitalia. It seems that the American is, each day, for one reason or another, becoming more Indian.

Could it be that the earth is exerting its domain over humans?

The Stand-Up Comedian and the American

In many ways, the stand-up comedian is *the* American.

Because the art form is so reliant on freedom of speech, individual points of view, and the benefits of a dynamic urban economic climate that include widespread literacy and ample leisure time, it could have come into being only in the United States, and only after the great changes of the late nineteenth century. And even though it flourishes in other lands, by and large, stand-up comedy remains a distinctly American expression, regardless of the comedian's country of origin. As he literally stands alone on stage, most often relying on only himself and the material he himself has written for a successful performance, the comedian represents an Emersonian hero of sorts. When George Carlin, for instance, reveals the humor of parental clichés like, "Well it just didn't up and walk away, did it?" "Get down off of there—you'll break your neck," or "I suppose if Johnny Finnegan jumped off the Empire State building, you would have to jump off the Empire State Building,"[69] he points out to us the unappreciated humor of our own childhood experiences. By doing so he has, willy-nilly, illustrated Ralph Waldo Emerson's dictum that "to believe your own thought, to believe what is true for you in your private heart, is true for all men,—that is genius."[70]

Similarly, just as Emerson points out that we that we hold Moses, Plato and Milton in high regard because they "spoke not what men wrote but what they [themselves] thought," we see Chris Rock in his act reject any kind of ethnic or jurisprudential loyalty in favor of providing his personal responses to what he observes. In his 1996 show *Bring the Pain*, for instance, Rock discusses how Marion Barry was re-elected mayor of Washington, D.C., after being caught smoking crack cocaine while in office a few years earlier. Rock says, "How the Hell did Marion Barry get his job back? Smoked crack, got his job back. How the Hell did that happen? If you get caught smoking crack at McDonald's, you can't get your job back. . . . They're not gonna trust you around the Happy Meals."[71] Even though it might have been more professionally advantageous for him to champion Black celebrities rather than speak out about such failings, Rock remains true to his convictions and openly questions why Barry has not been held accountable for his actions.

As this case illustrates, the comedian has the freedom, if not the duty, to say things great masses of people find offensive. Whether it is Lenny Bruce using words like "nigger" or "cocksucker" in his act (an utterance that got him arrested[72]), Carlin spitting out "shit, piss, fuck, cunt, cocksucker, motherfucker and tits"[73] in rapid succession, or Rock discussing at length the difference between "Black people" and "niggers,"[74] the comedian, like the person who burns the U.S. flag to demonstrate that the right to free expression is meaningless unless it is exercised, guards one of America's most cherished and fundamental rights.

Furthermore, the comedian also serves as the steward of the American paradise. To put the matter in more realistic terms, we can say that many comedians have, especially since the advent of the New Wave comedians of the 1950s, undertaken the task of pointing out exactly where and how the great American experiment is failing and of reminding us what is at stake. Consider, for instance, another bit from *Bring the Pain*. Here, Rock examines the gap between the American dream and the American nightmare,[75] saying:

Crack everywhere. Crack everywhere. You know what they say: "Crack is destroying the Black community. Crack is destroying the ghetto." Yeah, like the ghetto was so nice before crack. They say that like everybody in the hood had a mansion, a yacht and a swimming pool. Crack came by and dried it all up.

We always focus on the negative side of crack. . . . What about the good side of crack? What about the beauty of crack? What about the good things that crack has brought into our lives that were not here before? You know what the good side of crack is? If you are there at the right hour, you can get a VCR for a dollar-fifty.[76]

By simultaneously reminding us that the country is a nation of wealth and that crack sales are a function of poverty and desperation, Rock lets us know, in no uncertain terms, that the vision of the American Eden that has lived in the world's imagination since the days of Columbus remains a pipe dream and thus, the nation as a whole has a lot more work to do. Later on in *Bring the Pain*, while deep into a diatribe about the difference between "Black people" and "niggers," he hints at a remedy that seems right out of a Republican Party manifesto:

I see some Black people looking at me like, "Man, why you gotta say that? It ain't us, it's the media. It ain't us, it's the media. The media has distorted our image to make us look bad. Why must you come down on us like that, brother? It ain't us, it's the media." Please cut the fuckin' shit, okay? Okay? When I go to the money machine tonight, I ain't looking over my back for the media. I'm looking for niggers. Ted Koppel ain't never took shit from me. Niggers have.[77]

The implication here, as in so much of Rock's work, is that while social commentators—other comedians among them—can blame the country's long history of oppression and social inequality for its shortcomings, much of the responsibility for building and maintaining the American Eden also rests on the shoulders of the participants, from all sectors, who must be held accountable for their own actions.

And the comedian owes quite a bit to the nation's Puritan foundation. Despite the monumental and revolutionary accomplishments of those seventeenth-century American religious fundamentalists, one of their most important contributions to the American ethos was a restrictive, if not an oppressive, social climate, an attitude that is summed up by H.L. Mencken's hyperbolic comment that Puritanism is the "haunting fear that someone, somewhere, may be happy."[78] Since the arrival of the *Arabella*, virtually every American artistic statement expresses either support for or a reaction against Puritanism. Even into the twenty-first century, Americans, by and large and directly because of the Puritan influence, are likely to consider things sexual or corporeal as "dirty," while violence can be considered acceptable and perhaps even clean, an irony Bruce pointed out more than once. This, nevertheless, serves the comedian well. After all, jokes and comic bits more often than not explore areas of tension. With admonitions that, to this day, inform and shape American life, the Puritans set in place a strong foundation upon which comedy could be built. It is hardly surprising, then, that comedians so often joke about exactly those indulgences—indulgences in sex and liquor, for example—that the Puritans deemed supremely evil.

When Rodney Dangerfield jokes about adultery—for example, "With my wife, I never get a break. We made a rule that we only smoke after sex. I've got the same pack now since 1975. And my wife, she's up to three packs a day," or "My wife, she told me I was one in a million. I find out, she was right,"[79]—he takes us into dangerous territory, exploring the harsh potentialities of intimate relationships. Much of the power of these jokes, like so many others that are presented on the comedy club stage, is drawn from the way they challenge the Puritan spirit that hovers over the nation, reminding us that such sexual license is unconscionable and that such matters should not be discussed in public.

Finally, the comedian tells us that even though the United States has historically been a nation of "little men," the American nevertheless still roams among the gods. On the one hand, most vignettes emanating from the stand-up stage tend to be about the common plights of the common man. Consider, for instance, the great number of stand-up bits that concern the mundanities of daily life: Jackie Mason riffs about for four minutes about his getting a parking ticket; Jerry Seinfeld finds high comedy in his discovering a hair on a shower, riding in a cab or watching a parakeet flying into a mirror just as Roseanne discusses how, when her husband said, "Roseanne, I need my space" she, in turn, "locked him outside."[80] On the other hand, good comedy, like religious ritual, invites us into strange and magical realms filled with extraordinary occurrences—to places where Richard Pryor converses with a crack pipe, Bill Cosby tells us how Yahweh said to Noah, "How long can you tread water?" and where Flip Wilson's persona Geraldine Jones can negotiate with the Devil himself.

When taken as a whole, the corpus that is stand-up comedy becomes the most pluralistic and democratic of expressions. Jim Gaffigan, Brian Regan and Tim Allen provide for us glimpses into life in suburbia, just as Pryor, Steve Harvey and Eddie Griffin paint pictures of life in the inner city; Alex Reymundo and George Lopez discuss growing up in the barrio and Jeff Foxworthy and Ron White reveal the dysfunctions and secret fears of unsophisticated Southerners. Jonathan Winters, Emo Philips and Ellen DeGeneres, meanwhile, become America's court jesters, taking silliness to new levels, while Dennis Leary, Dennis Miller and Lewis Black take the opposite approach by building their acts around anger and venom. It seems that for every attitude, every societal sector and every political stance, there is at least one comedic spokesperson.

It is hardly surprising, then, that even though numerous theorists, both amateur and professional, have tried to isolate subconscious forces that might lead someone to the comedy club stage, no one has been able to convincingly identify any similarities beyond intelligence and a sense of humor. Comedy writer and historian Larry Wilde, for instance, once said that he "had a theory that all people go into professional comedy for one of three reasons: They come from poverty-stricken circumstances; they are members of a minority and/or they didn't get enough love as a child." When he posed this to Jerry Seinfeld, the comedian, who was on the verge of becoming a major star, responded with:

> If there is a psychological reason, I don't really know about it. I consider myself well-adjusted. I think there's a lot of unhappy people driving bread trucks and nobody cares about it. When it's a comedian, people find it very poignant if he's off-stage maybe not so happy and on-stage he's making everybody laugh. I don't think you can pin it down.
>
> It's really funny that God has chosen to give a sense of humor to a certain group of people. There is no rhyme or reason to it. I'm sure you've noticed this. If you put them all together, the shapes, sizes, personalities, loud, obnoxious, terribly introverted. I can barely see a thread of any kind running through this group. They have wonderful senses of humor. Some of them are in pain, but some are like everybody else—I don't really see a thread.[81]

The power of stand-up is that the performer is like everybody else—except a bit funnier.

Thus it seems that there is a very good reason the United States is the country that gave the world stand-up comedy and has continued to nurture it for more than a century: in addition to welcoming and including (at least in principle) a multiplicity of nationalities, ethnicities, jurisprudences, *Weltanschauungen*, ethoi and voices, it is a country that provides its denizens, as well as the rest of the world, plenty to disagree with while inviting (at least in principle) dialogue and free expression.

In short, we can say that because of this as well as the immediacy of the art form, stand-up comedy, when taken as a whole, is *the* great American chorus, one in which millions of voices can sing out as they may.

CHAPTER THREE
JOKE THEORIES

The Traditional Theories

One day I brought a video clip of comedian Sam Kinison, a gifted performer famous for screaming his punchlines, into my morning intro to literature class. The ten-minute segment was taken from a 1986 Rodney Dangerfield HBO special and involved a classic Kinison aside in which Kinison compares sex therapy to dog psychology. "I'd like to get in on some of that cash," the comedian says, and then proceeds to act out the part of a dog owner who is distraught because, "It's Rusty, man. I don't know. He used to be a sparky dog. He was a happy dude, man. He used to play with the Frisbee. And he hasn't been himself lately. He's losing his identity." Kinison then switches to the role of the dog psychiatrist, reassures the owner and heads into the therapy room where, using the microphone cord as a whip, beats the dog and screams, "You're a fuckin' dog! You understand that? You shit in the yard! Bark! Bark! Bark, you son-of-a-bitch." When the psychiatrist reemerges he tells the owner, "Rusty's all better now. We had a real good session. That'll be two hundred bucks."[1]

The students roared with laughter at this bit and talked about it for days, drawing connections between Kinison's act and the Freudian theory we had been discussing. When I showed the same clip to my afternoon introduction to literature class, the consensus was that Kinison was "obnoxious" and "annoying." Not a single person thought he was funny. I found the different responses both disconcerting and fascinating. What was the difference? Was it the time of day? Was it the mood in the room? If so, what influenced that mood? Was it the collection of people? While any one or even all of these factors could have played significant roles, it seems that a theorist would be hard-pressed to produce a system for accurately predicting such reactions.

The fact of the matter is that, even in a time when physicists are unraveling the secrets of the universe, producing a single theory that explains everything in nature from blips of energy that make up subatomic particles to an endless string of universes, laughter remains a mystery. Even though the worlds of psychology and psychoanalytic theory have produced almost ninety different theories of humor by one count,[2] in the literary world humor and laughter have received scant attention throughout the ages when compared with tragedy and pathos. Over the centuries, philosophers, theologians and literary critics have considered the subject to be trivial if not downright dangerous. Plato advised against laughter, warning that it "darkened the soul" and that what makes a person laughable is "self-ignorance,"[3] while Aristotle, the father of literary criticism, felt that laughter was little more than "educated insolence."[4] In the seventeenth century British philosopher Thomas Hobbes argued that laughter is a sign of cowardice and comes from "a sudden glory arising from some conception of eminency in ourselves in comparison with the infirmity of others, or with our own formerly" and could be harmful to a person's character.[5] Immanuel Kant commented, "In everything that is to excite a lively convulsive laugh, there must be something absurd (in which the Understanding, therefore, can find no satisfaction). Laughter is an affection arising from the sudden transformation of a strained expectation into nothing."[6]

Although other commentators, like Lord Shaftesbury in the seventeenth century and Arthur Schopenhauer two hundred years later, were more positive, it was not until Sigmund Freud and his 1905 study *Wit and Its Relation to the Unconscious* that the tide began to turn and humor and jokes began to be accepted as subjects worthy of study. Although there have been various informative contributions to the dialogue such as Eliot Oring's theory of "appropriate incongruity"[7] and Morreall's argument that laughter results from a "pleasant emotional shift,"[8] over the centuries three major theories have dominated the discussion of humor and laughter: Relief Theory, Superiority Theory and Incongruity Theory. Each of these is helpful and provides plenty of insight into the matter, although no single theory explains every laughter situation. In fact, when taken together, the three theories still cannot explain all laughter events.

Here is a summary of each.

Relief Theory

Without question, the most important voice regarding Relief Theory is Freud himself. In short, this theory posits that in order for an individual to live in a society, he or she must adhere to certain rules, some of which result in violence being committed against his or her own body. To put the matter another way, we can say that Freud argues that each human being is caught in a tug-of-war: part of us strains to live free as an individual, guided by bodily appetites and aggressive urges, while the other side yearns for conformity and acceptance. This results in every normal person's being continually steeped in psychic tension, mostly due to guilt and lack of fulfillment. This tension can be relieved, albeit temporarily, through joking.[9]

To illustrate, let's consider that a person has been lost in the mountains, has not eaten in three days and finally makes his way to a bakery in a nearby village. Even when in such extraordinary circumstances, this person cannot merely leap over the counter and begin wolfing down doughnuts. Instead, he must go through appropriate channels, such as waiting for the bakery to open, standing in line and paying for his food. A good joke, according to Relief Theory, gives a listener temporary entry into a different world, usually a world free of such constrictions. Comedian John Pinette, for instance, who builds a great deal of his act around his own obesity, takes his audience into a realm where rules such as those described above do not apply. He tells us, "I went to a Chinese all-you-can-eat buffet and, well, the owner—he got pissed. I mean, he was rude though—he'd come out every hour: 'Son-of-a-bitch still here!'"[10]

Relief Theory might also explain the success and popularity of the 2005 film *The Aristocrats*. The movie concerns a host of comedians giving individual takes on a single joke about a family of entertainers who walk into a talent agent's office, commit a variety of obscene, disgusting and brutal acts upon each other and then announce themselves as "The Aristocrats." The strength of such a joke lies not in the punchline, but rather in the extremes the joketellers can explore throughout the course of the set-up. What satisfies the audience, then, is the way the comedian violates taboos as he leads up to the punchline and allows the audience to vicariously experience a world free of restrictive social codes.

A good joke pierces the bubble of social tension, allowing the listener entry into a world liberated from the social restraints that Freud says weigh so heavily upon us.

Superiority Theory

In his 1951 study *The Origins of Wit and Humor*, classical literature scholar Albert Rapp argues that all laughter has developed from one primitive behavior, "the roar of triumph in an ancient jungle duel."[11] Essentially, Rapp argues that laughter is fundamentally a sign that one person (or a group) is dominating while another is being dominated. From this, we can extrapolate that jokes can be classified into three essential categories: (1) jokes that make fun of those more powerful than the joketeller, (2) jokes that make fun of those less powerful than the joketeller and (3) jokes that poke fun at the joketeller himself, thereby positioning the audience in a more powerful position. Or to put the matter in other terms, we can say that, implicitly or explicitly, a power structure exists within each joke.

A classic example of the first type can be found in the Jewish-American Princess cycle that has been popular in the United States over the last few decades, jokes such as, "Why did the Jewish-American princess refuse the colostomy? She couldn't find shoes to match the bag." The appeal of such a joke is that it allows those who have had to struggle financially to poke fun at, and therefore feel superior to, the super-privileged.

Examples of the second kind of joke are the Little Moron or Blonde joke cycles, jokes such as "Why did the Little Moron take a bong to class? It was high school" or "How do you know if a blonde has been using your word-processor? There's Wite-Out on the screen." Such jokes, by virtue of their narrative stance, allow both the teller and the audience to feel superior to the morons and the blondes—even though in such cases the characters are imaginary.

The third type of joke is the stock-in-trade of a great many comedians like Emo Philips and Rodney Dangerfield who build their routines about their hapless and desperate lives. Philips quips, "I'm a great lover, I bet,"[12] suggesting through his jokes and his freakish persona that he is someone to be laughed at, not merely because talks and dresses weirdly but because, as an adult, he is still a virgin. Dangerfield, on the other hand, with jokes such as "When my wife wants to have sex with me there's always a reason for it. One time she used me to time an egg," or "The other night I told my kid, 'Someday you'll have children of your own.' He said, 'So will you'"[13] casts himself as a cuckold and an inept, unloved father. By doing so, he invites his audience to feel superior to him.

Incongruity Theory
Perhaps the most useful, encompassing and comprehensive of the joke theories, at least as far as stand-up comedy is concerned, is Incongruity

Theory, which explains that jokes and laughter are produced through the juxtaposition of incongruous elements. A clear example of this is a common stand-up comedian's joke formula in which a comedian describes an act and then reveals that it is taking place in a grossly inappropriate setting. Comedian John "Hippieman" Novosad, for instance, tells how he likes to spend his Sunday mornings watching football in his underwear before revealing that "the people at the sports bar are getting pissed."[14] Another example is a joke such as "I walk out of church today and somebody tries to sell me a joint. I freak out and I say, as he's counting back my change, 'This doesn't feel right, Father Martinez.'" Obviously, what makes the joke work is that church is not a place where one would expect to buy illegal drugs from a priest.

Usually, a stand-up comedian will juxtapose two points of view. Take, for instance, the classic Emo Philips joke in which he tells how the "guy comes to our house and says, 'I'd like to read your gas meter.' I said, 'Whatever happened to the classics?'"[15] The set-up line provides a scenario that is in accordance with normal, standard behavior. The first story, involves a common everyday act, and that is the point of view planted in the mind of the audience. The punchline, however, shatters that initial image and draws us into a radically different world.

Perhaps this is another reason that the United States, since its very inception, has been fertile ground for humor and why so many of the top-shelf American literary masterpieces, books like *Moby-Dick*, *The Sound and the Fury*, *Tales of Mystery and Imagination*, *Walden*, *Catch-22*, *As I Lay Dying*, *The Sun Also Rises*, *The Adventures of Huckleberry Finn*, *A Good Man Is Hard to Find* and *The Catcher in the Rye*, no matter how dark and disturbing they may be, also work as comedies. America, after all, has historically been a place where various points of view challenge each other, clash, collide and cross-pollinate. This much has been discussed by American humor theorist Constance Rourke, who once commented, "there is scarcely an aspect of the American character to which humor is not related, few which in some sense it has not governed."[16]

A Hybrid Theory: Jokes, Farts and Feces

Let's consider, for illustrative purposes, what well may be a prototypical moment in human history: sometime before the advent of Homo sapiens, one orangutan is threatened by another. He defecates into his hand and hurls the dung at his aggressor.

Could this be the beginning of humor? Could this be the proto-typical, prehistoric version of the pie in the face? The cafeteria food fight?

Such an event has more than a little in common with modern joking. First of all, language throughout the ages has provided us with countless connections between jokes and excrement. The very word "humor," for instance, is derived from the Latinate root *umor*, which means "body fluid" and is associated with "humus" which means "the Earth"—and we are reminded that this is the stuff we are made of each time we defecate. The very word—which the ancient Greeks associated with fluids affecting the temperament—carries with it connotations of "wet, moist" and "becoming wet," [17] qualities that are very much those of fecal matter. Furthermore, a joke, as Kant argued, more often than not takes something of great importance and reduces it to nothing and is like excrement in that it reminds us that, despite the lofty ideals of religion or philosophy, Homo sapiens is an animal, is made of earth, has only a temporary stay on this planet and must participate in killing in order to survive.

The pitching of dung is a curious defensive measure, then, because of its multivalence. Unlike the pitching of a rock or a punch to the face, the act has little potential for long-term damage. Furthermore, feces are among those substances that literary theorist Julia Kristeva mentions in her discussion of "abjection." To Kristeva, "the abject" is "a psychic worrying of those aspects of oneself that one cannot be rid of, that seem, but are not quite, alienable—for example, blood, urine, feces, nails, and the corpse. The 'abject' . . . indicates what cannot be subject or object to you." [18]

If we accept this premise, the act is not only defensive but also quite intimate. Like the semen that is ejaculated during sexual intercourse, the thrown feces obscure personal boundaries, the wall between the subject and the object, or the "I" and the "you." To put it another way, we can say that by hitting the other ape with his own feces, the threatened animal is in a real and direct way giving a part of himself to his aggressor, much the way an infant might "gift" his feces to a parent. [19] This may be one explanation of why feces-throwing is often found in ritual clowning, as in the Kachina ceremonies of certain New Mexico Native American tribes.

Research also shows that apes themselves can be aware of the connection between excrement and jokes. In his thorough discussion, *Laughter: A Scientific Investigation*, Robert Provine tells how psychologist

Roger Fouts, a trailblazer in the field of human-chimpanzee communication, "reported that while riding on his shoulders, the chimpanzee Washoe urinated on him, signing 'funny' (touching her nose) and snorting."[20]

What is of primary interest to me here is that the reaction parallels the common delight that results when children are told stories about how they urinated, defecated or drooled on their parents. If we take the chimpanzee, the human's closest cousin, to be a glimpse into the human past, such an event lends great insight. As a social animal, the chimp instinctively senses that not only are mores being violated, but so are personal boundaries. Also, it appears that all three of the theories mentioned above help explain the reaction: Relief Theory tells us that Washoe laughs because, ironically enough, she is acting like an animal, Superiority Theory tells that it is because she is showing dominance over Fouts, that she is "taking possession" of him the way a wolf might urinate on a tree to mark territory, and Incongruity Theory tells us it is because she is doing the right thing at the wrong time and place.

And laughter, as Provine and Morreall have pointed out, is primarily a social phenomenon,[21] so much so that people often refer to "losing themselves" in mirthful paroxysms. Like the abject, the hurled feces and the act of coitus, laughter obscures the boundaries between the subject and the object, two subjects and, perhaps most important, the hostile and the intimate.

Feces, Flatulence, Speech and Jokes

Comedy giant George Carlin has suggested that we think of "farts as shit without the mess."[22] A fart, after all, is burst of intestinal gas that has much greater potential for obscuring personal boundaries than do feces, for a variety of reasons. First of all, the smelling of, that is, the inhaling of, another person's intestinal gasses immediately links the two bodies more directly and inoffensively than the hurling of feces. It is less offensive because the smell dissipates after a few seconds while the excrement must be scrubbed off. Self-proclaimed fartologist Jim Dawson puts the matter this way:

> A fart's molecules go to the mucous lining at the top of your nose, whereupon they are transported to millions of receptor cells in the membrane lining. There the farty molecules are transmuted into electrical signals that travel along a corridor of nerve fibers into your brain. You and somebody's stray fart have bonded and become one.[23]

Further complicating the issue is that flatulence oftentimes introduces a sonorous quality into a situation. Was it through the expelling of intestinal gas that human beings were introduced to the idea that the digestive tract produces sounds? Was it through the gift of flatulence that we first realized that sounds produced by the digestive tract could affect social circumstances? Is the fart the prototypical speech act?

The rectum and the mouth, after all, both involve mucous membranes and ends of the digestive tract. Each emits sounds and smells. Each is capable of uttering truths and has a tendency for metaphorically "talking shit." The mouth metaphorically "talks *shit*" when the speaker boasts, postures or feigns expertise. The rectum metaphorically "*talks* shit" when the offensive gases introduce fecal molecules into a conversation. Again, linguistic history provides plenty of evidence for such a connection. The word "fool" comes from the Latinate "*follis*," which means, literally, "a bellows" or a "windbag" and suggests a person who, for all the value of his words, may as well be passing gas.[24] In modern vernacular, the jokester is often referred to as an "ass," "asshole," "wise-ass," "smart-ass" or "butthead" and is often said to be "full of hot air," "talking out his ass," "talking shit out his ass" or making "wise cracks."[25]

For an illustration of how this might have developed, most of us need not reach further back than the years of our own adolescence, those days of social and physical awkwardness, times spent straddled between childhood and adulthood. Most of us can also remember those classmates who did not seem prone to the same difficulties as the normal teenager. Their clothes fit too well, their hair remained too perfect, their wit too quick. In ancient times such people were all too readily regarded as superhuman. Oftentimes such people came to be regarded as demi-gods and were granted special status as the emirs, pharaohs, emperors, kings, queens and goddesses who were a cut above the other flawed, imperfect humans. Let's say then, for illustrative purposes, that one of these beings is at the height of his or her glory, that she is performing a dance, that he is beating his chest or is about to be crowned, when suddenly the perceived demi-god breaks wind. Has the rectum spoken a truth? It has, after all, shattered the godly illusion and announced that the person so revered is also imprisoned by the life/death cycle, must participate in killing in order to survive and, most important, is a product of earthly substances. In his foreword to the 1913 reprint of John G. Bourke's study *The Scatological Rites of All Nations*, Freud addresses the matter directly:

[Civilized men] are clearly embarrassed by anything that reminds them too much of their animal origin. They are trying to emulate the "more perfect angels" in the last scene of *Faust*, who complain: "For us there remains a trace of the Earth embarrassing to bear. . . ." [We] have chosen to evade the predicament by . . . denying the existence of this inconvenient "trace of the Earth" and concealing it from one another, and by withholding from it the attention and care which it might claim as an integrating component of [our] essential being.[26]

If the flinging of dung is the prototypically humorous moment, then the breaking of wind may very well be the prototypical joke. After all, dung, albeit in a gaseous form, has been flung. As in the above example involving Washoe and Dr. Fouts, borders between two individual bodies and social mores have been transgressed.

Thus it seems that farts contain a beauty and wisdom all their own as they remind us of our temporary stay upon this earth. The more sonorous and well-timed among them are indeed "wise cracks."

The Conversation between the Id and the Super-ego

Some eight decades after Freud's death a great many scholars, philosophers and theorists (not to mention psychologists) dismiss his work altogether. What is undeniable, however, is that, at the very least, the premier psychoanalyst did present us with a vocabulary with which we could begin to discuss the workings of the human mind. Among his most important contributions to the lexicon are the terms for the layers of the subconscious he called the "id," super-ego," and "ego."

Even with such oversimplified divisions we can better understand the pools of tension a person encounters on a daily basis. As the internal infant or animal, the id is governed by the pleasure principle and seeks food when it is hungry, sex when it is aroused and intoxication for no other reason than to feel good. The super-ego, meanwhile, is the conglomeration of social pressures and internalized parental admonitions. It demands that, if we choose to live among others, we delay fulfillment, we do not fart in church or grab food from another's plate, even if our restraint results in self-inflicted suffering. Most of the time, the super-ego has the upper hand. Even when human beings do act like animals, as they might in the course of battle, coitus or a cafeteria food-fight, the animalistic impulses are always contained and relatively short-lived. The ego, meanwhile, mediates the demands of these two opposing forces.

Freud also approached very much these same conflicts with his observations on the Oedipus Complex, which was detailed in his 1899 book *The Interpretation of Dreams*. In short, Freud argues that an infant's first love object is the mother and, that consequently, the incident father is cast as the first enemy. The child, whether male or female, with its demands for instant gratification, is very much the id, while the parent, the being who slaps the hand when the child acts inappropriately, is the voice of the larger culture and societal decorum.

The conflict for these two forces serves as the wellspring for jokes. For an illustration of this we can turn to another of the stand-up comedian's close cousins, the ventriloquist, an entertainer whose roots also go back to ancient court jesters. The ventriloquist collapses the convention of team comedy in which one performer provides the straight lines and the other supplies the punchlines by providing both from the same source, albeit via different personas. In acts such as Otto and George from the 1990s we can see a very clear division between the two spheres. As the ventriloquist, Otto is the voice of propriety and societal norms. George, meanwhile, is a mealy-mouthed dummy who constantly talks about wanting to have sex with the women in the audience, objectifying his girlfriend, Turtlewaxing his penis and doing other things that would be socially unacceptable under normal circumstances. Throughout the course of their routines, George, of course, gets most of the laughs while Otto pretends to rein him in with scolding and admonishments.

This is odd, considering that nobody is really fooled. Everyone in the audience understands that a ventriloquist is someone who is paid to be two voices, to engage in a one-person conversation. The dummy, in fact, is very much the abject. He is not really subject, not really object. He is the uncensored voice for that which is base, objectionable and yet very much a part of the ventriloquist. Positioned upright on the ventriloquist's lap, he is in place to serve as a penile surrogate, the voice of bodily appetites or the "second head." While it would be inappropriate for Otto to stand on stage and say vile things about his girlfriend like, "My girlfriend gave me skull last night. When she was done my cock looked like a totem pole and her face looked like a glazed doughnut," it is acceptable for Otto to say it if he uses George as a vehicle.

Stand-up comedy also employs this kind of split, although it is more subtle. This can be seen in a typical joke such as this one from comedian Dwight York: "I woke up this morning and my joints were stiff. I shouldn't roll them so thick."[27] Here, the first part of the joke, the set-up, which generates the first story, is totally in accord with social decorum. In fact, it is such a mundane statement that it hardly draws attention to itself. It is the voice of the super-ego, that stuff we have been so steeped in since childhood that it almost becomes part of the background noise. When he comes through with the punchline and the second story reveals that what is of concern to him is not his health but rather his quest for convenient intoxication, then it becomes clear that another voice is speaking, the voice that seeks pleasure even at the price of violating mores and, in this case, civic laws. The power of this joke comes from the way it subverts social norms in favor of the pursuit of pleasure. It teases the super-ego by suggesting the rules will be followed, and then inverts the power paradigm and reveals the irrepressible presence of the id.

The great majority of jokes told on a stand-up comedy club stage seem to follow this pattern and when they do not they tend to be variations on the theme. Even the so-called clean jokes from the likes of Bill Cosby, Steven Wright and Brian Regan tend to pit the two forces against each other. One of the most popular routines of Cosby's early career, for instance, is "Noah," in which he recreates a conversation between the biblical patriarch and Yahweh, the ultimate super-ego. In a later bit, the famous "To Russell, My Brother, Whom I Slept With," a routine about two boys who tease and torment each other while they are sharing a bed, Cosby introduces the character of the father, who quickly becomes a version of the terrorizing super-ego. In later routines, Cosby plays with this theme. Sometimes the super-ego is his wife, sometimes his dentist and sometimes he acts the part while recounting conversations with his own children. Regan exploits the dynamic by consistently (and ingeniously) supplying the voice of the outer, sophisticated proper world and then acting out his childlike reactions to it. For instance, in one Comedy Central installment, he discusses modern physics, specifically Superstring Theory, saying, "I've been trying to get smart. I've been watching *NOVA*. . . . I started watching that thing at eight p.m. and at eight-o-three, my brain exploded. . . . If Albert Einstein don't understand it, me on the couch with a bag of potato chips don't have a shot."[28]

Sometimes, as with comics such as Mort Sahl, Lenny Bruce, George Carlin and Bill Hicks, the dynamic is reversed and the comedian becomes the voice of the super-ego. Consider this bit from the DVD *Bill Hicks—Totally*, recorded in 1994, in which the comedian becomes the super-ego chastising the administration of the President George H.W. Bush:

> Bush—trying to buy votes towards the end of the election, goes around, you know, selling weapons to everyone, getting that military industrial complex vote happening for him—sold a hundred-and-sixty fighter jets to Korea and two-hundred-and-forty tanks to Kuwait. Then goes around making speeches why he should be commander in chief, because [in a Bush voice] "We still live in a dangerous world." Thanks to you, you fucker. What are you doing? Last week the Kuwaitis had nothing but rocks. Quit arming the fuckin' world, man.
>
> You know we armed Iraq. I wondered about that, you know, during the Persian Gulf War those intelligence reports would come out: "Iraq, incredible weapons. Incredible weapons."
>
> "How do you know that?"
>
> [In a Bush voice] "Well . . . we looked at the receipt. But as soon as that check clears, we're going in."[29]

In such a case, and especially considering that Hicks' criticisms and observations were eerily apt and appropriate thirteen years after his death (not even the name of the president had to be changed), he has become the voice of the American conscience while the president and his administration are the entities that act like animals.

The Core of Human Neurosis

The single most recurrent theme in world literature is parental estrangement. A close second is the quest to heal that cleavage. In Greek mythology, for instance, Zeus and Poseidon fight and conquer their father, Cronos, just as Oedipus unwittingly kills his father Laius and marries his mother, Jocasta. Moses' mother puts him in a basket and sends him down the river in order to save his life, a trauma that sets in place his future role as the great liberator. Lao Tzu admonishes people of all ages to "learn to follow the Tao . . . the mother of the Ten Thousand Things"[30] and Adam and Even are expelled from Eden for disobeying their father, Yahweh—never mind that Yahweh put them in a position where failure was inevitable. Even Jesus, according to Matthew's Gospel, cries out with His dying breath that His father has abandoned him.[31]

Often this cleavage is overt, as with Pip in Dickens' *Great Expectations*, the tragedies of Hamlet and King Lear, *The Adventures of Huckleberry Finn*, *The Sound and the Fury*, *The Color Purple*, *One Hundred Years of*

Solitude, "Everything that Rises Must Converge," *The Old Man and the Sea, Tender Is the Night, Like Water for Chocolate, Death of a Salesman, Long Day's Journey Into Night* and movies like *The Godfather, Home Alone* and *Finding Nemo.* At other times, a surrogate parent is the centerpiece of the drama, as are the whale in *Moby-Dick,* the tycoon Dan Cody in *The Great Gatsby,* Randall Patrick McMurphy in *One Flew Over the Cuckoo's Nest* and the title character of Samuel Beckett's play *Waiting for Godot.* At the very least, it appears that even from this cursory examination, literature is a vehicle by means of which human beings can explore, entertain and, at least temporarily, heal this paternal rift.

If stand-up comedy has one advantage over the other literary forms, it is, at least as far as this particular neurosis is concerned, immediacy. While the novel, short story, movie, play and poem can ameliorate the parent/child cleavage through images, stories and wordplay, each of these maintains a certain amount of distance between the artist and the audience. The novel, poem and short story must be committed to paper and letters and the immediacy of the play is compromised by the fourth wall. Perhaps language theorist Walter J. Ong puts the matter best when he writes about the term "audience":

> it is really quite misleading to think of a writer as dealing with an "audience," even though certain considerations may at times oblige us to think this way. More properly, a writer addresses readers—only, he does not quite "address" them either: he writes to or for them. The orator has before him an audience which is a true audience, a collectivity. . . . But "readership" is not a collective noun. It is an abstraction in a way that "audience" is not.[32]

Like the orator, the comedian addresses the audience directly. Unlike the orator, however, the success of his performance is dependent upon his being emotionally accessible and available or, at the very least, cultivating the illusion that he is.

Limon takes up the matter in his seminal book *Stand-up Comedy in Theory or Abjection in America* as he builds much of his argument around the statement that "stand-up is the resurrection of your father as a child,"[33] an observation that is both simple and revealing. The comedian, after all, is in a fatherly role. He (or she, but most often he) faces the opposite direction of everybody else in the room, a situation which puts him at the head of the metaphorical table. He presides over meals and, because of the stage and the microphone, has an elevated stature, a booming voice and a phallic symbol. For the individual audience members, the situation recreates childhood in which the infant or toddler must submit himself to a parent who is infinitely more powerful in terms of both physical strength and vocal presence. Like the father, the comedian is not only the locus of attention, but also the locus of power. This much has been summed up by Dick Gregory, who once commented that "the more power you have, the funnier you are to the audience. You could walk out [as an unknown] and tell some jokes and if they're not funny, people aren't going to laugh. The president could come out and tell the same jokes and people fall off over the table."[34]

I am going to adjust Limon's theory, but only slightly, and argue that the stand-up comedian is your father resurrected as a thirteen-year-old. If we accept the premise that the set-up line is, usually, the voice of the super-ego and the punchline is the voice of the id, what we see is that the comedian is in constant vacillation between the two spheres through the course of a performance. With each joke, the comedian becomes an authority figure who consistently undermines the larger, societal authority. In other words, he is a father who is in command of the room, is emotionally available, unites his community and yet allows himself to be driven by his bodily appetites. Like a thirteen-year-old boy, the comedian has one foot in adulthood and the other in childhood. He is in constant vacillation between the two spheres, those internal longings and the need to "behave," if you will. With each set-up line he tells us that he is well-acquainted with how he is supposed to act. Each punchline, meanwhile, reminds us of his refusal to comply.

In the best-executed stand-up performances, when the audience members and the comedian meld into a single body and individuals transcend their solitary state, the central human neurosis is temporarily healed. The emotionally and physically abandoning father returns, undermines social pressures and brings a family—albeit a surrogate family—together.

CHAPTER FOUR
A STAND-UP PREHISTORY

My contention is that comedy grows out of a conversation, if not a heated argument, between base human instincts and the societal demand for propriety and decorum, between those two regions of the subconscious Sigmund Freud labeled the super-ego and the id. While the literary world has traditionally concerned itself with lofty ideals such as redemption, the eternal, ethics and heroism, comedy of all sorts has, by and large, concerned itself with matters such as bodily functions; pathological urges; physical, mental and emotional handicaps; and mortality. Thus it is hardly surprising that throughout the ages jokesters of all kinds have continued to pay homage to the voice of the base and bodily appetites, those animalistic longings for food, shelter, sex and natural and artificial pleasures, so much that comedians throughout history have often been associated with animals such as the rooster, pig, monkey or jackass.[1] Whether the jokester is considered a descendant of the trickster or a different manifestation of the trickster, he remains, as Joseph Henderson has argued, "a figure whose physical appetites dominate his behavior; he has the mentality of an infant . . . [l]acking any purpose beyond the gratification of his primary needs."[2]

Just like the bullied fourth grader who quickly learns to diffuse tension on the playground by making his aggressors laugh, humans more than likely learned early on—perhaps after the first few fist-fights were averted because of well-timed farts—the role bodily functions play in humor. Consequently, because of its effectiveness in building community, easing social anxieties and celebrating commonalities, joking was something humans had to learn to foster early on because at the very least, it made survival easier. At the very most, it made survival possible.

Thus begins the history of humor, a history that, after countless millennia, produced what we in the twenty-first century call stand-up comedy.

Trickster Tales (50,000 B.C.E–Present)

Virtually every spiritual or mythological system in the history of the planet involves humorous tales of comic deities, the chief exceptions, oddly enough, being among the most influential in recent times: Judaism, Christianity and Islam. Yet from China to the Americas, Tierra del Fuego to Ukraine, ancient myths tell of the comic antics of divine mischief-makers, virtually all of whom fall victim to their bodily appetites—appetites that are often symbolized by enlarged bodily organs such as penises, stomachs or buttocks. There is little doubt that in addition to providing instruction for children about mores and survival, these protostories were also meant to amuse. The preeminent psychoanalyst Carl Gustav Jung has commented that the "trickster has been a source of amusement right down to civilized times, when he can still be recognized in the carnival figures of the Pulcinella and the clown."[3] Ellen Rosenberg tells of the scope and influence of the trickster tale in the Americas, saying that

> trickster figures have been omnipresent since some point from 50,000 to 30,000 years B.C.E., when migrating people of or passing through Northern Asia brought to the Americas a range of shamanic religions and associated Emergence, Earth-Diver, and Trickster narratives. Figures such as Rabbit or Hare, Raven, Spider, Tortoise, Wolverine, and Coyote were ubiquitous in the performative and oral literary canons of the several hundred or so linguistically distinct cultures that were viable on the North American continent before the onset of Anglo-European cultural dislocation and supplantation in the fifteenth century C.E.[4]

A great many of these trickster stories tell of confrontations with body parts and base appetites. Wakdjunkaga, a character from the folktales of the Winnebago tribe of the Midwestern United States, for instance, is a trickster god who keeps his enormously long penis rolled up and stuffed in a backpack. He is known to have conversations with parts of his body and one story tells of how he instructs his anus to guard his food while he sleeps. When a thieving fox approaches, the anus tries to wake the rest of the body by repeatedly breaking wind. When Wakdjunkaga wakes and finds the food is gone, he punishes his anus by burning it.

One can only imagine the laughter elicited by raconteurs performing stories of Wakdjunkaga who, like the Norse god Loki, the god of pleasure and fun, always involved himself in mischievous antics that introduced chaos into ordered situations. Mythologist Tim Callahan tells how, "[c]ommon to many Amerindian tribes is the story of the laxative bulb. Trickster comes upon a talking bulb that says, 'Whoever eats me will defecate.'" In a typical story, Trickster eats the bulb, begins to break wind and at one point his farts become so powerful that they propel him several feet at a time. The story culminates when the Trickster is buried in his own feces.[5]

Despite the Puritan foundation of the American ethos, the trickster—with or without his overwhelming bodily appetites—is certainly not absent from American letters. Some of the most recent precursors of modern stand-up comedy were storytellers like Mark Twain and his contemporary, Artemus Ward, two performers who were not only fountains of trickster tales, but were tricksters themselves. Like so many modern comedians who appear in character even offstage—comedians such as Stephen Colbert, Carrot Top, Emo Philips, Larry the Cable Guy and Borat—Twain and Ward became living and breathing jokes, taking their antics into public life. Like their mythic counterparts, these characters have never been shy about dealing with bodily functions directly. Mark Twain, for instance, discusses a fart at length in his one-act play *Conversation as It Was by the Social Fireside in the Time of the Tudors*, just as the popular 2006 movie *Borat* contains a scene in which the protagonist carries a bag of his own feces to the table at a posh dinner party.

Others, however, take a more genteel route and deal with fecal metaphors or less offensive references to bodily functions. Philips approaches the matter obliquely with jokes like "the other day I was hanging dental floss out on the line to dry"[6] or "I woke up the other morning and went to the kitchen. My sister made some eggs. So we cooked them."[7] Colbert, meanwhile, satirizes the beliefs, attitudes and short-sightedness of American neo-conservatives, thereby revealing a more conceptual kind of excrement, i.e., that stuff that the nation as a whole does not want to acknowledge but is not able to deny. If we can define "shit" as that material that is a necessary but objectionable part of life, that stuff that we would rather not think about because it is a reminder of our mortality and that we must participate in killing in order to survive, then perhaps one of the most important modern shit slingers is Lenny Bruce, who made a career out of calling out America on its hypocrisies.

Thus we can chart a clear lineage from the ancient trickster myths to the social commentaries of Bruce, Mort Sahl, George Carlin and Chris Rock. In her article "Standup Comedian as Anthropologist," Stephanie Koziski makes a similar point:

> Many standup comedians jar their audiences' sensibility by making individuals experience a shock of recognition. This occurs as deeply-held popular beliefs about themselves—even the hidden underpinnings of their culture—are brought to an audience's level of conscious awareness. The standup comedian can elevate his audience to a new cultural focus.[8]

Whether it is a protean coyote god, Bugs Bunny getting the best of Yosemite Sam, Steve Martin closing his stand-up act by taking everyone in the audience to McDonald's or Bruce opening a performance by asking, "Are there any niggers here tonight?" the trickster has always been and remains a fixture within the human imagination, in no small measure because he always seems to find ways to shock us out of our respective comfort zones and make us look at our actual and metaphorical shit.

Court Jesters (23rd Century B.C.E–Mid 1600s C.E.)

In his seminal book *The Fool and His Scepter: A Study in Clowns, Jesters and Their Audience*, Jungian psychoanalyst and literary critic William Willeford discusses how humans throughout history have had a psychological need for contact with fools. He points out how the first jester on record was in the court of the Egyptian Pharaoh Pepi I in the twenty-fourth century B.C.E., roughly a thousand years before Moses. Willeford goes on to discuss the nature of the jester figure, documenting how "there were dwarf jesters in China in the earliest days, and in both areas of high civilization in pre-Columbian America dwarfs and hunchbacks served as court jesters." In fact, the need for the fool-like figures is so overpowering, reports Willeford, that "[a]rtificial dwarfing and other kinds of monster-making had been learned by the Greeks and Romans from the Orient; and in Greece . . . children were locked in special chests which made them into dwarfs able to pursue a profitable career."[9]

Like his cousin the fool, the court jester also has a direct connection to bodily appetites. Literary critic Daniel Hoffman in his analysis of Edgar Allan Poe's short story "The Cask of Amontillado," for instance, points out how early versions of the fool's cap involved a simple limp cone (later versions were a variation on this theme and included several limp cones), suggesting a limp penis, and thus marked the jester was the personification of "man's lustful nature made absurd and comical."[10] It is hardly surprising that themes of sex and obscenity were in the 1920s identified by anthropologist Julian Steward, in his studies of ritualized comedy, as one of the "four comic themes of universal occurrence."[11]

Another of these themes is the ridicule of the sacred, a function that also seems to be of primary importance to the court jester. Even though jesters were not practicing stand-up per se because their work was primarily physical rather than verbal and they did not employ a set-up/punchline format, it is clear that their impact has been felt throughout the ages. In much the same way that the jester mimicked the king, for instance, Bruce mimicked Catholic priests, David Letterman poked fun at presidents George H.W. Bush, Bill Clinton and, especially, George W. Bush and Richard Pryor performed burlesques on Protestant preachers. According to Todd White in his article "The Anthropology of Fools," this is in no small measure because, "[p]ersons of high social standing and prestige are perhaps most subject to ridicule, and it is common to find professional fool entertainers within the courts and circles of the highest social classes." He adds that "apart from providing a balance to the royal hubris, the primary function of the court jester is to provide comic relief from everyday stressers inherent to the throne."[12]

Clowns (23rd Century B.C.E–Present)

Etymologically speaking, the word "clown" emerges from various sources, such as the Icelandic *klunni* or the North Frisian *klönne*, both of which mean "clumsy fellow," or the Latinate *colonus*, meaning "colonist" or "farmer," and suggests an "unsophisticated or boorish country fellow."[13] Although the figure itself has obviously been created as the object of derision, as a character that virtually everyone else can look down upon, it is no secret that clowns play a particularly special role in human consciousness and have, like the trickster and the fool, had a place in virtually every culture at every epoch, in one form or another.

The modern clown, meanwhile, which P.T. Barnum once described as, along with elephants, one of the "pegs upon which circuses are hung,"[14] began not as a mainstay of the circus but grew out of theatrical traditions of Renaissance Europe, most especially Italy's Commedia dell'arte. The image was later embellished by English comedian Joseph Grimaldi, who invented the white-faced clown replete with red triangles on the cheeks, and thus served as the prototype for the modern circus clown.[15] The classical idiosyncratic features of the clown, namely the big nose and feet, provide a direct link to trickster deities. While the nose in many stories serves as a phallic substitute,[16] enlarged feet have throughout the ages been taken as a sign of a large penis and therefore suggest that clowns are also at the mercy of their sexual appetites.

The clown has been particularly important to the American imagination. For instance, *The Contrast*, a play written by American jurist Royall Tyler, appeared in 1787 and featured the Jonathan, a character that was essentially an American version of the clown or court jester, and which, according to humor anthropologist Constance Rourke, quickly established itself as the nation's "presiding genius" and "always the symbolic American."[17] Images of the Jonathan, a tall, thin, country bumpkin dressed in mismatched clothes and wandering lost in the city, are indeed profuse throughout American stories. He is Johnny Appleseed, Ichabod Crane, Uncle Sam, *The Sound and the Fury*'s Quentin Compson, *The Beverly Hillbillies*' Jethro Bodine, Steven Wright and *Seinfeld*'s Kramer.

The clown that plays most directly into the development of stand-up comedy is probably Dan Rice, a gray-bearded performer who, in the years just prior to the Civil War, was better known than Abraham Lincoln or Mark Twain. According to clowning expert Ron Jenkins, Rice, bedecked in a red and white striped suit, "used his one-ring circus as a comic forum for cultural and political debate. Surrounded by horses, pigs, and mules with names like Daniel Webster, Stephen Douglas, and Ulysses S. Grant, Rice turned his circus tent into a microcosm of antebellum democracy."[18]

Because the United States is so emotionally invested in the heroic efforts of the little man, whether it is the mythic hero like Jay Gatsby, the 1969 "Miracle" Mets, or the "little men" who never get ahead, the Walter Mittys, Willy Lomans, Charlie Browns, Rodney Dangerfields and George Constanzas, the clown, a caricature of the powerless and ineffectual, has always had particularly special status in American tales. He is the frontiersman facing off with the wild expanse, the pariah who is simultaneously comic and tragic, the loser who teems with potential.

Comic Actors (6th Century B.C.E.–Present)

Although several discussions of stand-up comedy list Groucho Marx, Bob and Ray and Abbot and Costello as among the greatest,[19] these folks were not really stand-ups. While noted for timing, wit, creativity and improvisational skills, none of them, with the possible exception of Marx, was particularly gifted when it came to reaching past the fourth wall—at least not when compared with the likes of Richard Pryor, Paula Poundstone or Jimmy Brogan. While Marx did his share of talking directly to his audience, this was usually in the guise of a game show host or talk show guest. Not only did he not have a worked-out act that can be considered stand-up, but there is no question that his genius involved his work on stage and in the movies in which he played characters, albeit characters who were very much like him.

This is not to say, however, that comic actors did not influence stand-up comedy or vice-versa. Although quite different animals—it has been said that a comedian wants only to play himself and that an actor wants to play anybody but himself—comic actors provide a vital chapter in the history of stand-up. The performance tradition not only has roots in comedic plays going all the way back to the ancient Greeks, but also has been informed by groups such as the Commedia dell'arte. Translating literally as "comedy of the actor's guild," this troupe was the direct forerunner of modern performance troupes such as Chicago's Second City and The Not-Ready for Prime-Time Players of *Saturday Night Live* fame. Like modern improv groups (and the Marx Brothers when they were filming their movies), the actors followed "a plot outline, called a scenario, rather than written dialogue."[20]

Nevertheless, it is important to note that there is plenty of cross-fertilization connecting the worlds of comedic acting, improvisation and stand-up. A good comedian, for instance, can often create a scene with several characters in which he acts out all parts. Consider, for instance, the work of Richard Pryor, who was probably *the* master. In his tour de force *Richard Pryor Live on the Sunset Strip*, the comedian acts out scenarios in which he plays all the characters. In one scene he is Gene Wilder, four prison inmates and himself, while in another he is a cheetah, a water buffalo and a lion. Ever the protean, Pryor easily steps out of one role into the other, bringing out the subtlety of each.

The Minstrel Show Stump Speech (Late 1700s–Early 1900s)
In the mid-nineteenth century, as America was coming into its own, the country began to create its own literature, its own styles of music and its own brand of popular entertainment. David Bushman writes that it was during the 1830s that

> American mass entertainment first flourished—in the form of minstrelsy, a coarse, frenetic breed of variety show in which white performers ap-

peared in blackface and spoke in exaggerated black dialects. And it is in minstrelsy that we see two of the earliest ancestors of the stand-up comedian: The end men and the stump speaker.[21]

According to historian Mel Watkins, the first act of the show was dominated by the flamboyant End Men who "dressed outrageously, mugged shamelessly, and fired off simplistic puns, quips, and riddles of the sort that would one day become a staple of burlesque houses and American adolescent humor." Act Two, meanwhile, "was highlighted by the stump speaker, whose monologues ranged from pure nonsense to lampoons of social philosophical issues"[22] and was usually "an oration delivered to the audience in Black dialect and filled with malapropisms."[23]

From the early 1840s until 1928, when it was overtaken by the more elaborate vaudeville show, the minstrel show comprised the "most successful theatrical spectacles in nineteenth century America,"[24] and it is from this tradition that the nation as a whole gets some of its most enduring jokes and joke prototypes, quips such as "Why did the chicken cross the road?" and "That was no lady. That was my wife."

Ironically enough, many of the early influences that led to the establishment of the minstrel shows involved slaves lampooning their masters, sometimes quite openly. In turn, White entertainers blackened their faces with burnt cork and began unwittingly lampooning the lampooning. In later years, the shows featured Black entertainers in blackface makeup. If we accept the premise that comedy is the voice from that part of the human psyche that is largely ignored because its contents are too objectionable, then it seems only fitting that the minstrel shows were a wellspring of humor directly resulting from two of the nation's most heinous sins, slavery and racism.

By the 1840s, the progression of the minstrel show was pretty much standardized and the show consisted of three parts. First, the ensemble of entertainers sat in a semicircle, with a white-faced "Interlocutor" in the middle. On either side of him were the End Men, "Tambo," who played the tambourine, and "Bones," who played bone castanets. The interlocutor posed questions and riddles to the End Men who responded with quips and buffoonery. The second part of the show was called the "olio," which "was really a variety show in which a medley of acts was presented."[25] According to Jan Harold Brunvand, each of the first two segments included a stump speech that was "an oration delivered to the audience in Black dialect and filled with malapropisms."[26] This, of course, had a profound influence on what would, within a few decades, become stand-up comedy. This kind of lampooning and the use of malapropisms were not only given new life in the comic lectures of Artemus Ward, but became mainstays of stand-up comedy throughout its history, perhaps most obviously in the work of Norm Crosby, Irwin Corey, Moms Mabley, Robin Williams and Larry the Cable Guy.

The Chautauqua (Early 1870s–Early 1930s)

If we were to compare popular entertainment in the early twentieth century to that of the early twenty-first century, three rough parallels would emerge. The most popular and defining phenomenon of the period, vaudeville, would easily line up with television sitcoms since both were designed to be quick, light and family oriented with very little, if anything, heavy-handed about them. The point was simply to keep people entertained. Burlesque shows, meanwhile, were that period's answer to HBO: they were essentially vaudeville with a satirical bite and some bawdiness thrown in, created to serve an adult audience. Finally, the Chautauqua, a variety show that featured lecturers, actors, plays, musicians, puppetry and impersonators, would be more akin to modern public television. The point was to educate, enlighten and generate discussion, as well as to entertain.

The Chautauqua phenomenon was begun in the early 1870s by the Methodist Episcopal Church near Lake Chautauqua, New York, as a program offering summer Sunday school adult education classes in the sciences and the humanities. By 1878, William Rainey Harper, who would go on to become president of the University of Chicago, would add a course of home reading, and the popularity of this and programs like it soon led to the Chautauqua becoming a national movement. By the early years of the twentieth century, the circuit Chautauqua, or "tent Chautauquas," as they were called, were enjoying enormous popularity with shows being organized by commercial lecture bureaus. The most successful of these was the Boston Lyceum Bureau, which was also called the Redpath Lyceum Bureau, because it was founded in 1868 by James Redpath.[27] Redpath himself had long been associated with education, history and social commentary. In the years before the war he was a lyceum lecturer, during the war he was a war correspondent and afterward he served as the managing editor of the *North American Review* and as general superintendant of education in Charleston, South Carolina. According to John E. Tapia, author of the book

Circuit Chautauqua: From Rural Education to Popular Entertainment in Early Twentieth Century America, the Redpath bureau had, by the end of the 1870s, put in place a program called "star lecture courses," which were designed to promote lectures that were both popular and expensive and featured lecturers such as Susan B. Anthony, Warren G. Harding, Theodore Roosevelt, Henry Ward Beecher, William Jennings Bryan, Mark Twain and even P.T. Barnum, although he was booked only once.[28]

At the turn of the century, with the movement growing, the next logical step was to take the programs on the road. Consequently, in 1903, the Repath bureau began "to sell a circuit program" on the basis that it was of higher quality and more cost-efficient than anything the smaller community chautauquas could offer.[29] Thus the Redpath bureau began to provide high-quality programs at affordable prices. The shows featured great collections of talent that circuit performer Gay MacLaren declared to be "the greatest aggregation of public performers the world has ever known" as it included "teachers, preachers, scientists, explorers, travelers, statesman, and politicians; singers, pianists, violinists, banjoists, xylophonists, harpists, accordionists, and bell ringers; orchestras, bands, glee clubs, concert companies, quartets, sextets, and quintets; elocutionists, readers, monologists, jugglers, magicians, yodelers, and whistlers,"[30] not to mention ventriloquist Edgar Bergen and his most famous dummy, Charlie McCarthy, and actress Ruth Gordon, who would years later star in the 1971 cult classic movie *Harold and Maude*. Even though the shows featured such notable lecturers as Anthony, Twain, Roosevelt and the hatchet-wielding anti-alcohol crusader Carrie Nation, perhaps the most sought-after was statesman and three-time Democratic Party nominee for the U.S. presidency William Jennings Bryan.

In the early decades of the century, when the Chautauqua stressed lectures over other kinds of entertainment, Bryan, who is probably best remembered for heading up the prosecution of the Scopes "Monkey" Trial of 1925, delivered speeches on social, religious, educational and political issues.[31] According to Robert Cherny in his biography of the American statesman, Bryan, while speaking on the Chautauqua circuit,

> seemed to extemporize. He delivered the same speeches over and over, honing the delivery, sharpening the metaphors, testing new phrases, and discarding those that failed to provoke the desired response. According to [Bryan's daughter] Grace, who often accompanied him on his tours, Bryan typically centered his comments around one or more of three in-

voluntary relationships experienced by every individual: to God, to society, and to the government.[32]

One of Bryan's most popular speeches was "Prince of Peace." First delivered in 1904,[33] the lecture promised listeners that "if they accepted and had faith in the teachings of Christ as the 'Prince of Peace,' their lives would be filled with 'purpose, earnestness, and happiness.'"[34] In other speeches, such as "The Value of an Ideal," Bryan pontificated about how in the United States, "the fundamental principle of government . . . is that people have the right to have what they want in legislation." Other times, however, he argued that it was the duty of the government to "restrain those who would interfere with the inalienable rights of the individual." Taking a cue from Jefferson himself, Bryan emphasized that the United States was built upon inalienable rights which, in addition to "the right to life, liberty and the pursuit of happiness" also included "the right to worship God according to the dictates of one's conscience," and that freedom of speech was "essential to representative government."[35]

Not all Chautauqua lecturers were quite so didactic, however. Others, such as Opie Read, author of some fifty-two humorous novels, often appeared on the Chautauqua stage in the guise of "Old Lim Jucklins," the protagonist of his best-selling novel, *The Jucklins*. According to Tapia, Read "was sort of a rural Plato who set up the dialogue so that Lim always got the best of anyone to whom he spoke." For instance, when Lim discussed the relationship between honesty and political success, he observed that

Success may after a while enable the candidate to tell the truth, but it seems that when a man breaks into politics he breaks in as a liar. . . . If your son-in-law is hesitating between politics and the penitentiary, remember that if he goes to the penitentiary you won't have to take care of him . . . a politician's smile may be bright, and so is a sunbeam when it falls on a puddle where the hogs have been wallerin'.[36]

Even though the Chautauqua remained popular into the 1920s, it too, like burlesque and vaudeville, eventually lost popularity due to motion pictures and radio. Yet because it was primarily a rural phenomenon, another factor figured into its demise: the automobile. With roads improving and access to urban areas thus becoming more affordable and feasible, the institution, which was heroic and noble in its own way, became less profitable and tenable. Within three years of the great stock market crash of 1929, the last two remaining Chautauqua bureaus were forced to close shop.

This is not to say, however, that the Chautauqua lecturer has completely disappeared. Certainly we saw his influence in the folksy philosophical musings of Will Rogers and his *Ziegfeld Follies* monologues, the shaggy-dog stories of Danny Thomas and certainly in the work of modern-day commentators like A. Whitney Brown, who wrote for and performed on *Saturday Night Live* from 1985 to 1991. His series of essays entitled "The Big Picture" were essentially Chautauqua lectures formatted for a television audience. The same is true of the work of Spalding Gray, whose monologue *Swimming to Cambodia* (which concerns his work in the Roland Joffe film *The Killing Fields*) is essentially a Chautauqua commentary on U.S. involvement in the Vietnam War.

The Medicine Show (Early 1800s–Early 1940s)

Even though hucksters, since the days of the Egyptian pharaohs, have touted cures for everything from the common cold to old age, there remains something distinctively American about the medicine show, an early form of variety entertainment that flourished during the nineteenth century. Today, the popular image of these spectacles involves characters like that of Allardyce Meriweather from Arthur Penn's 1970 film *Little Big Man*, a shyster who stands on the bed of his horse-drawn wagon between two gasoline torches prattling on about the bottle of miracle tonic in his hand. Such shows, which were a fixture of American popular culture and entertainment from about 1800 to just before World War II, blended free enterprise with the American promise for salvation—in this case salvation from ill health—as they supported the vision of the American Utopia, a place where all ills could be cured, whether they were diseases of a spiritual, political, technological or economic nature.

According to Ann Anderson, the medicine show tradition west of the Atlantic more than likely began in during the country's infancy with the character of the Yankee Peddler, who, though once quite real, soon became an American archetype and the stuff of legend. Depicted in tales as a "lanky loner with a pack full of notions, herbs, pots, shoes, and clocks," the peddler preferred hawking his products door to door to displaying them in the village square. He played an instrument to announce his arrival and, to amuse a backwoods housewife, he was wont to perform magic tricks.[37] Like his descendant, the medicine show huckster, the Yankee peddler took advantage of obscure technical terms as well as the human propensity to imagine the miraculous. In his 1939 book *The Power of the Charlatan*, Grete de Francesco discusses the allure of the snake-oil purveyor, saying that he

> achieves his great power by simply opening a possibility for men to believe what they already want to believe. His choicest audience would be composed of the semiliterate, those who had exchanged their common sense for a little distorted information and had encountered science and education at some time, though briefly and unsuccessfully. This was the audience, easily intoxicated by visions, that sought the charlatan quite as eagerly as he looked for it.[38]

By the 1880s and 1890s, just as vaudeville entertainment was coming into its own, the American medicine show was in its heyday, playing in frontier towns and offering its audiences soft shoe dances, team comedy, magic acts and, of course, direct-address spiels that were part comedy, part sales pitch and part pure hucksterism, as the performers usually sold products that were made mostly of alcohol, water, Epsom salts and just about anything that could give them a pungent, disagreeable flavor. Once such concoction, The Seven Barks Tonic, for instance, contained "hydrangea, poke root, Culver's root, dandelion, Lady's slipper, colocynth, bloodroot, blue flag, stone root, goldenseal, mandrake, black cohosh, butternut, aloes, capsicum, sassafras, and ginger."[39] According to Owen Tully Stratton, who worked the medicine show circuit before becoming a bona-fide pharmacist and physician, the medicine he and his partners sold "tasted like hell, which attested to its strength."[40]

Stratton tells how he entered into the business upon the suggestion of his friend, Jim Ferrell, after Ferrell had teamed up with Dr. J.L. Berry, who was hawking a tonic called Dr. Berry's Mineral Water Salts along the Pacific Coast. In a manuscript published in 1989, some thirty-five years after the author's death, Stratton recounts his four years in the medicine show business and tells how, despite his initial stage fright, he was able to piece together an effective spiel. He tells how "most spielers began with a story, and the less truth the story contained, the better, since it was a foundation for bigger lies"[41] Like the modern stand-up show, the medicine show was also wont to include characters who, like Emo Philips, Carrot Top or Bobcat Goldthwait, appeared in costume. Stratton tells how, for a while, the performers in Dr. Berry's productions wore suits

which were modeled after what [Dr. Berry] thought Quakers wore. . . .
The reason for the get-up was that the panaceas Jim and Berry were selling bore labels of the Quaker Medicine Company, an organization that
owed its existence to Jim's imagination. The Quaker suit consisted of a
long-tailed coat, a vest that buttoned on the side and came up to the
throat, and barn-door trousers, topped off by a wide-brimmed, flat-
crowned hat. All in Quaker gray of course.[42]

The sales pitch for these particular remedies, meanwhile, involved
a complicated tale of how they were made in Bucks County, Pennsyl-
vania, or sometimes in the outskirts of Cincinnati, and how the production of each was supervised by "old Dr. Josiah Baker, a Quaker
Botanist one hundred and four years of age, as hale and hearty as a
man of forty."[43]

While the performer's job was, first and foremost, to sell bottles of
liquid that looked and tasted like medicine, a part of his job was keeping onlookers interested. After some ballyhoo to rally a crowd and
arouse interest, the performer launched into a spiel that oftentimes
employed a set-up/punch line format. Stratton, for instance, recalls an
instance in which he advised the adults in the crowd before him that
"parents should never punish your little ones when they are cross, crying, and fretful. It is natural for them to be happy and playful like little
lambs on a hillside." He then interrupted the flow of the presentation
by roaring "in a voice like thunder" at children playing in the adjacent
field: "Here! Here! If you boys don't stop that noise, I'll break your
necks!"[44]

One of the most legendary and successful of the medicine shows
was that of Thomas P. Kelley, who was also known as the Fabulous
Kelley, a former tightrope walker who performed in and produced
shows between 1885 and 1930 and made more than two million dollars
selling his tonics. Usually held in a playhouse tent with no fewer than
six thousand seats, Kelley's shows charged no admission as they
treated audiences to his hour-long lectures sandwiched between songs
and skits, often performed by some of vaudeville's best acts. Kelley's
formula for a successful show can still be considered sound advice to a
comedian working clubs in the twenty-first century: "a smash opening,
a crash finish, and keeping them close together."[45]

In the middle 1920s, when the medicine show was losing business
to new entertainment forms allowed by new technologies, the Doc
Lewis troupe picked up a twelve-year-old, carrot-topped comedian
when it made a stop in Vincennes, Indiana. That child was Richard

"Red" Skelton. According to Skelton biographer Arthur Marx, Skelton approached Doc Lewis after one of the shows and asked for a job, assuring Lewis that he could sing and dance. After failing an impromptu audition and taking a job hustling tonic on street corners, Skelton ran up the stage in the middle of one show, tripped on a step and tumbled into a supply of medicine bottles. The audience loved it, and Lewis took the boy on tour with him, paying him to fall off the stage.[46] So began the show business career of one of the most beloved comedians in American history.

Consequently, there can be little doubt as to the enormous influence the medicine show has had on the development of stand-up comedy: in the years to come, the gasoline torches would be replaced by stage lights, the miracle tonic by the beer, cocktails and nachos, the ballyhoo by the emcee whose job it is to prepare the audience for the rest of the show. Just as the snake oil purveyor's livelihood was built upon his ability to spin tales, overwhelm his audience with hyperbole and to manipulate them into believing the extraordinary, the stand-up comedian—like Woody Allen telling us he created a rainstorm in his apartment or Richard Pryor acting out his conversation with a heart attack—pulls the audience into magical worlds where all involved explore various frontiers and contemplate the impossible.

The Victorian Music Hall (Late 1840s–Mid-1920s)

By the middle of the nineteenth century, both England and the United States were enjoying the benefits of the Industrial Revolution as increasingly more urbanized people began finding themselves with extra money in their pockets and the desire and opportunity for cheap entertainment. By the 1840s, as the concert saloon of early vaudeville was becoming increasingly popular west of the Atlantic, London was creating a similar type of variety entertainment called the music hall. In her book *Victorian Music Hall: Class, Culture and Conflict*, Dagmar Kift discusses how the first music hall began when the Canterbury Arms, a public house owned by entrepreneur Charles Morton, evolved into a "Free-and-Easy," that is, a site of weekly "singing meetings" that were "attended by tradesman and mechanics who amused themselves by singing." Shortly thereafter, Morton's public house became so popular that customers urged him to open the room more often and "to employ professional singers and to allow that their wives be admitted." By 1852, Morton transformed "an ordinary public house" in south London into the city's "first music hall."[47] Kift writes that

Morton soon found his room was not large enough. He then obtained some ground at the back of the premises, and built a handsome hall, capable of holding about 400 or 500 persons, and having succeeded in getting a licence from the magistrates, he opened a concert room. The entertainment was by professional singers from a platform, and consisted of glees, madrigals, choruses, songs, and comic songs.[48]

By the 1860s, the music hall had become a vital part of the London entertainment scene and soon

Morton's enterprise was matched and in part anticipated by other publican-entrepreneurs, not only in London but in the industrial north and midlands where growth was similarly rapid, extensive and dramatic. Within little more than a decade or so, the music hall had entered its first major boom, displaying all the elements of a prototype modern entertainment industry in terms of scale, investment and ethos.[49]

Although it began with musical entertainment, the music hall soon found itself incorporating dancers, comic skits and, on occasion, comic monologues. Among the most famous of its stars was Dan Leno, a singer, comic actor, pantomimist, impressionist and, in his youth, a champion clog dancer. According to biographer Gyles Brandreth, Leno, who was born George Galvin, "made his first professional appearance at the Cosmothica Music Hall on Bell Street, Paddington. . . . at the age of four" when he was billed as "Little George, the Infant Wonder, Contortionist and Posturer."[50]

By the 1880s, Leno would become one of England's most popular entertainers, appearing at three or four music halls a night and earning more in a year than most "most of his contemporaries did in a lifetime."[51] At the height of his fame, Leno came on stage dressed as a woman and performed what he referred to as "songs," but which, according to Brandreth, were

actually extraordinary monologues with a snatch of song at top and tail . . . by the time he had reached the height of his fame and popularity, he had so perfected his style and honed it down to the essentials, that he simply used one verso of a song to get him onto the stage and one quick chorus to get him off. The burden of his act was this patter, which he rattled off as though he were having cosy gossip with each and every member of the audience individually.[52]

One of Leno's most memorable characters was a woman who was determined to marry a reluctant suitor named Jim Johnson, a man who worked in the building trade. After an opening verse in which the character sang of chasing Johnson for some twenty-five years and declaring that "I really think Jim's very partial to me/Though never a word he has said/But this morning I passed where he's building a house/And he threw half a brick at my head,"[53] Leno would launch into a monologue and take off on a tangent and introduce the character of Mrs. Kelly:

> You see, we had a row once, and it was all through Mrs. Kelly. You know Mrs. Kelly, of *course*—Mrs. Kelly—*Mrs.* Kelly!! *You* know Mrs. Kelly? Of course, you *must* know Mrs. Kelly! Good life a-might! Don't look so simple. She's a cousin of Mrs. Niplett's, and her husband keeps the little what-not shop at the—oh! You must know Mrs. Kelly. Everybody knows Mrs. Kelly.[54]

According to Brandreth, the monologue, which had little to do with the Jim Johnson bit, was delivered with such deftness and "with such conviction that, in a moment, he managed to convince his audience that they knew her quite as intimately as he did."[55]

Upon Leno's death from a brain tumor in 1904, no less a figure than Charlie Chaplin, another music hall veteran, described Leno as "the greatest comedian since the legendary Grimaldi"[56] while Leno's obituary in *The Times of London* declared that "to find anything like a close parallel to his style we should probably have to go back to the Italian commedia dell'arte."[57] Because of the way in which he was able to translate the common plights of the "little man" into comic art, Leno's influence can easily be detected in the work of comedians such as Chaplin, Buster Keaton and the Marx Brothers.

Even though the music halls also produced the likes of Laurel and Hardy, Gracie Fields, Albert Chevalier, Marie Lloyd, Julie Andrews and Peter Ustinov, and produced songs like "It's a Long Way to Tipperary," the influence of this particular brand of variety entertainment, as with that of vaudeville, began to fade in the years surrounding World War II. In the note that precedes *The Entertainer*, a 1957 play that is essentially a requiem for the Music Hall, John Osbourne comments, "The music hall is dying, and with it, a significant part of England . . . some of the heart of England has gone; something that once belonged to everyone, for this was truly a folk art."[58]

Indeed, the music hall belonged to everyone—not just everyone in England, but everyone in the world. It was folk entertainment at its best.

Mark Twain (Nov. 30, 1835–April 21, 1910)

On January 17, 1856, at a meeting of printers celebrating Benjamin Franklin's one-hundred-and-fiftieth birthday in Keokuk, Iowa, a twenty-year-old newspaper writer delivered an after-dinner speech that would change his life, American literary history and American entertainment. The speaker was Samuel Langhorne Clemens, who would later be better known by his pen name, Mark Twain. More than a decade before he would publish his first novel, Twain learned that audiences "across American hungered for edification and entertainment from traveling lecturers, and [he] had a rare talent for supplying both."[59] Nevertheless, it would take the young writer and performer another eight years to build up the confidence to compare himself to Artemus Ward, who in the interim had become the most popular comic lecturer of the time, and deliver a multi-night performance at the burlesque Third House in Carson City, Nevada. It would take another two years for Twain to learn that people were willing to shell out money to see him exclusively.

For the next half century, Twain toured the country as a comic lecturer, delivering monologues of various lengths on various subjects and freely employing both his famous wit and gift for satire. According to Robert Stebbins, "Twain would lounge on stage, drawling out tall tales and anecdotes, pausing skillfully while his audience roared with laughter at certain passages."[60] Unlike other so-called "platform lecturers" of the time, performers such as Ward and Petroleum Vesuvius Nasby, who relied on "malapropisms," "puns," and "atrocious grammar,"[61] Twain spun exaggerated yarns laced with biting witticisms to keep his audiences interested.

Chapter 78 of *Roughing It*, Twain's second major book, deals exclusively with the fears and stage fright of one of his early speaking engagements. In this more or less autobiographical novel, Twain tells us how, after five and a half years' sailing in the Far West, he finds himself "home again, in San Francisco, without means and without employment."[62] He decides, after "torturing his brain," to present a public lecture, writes a draft of it and shows it to his colleagues, only to have them all scoff at it. Finally, after someone suggests that he rent out "the largest house in town, and charge a dollar a ticket," Twain em-

barks on the business venture. For this he finds "a handsome new opera house at half price" and spends a hundred and fifty dollars on
printing and advertising, all the time worrying himself sick that the enterprise will be a flop and that few, if any, people will attend. He is so
fraught with anxiety that he is unable to sleep or eat and even considers fleeing town, feigning illness or committing suicide. On the day of
the performance, he arrives at the venue two hours early in an attempt
to "face the horror." Twain tells how he

> entered the theatre by the back door. I stumbled my way in the dark
> among the ranks of canvas scenery, and stood on the stage. The house
> was gloomy and silent, and its emptiness depressing. I went into the dark
> among the scenes again, and for an hour and a half gave myself up to the
> horrors, wholly unconscious of everything else. Then I heard a murmur;
> it rose higher and higher, and ended in a crash, mingled with cheers. It
> made my hair raise, it was so close to me, and so loud. There was a
> pause, and then another; presently came a third, and before I well knew
> what I was about, I was in the middle of the stage, staring at a sea of fac-
> es, bewildered by the fierce glare of the lights, and quaking in every limb
> with a terror that seemed like to take my life away. The house was full,
> aisles and all!
>
> The tummult [sic] in my heart and brain and legs continued a full
> minute before I could gain any command over myself. Then I recognized
> the charity and the friendliness in the faces before me, and little by little
> my fright melted away, and I began to talk. Within three or four minutes
> I was comfortable, and even content. . . . Presently I delivered a bit of se-
> rious matter with impressive unction (it was my pet), and the audience
> listened with an absorbed hush that gratified me more than any applause;
> and as I dropped the last word of the clause, I happened to turn and
> catch Mrs. —'s intent and waiting eye; my conversation with her flashed
> upon me, and in spite of all I could do I smiled. She took it for the signal,
> and promptly delivered a mellow laugh that touched off the whole au-
> dience; and the explosion that followed was the triumph of the evening.[63]

At this, his fate as a performer was sealed. The great American
humorist was about to make history again.

Anyone with even moderate exposure to Twain's work can appreciate his gift for humor. It is easy to imagine how when he took to the
stage he brought with him countless yarns, quips, observations and
comments, much of the material that had or would appear in his published stories. Consider, for instance, this passage from the final chapter of *Life on the Mississippi*, the opening lines of which actor Hal Hol-

brook has utilized in the introductory bit in his recreation of the writer in the one-man show *Mark Twain Tonight!*:

> How solemn and beautiful is the thought, that the earliest pioneer of civilization, the van-leader of civilization, is never the steamboat, never the railroad, never the newspaper, never the Sabbath-school, never the missionary—but always whiskey! Such is the case. Look history over; you will see. The missionary comes after the whiskey—I mean he arrives after the whiskey has arrived; next comes the poor immigrant, with ax and hoe and rifle; next, the trader; next, the miscellaneous rush; next, the gambler, the desperado, the highwayman, and all their kindred in sin of both sexes; and next, the smart chap who has bought up an old grant that covers all the land; this brings the lawyer tribe; the vigilance committee brings the undertaker. All these interests bring the newspaper; the newspaper starts up politics and a railroad; all hands turn to and build a church and a jail—and behold, civilization is established for ever in the land. But whiskey, you see, was the van-leader in this beneficent work. It always is.[64]

Full of irreverent observations about the human's continual pursuit of intoxication, this bit of monologue certainly forecasts one of the obsessions of the modern comedian: pleasure through the use of drugs.

Twain's motivations for staying on the lecture circuit—which took him across America, across Europe and into Australia—have been the subject of quite a bit of speculation. While there is little doubt that the money he earned from lecturing kept him out of bankruptcy and that tours distracted him from his grief after the death of his children (his nineteen-month-old son Langdon in June 1872 and his twenty-four-year-old daughter Susy in 1896), there is also clear evidence that Twain enjoyed the art form and began developing these talents while still a boy. According to Rasmussen, "Twain's bent for public speaking may have begun in his boyhood, when the only school routine that he enjoyed was the weekly spelling bee. A star performer, he relished being a center of public attention and began learning how to play before audiences."[65]

Whatever his motivation, it seems clear that Twain has a unique role in American literary history: not only did he change the language and re-engineer the novel and short story so that they were more enjoyable, less pretentious and certainly more honest, but his spirit continues to hover over the world of stand-up comedy.

Will Rogers (Nov. 4, 1879–Aug. 15, 1935)

If Mark Twain had one immediately identifiable heir, it was Will Rogers. An Oklahoma cowboy of Cherokee ancestry, Rogers won fame early in life as a lariat spinner and horse rider, skills he perfected while working as a gaucho in Argentina. His love of exotic adventures, which lasted throughout his life, eventually took him to South Africa, where he began his career as an entertainer by joining a Wild West show. [66] He would go on to show off his remarkable roping skills—he could lasso three galloping horses simultaneously[67]—in Japan and China before making a name for himself in the United States. According to his biographers, Rogers first claimed national fame in 1905 when, at the age of twenty-six and while performing as the star roper in the Mulhall Show at the Horse Fair in Madison Square Garden, he roped a steer that had charged into the stands and managed to lead the beast back into the arena.[68]

For the next four years Rogers worked in various capacities, spinning a lariat on vaudeville stages and participating in an elaborate act that included several horses and other riders. While performing with the Orpheum Circuit, a Delaware-based theatrical organization, Rogers decided, upon the urging of a theater manager, to simplify his act and appear on stage with just his rope and patter with the audience. This, according to biographer Richard M. Ketchum, was the "decision that was probably the most important one of his theatrical career."[69]

After years of playing vaudeville houses, performing in other Wild West shows and taking his act to England and Germany, the Oklahoman got another big break. In 1915, Gene Buck booked him to perform in the *Midnight Frolic*, a show held on the roof of the New Amsterdam Theatre, a swanky New York nightclub upstairs from the auditorium in which the *Ziegfeld Follies* played. For Buck and owner Florenz Ziegfeld, the "frolic served as an experimental theater where Ziegfeld tested new talent, skits, songs, and scene designs on a stage similar to the main one downstairs."[70] Even though Ziegfeld himself was not particularly impressed because he felt that the cowboy who made gum-chewing a signature part of his act "did not fit in with the café's cosmopolitan atmosphere," Rogers nevertheless would go on to become a fixture of the *Frolic* and, eventually, one of the *Follies'* biggest stars. Appearing with the likes of Eddie Cantor and W.C. Fields, Rogers won over audiences while "performing rope tricks and pausing now and then to drawl amusing comments on current events."[71]

Because those who attended the two Ziegfeld venues tended to be regulars, Rogers was pressured to come up with new material. To do so, he turned to the newspapers and began making topical jokes an increasingly large part of his act. Once, when an interviewer asked who wrote his material, Rogers responded:

> Why the newspapers write it! All I do is get all the papers I can carry, and then read all that's going on. I use only one set method in my little gags, and that is to try to keep to the truth. Of course you can exaggerate it, but what you say must be based on truth. Personally I don't like jokes that get the biggest laughs, as they are generally as broad as a house and require no thought at all. I like one where, if you are with a friend and you hear it, it makes you think and you nudge your friend and say, *he is right about that!* I would rather have you do that than to have you laugh— and then forget the next minute what you laughed at.[72]

Nevertheless, with quips like "grammar and I get along like a Russian and bathtub," "Diplomats are nothing but high-class lawyers— some ain't even got high class"[73] and "asking Europe to disarm is like asking a man in Chicago to give up his life insurance,"[74] Rogers would always be ready with a quip, a wisecrack or an amusing comment, regardless of the medium he happened to be working in.

Even though he would go on to star in motion pictures, both silent and talkies, do radio commentaries, star in the Broadway production of Eugene O'Neill's only comedy, *Ah, Wilderness!* and become the "the country's most widely read columnist,"[75] perhaps the most important element of Rogers' legacy was the way he stated, implicitly but unequivocally, that the nation's most respected icons were oftentimes the best sources of humor. One of his favorite targets was the lawyer, statesman and candidate for the U.S. presidency William Jennings Bryan. While performing in a benefit in 1916, for instance, the cowboy comedian found himself with a bad case of stage fright when he learned that President Woodrow Wilson and his wife were in the audience. Despite his nervousness, he still managed to poke fun at Bryan's longwindedness and the way he was fading from the spotlight, saying, "I'm kinder nervous here tonight. . . . I shouldn't be nervous. . . for this is really my second Presidential appearance. The first time was when Bryan spoke in our town once, and I was to follow his speech and do my little Roping Act. . . but he spoke so long that it was so dark when he finished they couldn't see my roping." After a pause he added, "I wonder what ever became of him."[76]

In his 2006 dissertation, Peter McClelland Robinson noted that "Rogers opened the presidency to ridicule but with such even-tempered goodwill that millions of Americans were willing to laugh along."[77] For instance, after the stock market crash of 1929, Rogers, ever the regular guy, did what he could to help an ailing nation and tried to help President Herbert Hoover "restore confidence." Nevertheless, he wondered, "But you will have to give me some idea where 'Confidence' is . . . and just who you want it restored to."[78] Furthermore, when Hoover responded to the crisis by invoking the "Spirit of Valley Forge," Rogers pointed out, "He found somebody that was worse off than we are, but he had to go back 150 years in history to do it."[79] Later on he commented on the irony of the Depression, saying that the United States is

> a country with more wheat and more corn and more money in the bank, more cotton, more everything in the world—there's not a product that you can name that we haven't got more of than any other country ever had on the face of the earth—and yet we've got people starving. We'll hold the distinction of being the only nation in the history of the world that ever went to the poor house in an automobile.[80]

In August 1935, after it was learned that Rogers and his friend Wiley Post had died in an airplane crash near Point Barrow, Alaska, the nation responded with an outpouring of grief that was virtually unprecedented for an entertainer. Before the modest last rites, Rogers' "casket lay in state in Forest Lawn Memorial Park, where fifty thousand people—many of whom had been standing in line since the previous night—filed by in silence under a scorching sun" while other "memorial services were held in the Hollywood Bowl, in Beverly Hills," and in his hometown of Claremore, Oklahoma, "while in many towns the flags were at half-mast; the nation's motion picture theatres were darkened; the CBS and NBC networks observed a half-hour of silence; and in New York a squadron of planes, each towing a long black streamer, flew over the city in final tribute."[81]

There is little room for doubt that Rogers had a profound impact on stand-up comedy. In addition to being one of the first comedians to "engage in those witty and sometimes teasing exchanges so frequently used by contemporary performers," he was also among the first "to organize his act around an identifiable 'hook'—a special talent, social role, or physical feature used to the performer's advantage in eliciting laughs,"[82] which, in his case, was rope-twirling.

Despite their profound impact, still, neither Rogers nor Twain can really be considered practitioners of "pure stand-up," as "Twain worked outside vaudeville as a monologist" and was really more of a "comic lecturer who was often funny, not an entertainer," and Rogers "was a mixed stand-up comic of the prop variety."[83] Nevertheless, the two most important nineteenth-century American wits, along with vaudevillian Charley Case, led a Charge of the Everyman, and Ed Wynn, Eddie Cantor and Beatrice Hereford followed close behind.

The era of stand-up comedy was about to arrive.

CHAPTER FIVE
A HISTORY OF STAND-UP

The changes the United States underwent during the last decades of the nineteenth century are indeed legendary: in a mere three decades, the country's population went from slightly more than 31 million to about 75 million, the railroad revolutionized transportation and even though Eli Whitney had patented the cotton gin in 1794, it was not until the decades following the Civil War that the country began to feel the real impact of the Industrial Revolution. As industry shifted from water power to steam and coal power, the city became more important than ever as the locus of economic and cultural activity. Industry meant jobs, jobs meant a thriving economy and a thriving economy meant the United States was becoming unique in world history. More people than ever were becoming prosperous enough to have their basic needs met, so much so that two previously uncommon luxuries were becoming increasingly widespread: literacy and leisure time.[1]

With a new urban population that was largely working class, immigrant and affluent when compared to the rest of the world came a need for new kinds of entertainment. Even though the minstrel show had been popular for some time, something else was needed. Before long, various offshoots of the Victorian music hall would come into being west of the Atlantic. Burlesque shows would offer bawdy satire and risqué productions; vaudeville shows would come to dominate the entertainment landscape and essentially set the standard for American entertainment and the "Borscht Belt" resorts of Sullivan County, New York, would serve as training grounds for some of the nation's most important stars. Within a few years, these modes would all but disappear, but not before having a major impact on virtually every sector of American entertainment.

Building upon traditions going as far back as the first trickster tales, each of these arenas played a significant role in the development of the literary form we have come to call stand-up comedy. Despite claims from many a Borscht Belt comedian that he is a practitioner of "the world's second oldest profession," the art form is essentially American, one that was enabled by the newfound prosperity of the late nineteenth century and the distinctly American values of freedom of expression and sanctity of the individual. This is not to say, however, that it appeared suddenly, that some vaudevillian simply had an epiphany one afternoon and took to the stage that night to tell jokes directly to the audience. Rather, stand-up comedy was eons in the making, and once it was introduced to the American stage in the late nineteenth century, things were never quite the same.

Vaudeville (Mid-1800s–Mid-1930s)

If the Civil War was America's adolescence, then those decades that followed served as its entry into adulthood. In the latter half of the nineteenth century, the country was undergoing more than a few trials by fire. Not only was the young nation still reeling from the Civil War, but the Industrial Revolution brought with it dramatic shifts in demographics, a more dynamic economy and a new kind of urbanite with a very different way of looking at the world. While in 1840 nine out of ten Americans lived in the countryside, within a few short decades nearly half would live in the city. Immigrants flooded the country—5.5 million in the 1880s alone[2]—the vast majority coming from places like Germany, Ireland and Italy, bringing with them concepts of morality that did not jibe easily with those the Puritans had set in place early in the seventeenth century. Certainly, for a great many European transplants, the idea of "a good time" quite often involved "beer, ale, music and dancing."[3] Post-Civil War America was in search of entertainment that was cheap, light and accessible.

Enter vaudeville.

Weaving together various entertainment traditions such as the Commedia dell'arte, circus and street performing, miming, and the lavish theatrics (replete with cross-dressing comedic acts) of the Victorian music hall, and taking its name from the Val de Vire, the French river valley that was known for its tradition of bawdy songs, vaudeville offered the new urbanites exactly what they were looking for. The diversion was "freer than the more fully scripted Broadway show"[4] and featured dancers, singers, jugglers, magicians and sketch and team comedy. More rapid, elaborate and professional than the minstrel show and less salacious than the burlesque show, vaudeville was more or less family entertainment (even though, especially in the early years, the audiences were mostly male) and catered to crowds that were rapidly becoming more affluent, sophisticated and literate. Yet, unlike plays, operas and burlesque, it brought together a series of unrelated acts—sometimes as many as ten or twelve—on a single bill.[5]

Although vaudeville officially began in 1840, when the Boylston Hall in Boston opened its summer season,[6] its momentum, like that of most things American, was compromised by the Civil War. Once the nation did recover in the last decades of the nineteenth century, vaudeville was on its way to becoming the dominant American entertainment form, and its popularity lasted until the late 1920s, when it began to be supplanted by radio and "talkie" motion pictures. Between 1910 and 1925, there were as many as 2,000 dedicated vaudeville theaters in the United States, most of which put on at least two shows a day and some of which ran as many as nine shows a day[7]—not to mention other venues such as grange halls, tents, auditoriums and converted churches. Furthermore, as many as 50,000 entertainers played vaudeville stages while countless pit musicians, stage managers, ticket takers, costumers, make-up technicians, scene painters, bookers and agents worked the peripheries.[8]

It was in vaudeville that stand-up comedy was born. Even though Mark Twain had worked with direct-address entertainment since 1857 and had been lecturing regularly since October 2, 1866, when "he spoke for the first time before an audience that had paid solely for the privilege of hearing him,"[9] it was not until sometime between 1880 and 1890 that stand-up comedy actually came into being. According to Martin and Segrave, it was during this time that Charley Case, who some sources suggest was an African-American who could pass for White, took to the stage for the explicit purpose of telling jokes directly to the audience so as to elicit laughter. Robert Stebbins writes that unlike Will Rogers, who used props, and Mark Twain, who was essentially a comic lecturer, Case was the "first pure stand-up comic"[10] and during the 1880s and 1890s, "pioneered the monologue." When Case performed he simply "came on stage dressed normally and with no props. . . . He told jokes and funny stories to the audience. It was an unusual style for the time, even for men."[11]

Even though some of his monologues have been preserved and he is credited with writing the song "The Fatal Glass of Beer" that W.C. Fields sang in a movie short of the same name, Case's story remains somewhat mysterious. Even vaudeville historians can't seem to agree on the facts. While Douglas Gilbert reports in his book *American Vaudeville: Its Life and Times* that Case was African-American,[12] Joe Laurie Jr. in *Vaudeville from Honky Tonks to the Palace* tells us that Case's father was Irish and his mother African-American.[13] What it is clear, however, is that Case "was a product of the beer halls," which were "a curious nursery for his talent," that he was a superb comedian and that "he made good before stage audiences, compelling attention through sheer perfection of comedy and personality."[14] Gilbert writes that Case's quiet monologue was "one of the most entrancing acts in vaudeville." Described as a "quiet neurotic," Case performed only if he had a string or a handkerchief to "twiddle in his fingers." On at least one occasion when he had forgotten his string and when no suitable replacement could be found, he reportedly "quietly took his hat and slipped away."[15] That the following bit, preserved by Gilbert, does not read too well is testimony to the brilliance of Case's delivery:

> Father was a peculiar man. Us children didn't understand him. Mother understood him. Mother could always tell when father'd been drinking. We couldn't tell. We used to think he was dead. Father was a great hand for finding things. I remember him coming home one night. He picked up something. He couldn't see just what it was, but he brought it home. When he got to the house he found it was an arm-load of wood. Father didn't mean to take anybody else's wood, of course. We already had a lot of our own just exactly like it.[16]

While in his early days, Case wore blackface, as was the custom at the time, he abandoned the practice by the early years of the twentieth century. Though an entertainment pioneer, Case usually worked small-time vaudeville houses even when younger African-American comedians like Bert Williams and Ernest Hogan were performing in the *Ziegfeld Follies* or starring in musical comedies. While it is pretty much agreed upon that Case was "easily depressed" and that he died in 1916, the exact cause of his death is also the subject of dispute. While Gilbert says that "Case died of tuberculosis," Laurie writes that he died "in his midtown Manhattan hotel room" and "the official report stated Charlie [sic] was killed while cleaning his revolver," which was "often a cover for suicide" and that upon hearing the news, his wife dropped dead at their home in Larchmont, outside New York City.[17]

Another pioneer of direct-address comedy, and arguably history's second stand-up comedian, was the Englishwoman Beatrice Hereford. While the exact decade of Case's first monologue may never be known, there is clear evidence that sometime in 1895 Hereford began earning a reputation for her direct-address comic performances. According to Martin and Segrave, Hereford's first formal monologue took place in London, with George Bernard Shaw and Henry James in attendance. Even though Hereford performed in comic plays and, later on, after moving to Massachusetts with her husband, starred in vaudeville and Broadway revues, she continued to perform her monologues into the 1930s. In skits such as *A Professional Boarder*, for instance, Herford presented a breakfast conversation with a host of characters, all of them imaginary, saying things like, "Oh, going to have your picture taken; Is that so? Where do you go, Mrs. Watson? Oh, no. I don't care for his pictures at all. I had mine taken there, and I wanted to burn them all up, but they cost so much, so I gave them all away to my relations."[18]

Even though the modifications Case and Hereford introduced to the stage did not immediately open up a floodgate of stand-up comedy, when their innovation did take hold it became a mainstay of American entertainment. By the early years of the twentieth century a new chapter in stand-up had begun with the introduction of Ed Wynn, who had also perfected his craft on the vaudeville stage, usually as an emcee. A natural comedian who was wont to quip that, "I never wanted to be a real person,"[19] Wynn would eventually become one of the biggest draws on Broadway and years later would star in his own (although short-lived) television show and be featured in the 1964 Disney film *Mary Poppins*, in which he played Uncle Albert, a character who loves nothing more than laughing. Known for his "punning jokes," "addled-brained observations," lengthy, pointless anecdotes, comic introductions to the other acts and pedestrian jokes such as "The difference between a Scotchman and a canoe is that a canoe tips,"[20] and even for the way he improvised jokes when stage crews needed more set-up time behind the curtain, Wynn was a savvy entertainer and businessman who went on to write and produce numerous Broadway shows. Wynn's stage persona foreshadowed the emotional honesty of Richard Pryor and Bill Hicks as he "did everything possible to make each individual in the theatre feel as if he were a friend being personally guided through a singularly lunatic, hilarious world."[21]

Although the traditional vaudeville stage would become an anachronism by the depression years of the 1930s, the entertainment form was kept alive by television variety shows such as *The Hollywood Palace*, *The Ed Sullivan Show* and, later on, *Saturday Night Live*, and would come to serve as the foundation upon which American entertainment is built. It would not only supply the country with some of its biggest stars, notables such as the Marx Brothers, Red Skelton, George Burns and Gracie Allen, Jack Benny, Judy Garland, Abbot and Costello and Bob Hope, but also would spawn numerous descendants. Among the most important of these were the Theater Owners Booking Association, which was more commonly known as "The Black Vaudeville" or "The Chitlin' Circuit," and the Borscht Belt, or the Jewish vaudeville circuit that included the resorts of Sullivan County, New York.

There is no question that into the twenty-first century, when the old vaudeville halls, if standing at all, remain downtown relics and venues for punk and metal band dances, vaudeville's vestiges live on in radio, television and comedy clubs.

Burlesque (Mid-1800s–Mid 1930s)

A direct descendant of the Victorian music hall was the burlesque show, a form of adult entertainment that was designed, perhaps unwittingly, to shock spectators, if not all Americans, out of their comfort zones. Like the literary comedies from which its name is derived, burlesque was built upon exaggeration and parody; was invested in the mocking of social, cultural and political trends; and was grounded in the "aesthetics of transgression, inversion and the grotesque."[22] The productions mocked Victorian sanctimoniousness and hypocrisy and questioned the roles of women and what could be considered licentious. According to Robert C. Allen, author of the book *Horrible Prettiness: Burlesque and American Culture*, a typical example of these shows was *Ixion*, a theatrical piece which was "a general lampoon of classical culture and mythological allusion composed in punning rhymed pentameter"[23] and involved a parody of the cancan dance, which had just recently been imported from the cabarets of Paris.[24] And of course there were the shows' most notorious element, the scores of unruly women.

As with rock 'n roll, hip-hop, bebop jazz and Beatnik poetry, all this bawdiness, irreverence and satire was, to many people, a sign of a morally decaying culture. Writer and literary critic William Dean Howells, for instance, once commented that burlesque set out

> respecting nothing—neither taste, propriety, virtue, nor manners. Its design is to be uproariously funny and glaringly indecent. It seeks to unite the coarsest fun with the most intoxicating forms of beauty. It presents women garbed, or semi-garbed, in the most luxurious and seductive

dresses possible, and makes them play the fool to the topmost bent of the spectator. One is dazzled with light and color, with gay songs, with beautiful faces and graceful limbs, and startled at the coarse songs, the vile jargon, the low wit, and the abandoned manners of the characters. The mission of burlesque is to throw ridicule on gods and men—to satirize everybody and everything; to surround with laughter and contempt all that has been reverenced and respected.[25]

In spite of such finger-wagging, there were those who appreciated the art form for what it was. Alan Trachtenberg, for instance, has commented that the productions "took wicked fun in reversing roles, shattering polite expectations, and brazenly challenging notions of the approved ways women might display their bodies and speak in public."[26] Similarly, none other than Red Skelton, who worked the circuit as a young man, took delight in the fact that the productions were "burlesque in the literal sense of the word. We burlesqued Broadway shows."[27]

Besides that, the country as a whole was ready to accept these bawdy stage productions when they first began appearing in the middle of the nineteenth century and has maintained them, in various forms, ever since. Even after it too had its momentum interrupted by the Civil War, burlesque managed to quickly regain its popularity. Between 1890 and 1920, burlesque was in its heyday and "troupes toured every part of the United States and its territories, from New York to Klondike mining camps."[28] In fact, this particular mode of entertainment rode a wave of popularity that did not wane until the 1930s when, as with vaudeville, the Chautauqua circuit and medicine show, its viability was compromised by the advent of radio, motion pictures and a harsh economic climate.

Burlesque's most popular acts, of course, were its women, performers such as Sally Rand, who danced naked on stage behind giant fans, never revealing too much of herself; Lili St. Cyr, whose act involved taking a bubble bath on stage; and Dixie Evans, who was billed as "the Marilyn Monroe of Burlesque."[29] Yet, despite the countless temptresses who peeled off their gloves and stockings to the delight of rooms full of spectators who were, for the most part, male and working class, only one, Gypsy Rose Lee, would ever go on to be considered anything close to a household name.

Even though there can be little doubt that into the twenty-first century the tradition lives on in what are now called "gentleman's clubs" that feature acts that are performed by women who are referred to as "exotic dancers" rather than "strippers," burlesque's great legacy is its comedians. Unlike their counterparts in vaudeville, these jokesters took to the stage in an environment where they were virtually required to challenge established norms. Even though they were not the main attractions, future movie stars such as W.C. Fields, Red Buttons, Robert Alda, Mae West, Bud Abbot and Lou Costello, Bert Lahr and Joey Bishop, to name but a few, were comedians who honed their comedic skills on the burlesque stage. Other veterans such as Don Adams, Pinky Lee, Jackie Gleason, Phil Silvers and Skelton, meanwhile, would go on to become major television stars.

Aside from the jokes that were designed to keep audiences entertained between acts, burlesque added two other dimensions to stand-up comedy, both of which involved introducing into the performance a familiarity that had been absent from conventional acting, sketch comedy and team comedy. According to Allen, "[i]ntimacy with the audience was an expected part of the burlesques and acting styles of [performers such as] William Mitchell, John Brougham, and their male colleagues." Such familiarity was something few were accustomed to. *New York Herald* writer Leland Croghan wrote that Brougham, an Irish immigrant who wrote and produced plays as well as took on character roles, during his performances "interpolates a joke bearing a reference to some political topic of the day, now he talks confidently to the leader of the band and to an extent which, sublimely violating all the principles of illusion, produces an amiable fraternity between stage and audience."[30]

The second way in which this was done was through the dancers themselves as they learned of the great power that comes with making each spectator feel special. Olive Logan, an anti-burlesque crusader, actress and feminist, once railed against the female performers and by doing so identified much of what the productions had to offer to the world of show business. In one tirade she said that the dancer was "always peculiarly and emphatically herself,—the woman, that is, whose name is on the bills in large letters, and who considers herself an object of admiration to the spectators."[31] Such observations sound rather like that made by John Limon, who more than a hundred and thirty years after Logan's diatribes would comment on the magic of stand-up by saying that "all stand-ups . . . give themselves over to the stand-up condition, which is a non-condition between nature and artifice. (They are neither acting nor conversing, neither in nor out of costume.)"[32]

Although stand-up comedy first appeared in its pure form in vaudeville, it would, in many ways, chase the burlesque aesthetic well into the

1950s. It was not until then, when Lenny Bruce and Mort Sahl introduced two new standards to the world of stand-up—the conversational,
improvisational delivery and the topical joke that called out sacred cows
such as the president, Congress, corporate bigwigs, national hypocrisy
and neo-Victorian values—that stand-up comedy began to come into its
own.

It is no accident then that Bruce, who is often considered to be
among the most influential stand-ups, honed his skills while introducing
strippers in clubs such as Los Angeles' Strip City and The Colony Club.
There, the young comic, who was the son of a dancer/comedian and the
husband of a stripper, found himself inspired by the antics of burlesque
house comedians like Buttons and made his show business bones. In
such venues he learned to "loosen up onstage to hold the attention of
horny guys who couldn't wait for him to bring on the girls and get off so
they could get off" and that he "was forced to dirty up his act to com-
pete with the strippers."[33] To put the matter another way, we can say
that burlesque gave birth to Bruce and Bruce gave birth to a style of
comedy that, like burlesque, not only entertains us with genuine talent
and risqué language and behavior, but is dedicated to challenging a culture's illusions about itself.

Ultimately, despite Howells' warning that burlesque spread a "chaos-
inducing disease" through its celebration of female sexuality, the shows
were in many ways quintessentially American. In the nineteenth century,
the United States was a nation that celebrated its extremes. On the one
hand, it was the great socio-political experiment inspired by the lofty
ideals of John Locke, David Hume and Thomas Jefferson—not to mention the God of Reason Himself—and championed itself as having a
distinctly new breed of people with a new and radical ethos. On the other hand, it was a nation and people that were increasingly defined by the
anarchy of the frontier and the Wild West. It was a country that had at
its core great progressive thought while its inhabitants had to recreate
millennia of human history, to go from the very primitive to the very
modern, within a few centuries. In this way, America was very much like
the burlesque show as it mixed the ultra-sophisticated with the bawdy
and carnal.

Dada (Early 1900s)
The early years of the twentieth century were hard on dyed-in-the-wool
Victorians still clinging to visions of an ordered universe. Friedrich
Nietzsche claimed that "God is dead and we have killed him" and

Sigmund Freud's essay on the Oedipus Complex called world religions into question by suggesting that punishing deities were more the manifestations of suppressed childhood neuroses than they were mystical truths. Albert Einstein suggested that everything was relative, World War I resulted in unprecedented and unimagined carnage and morals and mores had to be reinvented as more people found themselves living in industrialized cities. All this left the average Joe reeling.

Nevertheless, more than a few artists and intellectuals were quick to embrace the chaos. The century's early decades saw an ever-increasing interest in abstract art as well as in the Cubism of Pablo Picasso and Georges Braque, art which chopped up the human form and reassembled it so that it was hardly recognizable. Another direct response to the times came from Marcel Duchamp, "a handsome, charismatic man of astonishing intellect" who "devoted a lifetime to the creation of art that was more cerebral than visual."[34] According to H.H. Arnason, Duchamp's first inquiry into the nature of art came in 1912 with paintings like *Nude Descending a Staircase*, which made use of Cubistic techniques—that is, it showed the same object from multiple points of view simultaneously—to present a "static representation of movement."[35] A year later, the artist made his "most outrageous assault on artistic tradition" with the invention of the "readymade" (everyday objects which were simply designated as art) and the "assisted readymade" (everyday objects which required a small degree of manipulation). Among the most famous examples of this "artistic choosing" were the assisted readymade *Bicycle Wheel*, which was a bicycle wheel mounted on a painted wood stool, "his famously irreverent addition of a mustache and goatee to a reproduction of the *Mona Lisa*" and perhaps his most famous piece, a readymade which was a urinal which he inverted, signed with the name "R. Mutt" and entered in a 1917 New York art show.[36]

Like so many other artists at the time, Duchamp was responding to chaotic times with chaotic art. This movement, which was nourished by intellectuals who "felt that reason and logic had led to the disaster of world war, and that the only way to salvation was through political anarchy, the natural emotions and, the intuitive and the irrational," was termed "Dada." The name, which means "'yes, yes,' in Rumanian," and "'rocking horse' and 'hobby horse' in French," was chosen by artist Richard Huelsenbeck and writer Hugo Ball, both German. Ball noted in his diary that for "Germans it is a sign of foolish naiveté, joy in procreation, and preoccupation with the baby carriage."[37]

While such "reverence for the absurd" took hold in art galleries and intellectual circles west of the Atlantic, its influence could also be felt in less pretentious settings such as vaudeville theaters. Gilbert Seldes, in his book *The Seven Lively Arts*, argues that the art of vaudeville was also a response to the new urban realities of the post-World War I world. He identified the "inconsecutive" and "pointless" art of vaudevillians like Joe Cook, James J. Morton and Charley Case as the American answer to Dada, arguing that the art of vaudeville was an understandable and even expected response to "the bewildering confusion of the modern city."[38]

And it was the adjustment to city life and life in an increasingly industrialized world from which Case drew his material. His monologues told of the perils of urban life, not the least of which involved the constant struggle to eke out a living. Consider, for instance, this bit preserved in the book *Monologues, Epigrams, Epitaphs and Parodies* from 1910 and its "country boy lost in the city" theme that recalls the New England Jonathan:

> You know my brother Hank and I slept in the next room to father, and there was only a thin partition between. Well, one night father thought he heard burglars in the house, so he rapped on the partition and said, "Boys, I think there are burglars in the house, go downstairs and see if you can find them." I said: "father's talking to you Hank," but Hank said he hadn't lost any burglars and for me to go down and find them. Well, Hank and I finally went down but we couldn't find any burglars, so we went down to the police station and I told the police that there were thieves in our house, and they said, "yes, we've been onto it for some time." The police told us to go back home and when we got there, the thieves would be there.[39]

Another bit also tells of the travails of going from city to city on the vaudeville circuit:

> My brother Hank and I joined a theatrical company once, and we had to sing a song. When we got through, the audience made an awful racket and I asked the stage-manager if they wanted us back. "Yes, back there," said he. Well, when the show was over the manager said to us, that a large portion of the audience was waiting for us at the stage door with clubs. So Hank says to me, "if we go sneaking down there they'll think we are afraid of them, so we'll just walk boldly out this side window." When we got to the depot I sent Hank out to get enough cigars to last us on the trip. In a little while he came back with both hands full—a quarter

a piece. One of them was nearly whole. Hank is a good judge of cigars, although nobody ever told him anything about it. He just picked it up himself.[40]

Today, we can see a clear connection to Dada in the work of comedians like Steven Wright and Mitch Hedberg who, much like Duchamp and his ilk, have made a sport of dissecting the world and reframing it so that it is hardly recognizable. Vaudevillian monologists and modern stand-ups to no small degree have been invested in juxtaposing the incongruous and revealing a world that is chaotic and filled with arbitrary values. Wright does this by making declarations such as "I'm going to get a tattoo all over my body of me but taller"[41] and "I used to work in the factory where they make hydrants but you couldn't park anywhere near the place." Hedberg, meanwhile, defamiliarizes the minute and unimportant in order to separate them from the rest of the world and infuse them with monumental importance. Hedberg's jokes often run along the lines of

> I bought a doughnut and they gave me a receipt for the doughnut. I don't need a receipt for a doughnut. I just give you the money, you give me the doughnut. End of transaction. We don't need to bring ink and paper into this. I just cannot imagine the scenario where I'd have to prove that I bought a doughnut. [Like I would say to] some skeptical friend, "Don't even act like I didn't get that doughnut. I got the documentation right here. Oh wait. It's back home in the file. Under 'D,' for doughnut."[42]

Like a Zen master with his koans, Hedberg with his jokes forces his audience to see everyday objects out of context, and when it does so the rest of the world fades away. We are thus drawn, at least temporarily, into a world where items like the doughnut and its receipt become the most important objects in the world. Like Duchamp and Picasso, comedians like Wright, Hedberg, Jerry Seinfeld, Emo Philips, Robert Townsend, Brian Regan, Margaret Smith, Harlan Williams and Jim Gaffigan reveal to us a chaotic universe as they cut, paste and recreate worlds that we can recognize, but that nevertheless remain hauntingly unfamiliar.

The TOBA (1920s–1930s) and
Moms Mabley (March 19, 1894–May 23, 1975)

In the 1920s and 1930s, notable venues like the Cotton Club and the Apollo Theater in Harlem featured almost exclusively African-

American talent while denying Black patrons entry into their showrooms. Indeed, in a time when Jim Crow laws were widely considered reasonable and both the U.S. Army and professional baseball saw fit to keep Blacks and Whites separate, it seemed to make sense to America as a whole that Blacks should have their own vaudeville circuit. In 1907 a network of theaters and theater owners established the Theater Owners Booking Association, or TOBA, to showcase African-American talent. Sometimes called the Chitlin' Circuit,[43] the TOBA flourished into the 1930s, when it too fell victim to the Great Depression and technological advances.[44] During its run, however, the TOBA was able to prepare more than a few entertainers for entry into a show business world that—though years away—would be less concerned with skin color than it was with the performer's ability to satisfy audiences.

Among the most famous of the TOBA comedians was Dewey "Pigmeat" Markham, who worked as house comedian at the Apollo Theater. Originally a tap dancer, Markham has been credited with creating several dances, "including the 'Boogy Woogy' and 'The Chuck.'" As a comedian, however, his most famous line was introduced to the nation by Sammy Davis Jr. on the television show *Rowan & Martin's Laugh-In*, when Davis trucked across the stage chanting, "Here come de judge, here come de judge," an event that brought Markham national attention—never mind that he had written the line some forty years earlier.[45] With a high-energy act that that featured dancing, clowning, blackout sketches and double entendres, Markham had been a favorite performer among audiences at the Apollo and places like it for some time. In 1944 *Variety* noted that Markham "has much talent and could get by with much cleaner stuff. However his blues gags garnered the biggest bellies and that's probably what's keeping him in that groove."[46]

Arguably the most influential of TOBA veterans, at least as far as stand-up comedy was concerned, however, was Jackie "Moms" Mabley, the granddaughter of a slave.[47] Born Loretta Mary Aiken in Bravard, North Carolina, in 1894, Mabley was of mixed Black, Cherokee and Irish lineage. She got into show business while still in her teens because she was "pretty and didn't want to become a prostitute." Eventually she took the name of a boyfriend who deserted her, saying, "He took a lot off of me. . . . The least I could do was take his name." Soon after that, "Louis Armstrong, Duke Ellington, and Sophie Tucker dubbed her 'Moms' because of her willingness to help struggling actors and comics."[48] The moniker fit in other ways, however. While still in her twenties she had begun to cultivate the character of Moms, an oversexed yarnspinner full of common-sense wisdom who appeared on stage in "hats that were designed *not* to match the drooping sweaters and the too comfortable and too vividly patterned housedresses she tossed on her frame in public defiance of all claims to feminine fashion," not to mention her "knee-length Argyle socks, again in brilliant colors" that "gave way to striking, oversized men's slippers that were as much a trademark of Moms as her toothless delivery of jokes." Also, she had had three children—one before she was twelve—all of whom were eventually kidnapped by their caretakers. Moms was not to see them until they were adults. [49]

Furthermore, Mabley herself said the creation of the "Moms" character was motivated by respect and admiration for her own grandmother, commenting that "I had in mind a woman about 60 or 65 years. She's a good woman with an eye for shady dealings . . . she was like my granny, the most beautiful woman I had ever known. She was the one who convinced me to go and make something of myself. . . . She was so gentle, but she kept her children in line, best believe that."[50]

On and off stage, Mabley was an iconoclast. Even though she shared stages with some of the biggest names in show business— giants like Armstrong, Ellington, Tucker, Nancy Wilson, Cab Calloway and Cannonball Adderley—she nevertheless deliberately cultivated physical ugliness while speaking openly about her sexual appetites. Trudier Harris writes, "one observer commented that she could take the most taboo of subjects and deliver jokes about them in lines as clean as new-fallen snow."[51] For instance, jokes like "The only thing an old man can do for me is bring me a message from a young man" and "A woman is a woman until the day she dies, but a man's a man only as long as he can"[52] announced to the world that though Black, homely, toothless and disheveled, she was still a sexual being. In addition, her very appearance satirized the "legitimacy of class and social distinctions as defined by the proper look."[53]

Beyond this, there was an archetypal dimension to her character as she made "extensive use of folk themes that were commonly known by the Afro-American community, a body of lore that points to the perpetuation of a cultural tradition from the 'woman of words' to the community and, equally, from the community to the 'woman of words.'" Consequently, Mabley's comedy often grew out of "a laughter of recognition which established bonds of identity and friendship with her audience."[54] Certainly, there was plenty of good old-fashioned folk wisdom in Mabley's jokes, in lines like "It ain't the depths of the river that drowns a man; it's the water," "I'd rather be a young man's fool than an old man's darling," or (while advising children about crossing the street) "Damn the lights; watch the cars; the lights ain't never hit nobody."[55]

When Mabley died in 1975 she left nothing less than a treasury of great comedy that included fifteen record albums, appearances on hit shows like *The Smothers Brothers Comedy Hour*, *The Merv Griffin Show* and *The Flip Wilson Show* and two Top-40 hits—the serious anti-Vietnam War commentary "Everything's Gonna Be Alright" and the funky "It's Your Thing" (which she performed on the October 13, 1969, edition of the show *The Music Scene*, with Lily Tomlin looking on in admiration)—not to mention an enormous influence on the world of stand-up.

The Borscht Belt (Early 1900s–Mid-1970s)

In the last decade of the nineteenth century, New York's Ulster and Sullivan counties were beginning a slow transformation. And no one could have predicted how the changes in this area less than a hundred miles from New York City would impact American entertainment.

Home to a great many Jewish farm families, this region in the southern Catskill Mountains had, since the end of the 1890s, been a great producer of milk and eggs because "not much else grew well in the region."[56] As transportation—most notably the O&W railroad, which carried the commodities into New York City—became more widely available, the farmers learned that they had a more lucrative product at their disposal: vacation time for middle-class city-dwellers. In an epoch in which upstate hotels were wont to display signs reading "No Hebrews Accommodated,"[57] these homes could offer to "Jewish shop workers and small store keepers from the city" affordable leisure activities along with "a whiff of fresh air."[58] Before long, more residents, farmers and entrepreneurs got in on the act. Dedicated boarding houses sprang up, then kuchalayns, which were boarding houses in which renters shared kitchen facilities. After that came bungalow colonies and hotels.[59]

By the 1940s, this area which would be informally known as "the Borscht Belt"—a reference to the hearty beet soup that was a staple of many first-generation Jewish families—would be home to "literally hundreds of small boarding houses" and more than five hundred hotels. During "The Season," which ran from Memorial Day weekend to Labor Day weekend, the resorts were places where "Jews could have a proper vacation like regular Americans but they could do it in Yiddish if they wished, and with kosher food, varying degrees of religious observance, and a vibrant Jewish culture of humor, theater and song."[60] Guests were offered activities like tennis, swimming and Canasta games during the day and entertainment at night, which meant that more than a thousand stages required entertainment every night of the week throughout the summer.

Because "[t]hese places" as Stebbins has noted, "did not offer variety shows," but rather were arranged so that a "comic or some other single performer would present the entire show, possibly all shows, on a given evening" and sometimes "did so for several successive nights,"[61] the Borscht Belt venues required a new kind of entertainer, the toomler. According to comedian Joey Adams, a veteran of such venues, the title was taken from the Castilian Yiddish word for "fool or noisemaker" and the toomler was essentially a jokester who both on and off stage "does anything and everything to entertain the customers so that they won't squawk about their rooms or food"[62] and was responsible for "keeping guests laughing not just during performances onstage, but all day every day and everywhere—poolside, at card games, in dining rooms."[63] According to Phil Brown, the toomler's humor "was often developed out of the daily life of the people he associated with, so that much of the Catskills comedy was an organic product of its own fermentation."[64]

Perhaps the most famous of these entertainers was Jerry Lewis, who got his start when, at age fifteen, he signed on with the Majestic Hotel in Fallsburgh. Born Jerome Levitch to a husband-and-wife musical team, Lewis seemed ready-made to play before audiences who, according to Joyce Wadler, demanded antics like "comics throwing themselves, fully clothed, into the pool."[65] While working as a tearoom boy at Brown's Hotel, Lewis "would drop a whole tray of peach melbas or make a three-point landing in a pot of mashed potatoes just for a snicker. On a cold night he might even start a fire in the tearoom— and it didn't have a fireplace."[66] Later on the future movie star was wont to pour a bowl of soup on his head in the main dining room, just "to get a few laughs."[67]

Even for the likes of natural physical comedians like Lewis, toomling was demanding work. Red Buttons, for instance, while working at Beerkill Lodge in Greenfield Park, for a while "quadrupled as an enter-

tainer, bellboy, prop boy and waiter on busy weekends," earning a sala-
ry of "a dollar and a half each and every week."[68] Danny Kaye, who
eventually became known as "King of the Catskills,"[69] spent some time
as one resort's social director, which meant that he served as "producer, director, writer, actor, song-and-dance man, emcee, comedian, scen-
ic designer, electrician, stage manager, stagehand and sometimes waiter."[70] According to Adams, "[m]ost of the 'stars' got paid off in meals
and places to sleep, usually cozily situated in a basement storeroom
or—if they were at the top of their profession—in a stuffy attic. Alan
King's bedroom at the White Roe Hotel was a cot onstage."[71]

Between the 1930s and 1950s, however, the Borscht Belt resorts
were in their heyday and proved to be a training ground for some of
the most important comedy acts of the forthcoming decades with the
likes of Joan Rivers, King, Buttons, Milton Berle, Don Rickles, Jack
Benny, Jack Carter, Jackie Mason, Dick Shawn, Sid Caesar, Mel
Brooks, Buddy Hackett, Kaye, Don Adams, Morey Amsterdam, Lenny
Bruce, Myron Cohen, Phyllis Diller, Shecky Greene and Henny
Youngman—to name but a few—cutting their performing teeth on
those stages. The influence of the Borscht Belt comedian is so pervasive, in fact, that by the 1970s the image of the cigar-smoking, tuxedo-
clad comic who laces his jokes with Yiddish witticisms had become a
cliché and the stuff of parody.

By the 1970s, the Borscht Belt was only a shadow of its former
self. According to Bushman, the decline was essentially economic in
nature as more people could afford jet travel and more exotic vacations.[72] Nevertheless, for decades to come, the imprint could be found
in virtually every American television variety and talk show, a great
many nightclubs and, of course, the innovation that was the dedicated
comedy club.

Although the exact reasons that Jewish comedy in general and
Borscht Belt comedy in particular have had such an impact on American stand-up have been the subject of much theorizing, there is general
agreement that the impact has been dramatic if not mind-boggling. As
recently as 1978, *Time* magazine reported that while "Jews constitute
only 3% of the U.S. population . . . 80% of the nation's comedians are
Jewish."[73] One reason might be that Jewish humor has resonated with
America as a whole because American mythology so closely parallels
Jewish mythology. Just as Yahweh promised freedom and prosperity
for the enslaved Jews living under Egyptian rule during the time of
Moses, America promises freedom and prosperity for the poor, en-

slaved and downtrodden people throughout the world. And it was this very promise that, during the late nineteenth and early twentieth centuries, brought the country's largest wave of immigrants to New York's Ellis Island. Furthermore, just as the Promised Land mentioned in the Mosaic books is said to be "a land flowing with milk and honey," or a land of fertility and abundance,[74] the United States has been historically and mythically a land where prosperity and opportunity are found and nurtured. Finally, Americans, like Jews, have had little trouble seeing themselves as "God's chosen people." Even the Puritan's initial venture to the New World was modeled after the stories of Adam and Moses.[75]

Still another explanation might be that the Jewish intellectual tradition, especially the study of the Talmud, the ancient rabbinical commentaries on the Torah which are said to contain the answers to every moral problem, has historically served as a template for the comedic creative process. Just as a Talmudic scholar might take a moral dilemma—for instance, a man's stealing a chicken to feed his family—and examine it from various points of view to determine whether the actions were ethical, much of the art of stand-up revolves around taking mundane events and examining them from various angles.

A clear example of this can readily be seen in the work of former Borscht Belter Jackie Mason. Described by Phil Berger as "a Talmudic scholar from the Lower East Side" of New York and "a quizzical kid who gave up the rabbinate to be a comic,"[76] Mason builds his comedic routines by examining events and situations from multiple angles. In one of his most enduring and successful bits, for instance, Mason analyzes a trip to his psychiatrist's office from several points of view almost simultaneously, saying,

> There was a time that even I didn't know who I was. . . . Luckily, my psychiatrist told me who I am. [If] not for him, to this day I wouldn't know who I am. . . . As soon as I came into his office, the first thing he said to me is, "We're gonna have to find out who the real you is. Otherwise you'll never be happy." . . . I said to myself, "I need him to find out who I am? If I don't know who I am, how's he gonna know? He never met me."
>
> He said, "We both don't know. That's why we have to look for the real you."
>
> I said to myself, "If I don't know who I am, how do you know who to look for? And even If I find me, how will I know it's me? Besides, if I want to look for me, [why] do I need him? I could look myself. . . .

He said, "The search for the real you will have to continue. That will be twenty-five dollars, please."

I said to myself, "This is not the real me. Why should I give him the twenty-five dollars? I'll look for the real me. Let *him* give him the twenty-five dollars. What if I find the real me and he doesn't think it's worth twenty-five dollars? Then I've stuck my money with the real him."

I said to myself, "For all I know, the real me might be going to a different psychiatrist altogether. Might even be a psychiatrist himself." . . . I says, "Wouldn't it be funny if *you're* the real me and you owe me twenty-five dollars? . . . I'll tell you what, I'll charge you ten dollars, we'll call it even." [77]

Judging by this kind of material, it seems that Mason's transformation from the pulpit to the Catskills and then onto the nightclub stage, *The Ed Sullivan Show* and finally to his acclaimed one-person shows like *The World According to Me*, *Freshly Squeezed* and *A Night at the Opera*, is only natural, logical and organic.

Although stand-up comedy is an innovation that was most directly inspired by the White Southerner Mark Twain and the Cherokee Will Rogers and was introduced to the world by the African-American Charley Case, there can be no question that Jewish comedians as a whole and Borscht Belt comedians in particular changed the profession like no other single group.

Nightclubs (Early 1900s–Present)

Yet another response to America's newfound prosperity was the New York nightclub or, as it was sometimes called, the cabaret. Unlike the saloon, which catered almost exclusively to working-class men, or the rathskellers, which were basement establishments that served as "hangouts for newspapermen, entertainers and bohemians,"[78] nightclubs in the early decades of the century emphasized sociability for "late-night crowds still bent on enjoying themselves"[79]—which in New York City meant after Broadway shows let out. According to Lewis A. Erenberg, although "the cabaret's early days are clouded in murky origins," sometime around 1911 "cabaret-style entertainment had spread from the segregated vice districts and theatrical-sporting communities of the rathskellers to the Broadway restaurants."[80] This meant that, in no small measure, Victorian mores were loosening up and that which "had been permitted only in the dark now did not seem quite so wicked. The cabaret had made a symbolic evolution from a hidden aspect of life to one accepted as a phenomenon of human existence."[81] The cabarets, for example, were the "first public drinking institutions to admit well-to-do women because their approach to drinking differed from that of the male saloon."[82]

As increasingly more intimate spaces began featuring entertainment, the entertainers seemed to have less trouble reaching past the fourth wall. After all, the nightclub was built around the oxymoronic concept of public intimacy. Nightclub entertainment meant that patrons sat at their own tables rather than in a theater full of seats, and that the entertainers themselves were part of the crowd. Even though sometimes these establishments brought in other kinds of expanded entertainment such as chorus girl revues, most of the time the entertainment was brought in straight from vaudeville, and seldom were more than two people on stage at a time. One of the first such headliners to "move into the cabaret with any regularity" was a hefty singing comedian named Sophie Tucker. Born Sophie Abuza to Russian-Jewish parents who immigrated to Hartford, Connecticut, shortly after she was born in 1887, Tucker entertained patrons of her parents' restaurant in between waiting on tables. From an early age, she was bound and determined to get into show business.[83] She took the name Tucker in 1906 after she ran away to New York, where at first she found work singing in modest restaurants. Eventually she was accepted into an amateur show at the 116th Street Music Hall on the condition that she appear in blackface because the manager felt she was so "big and ugly."[84] In 1909, after working in vaudeville and burlesque theaters, Tucker was offered a part in the *Ziegfeld Follies*, the lavish revues that would remain a fixture on Broadway into the 1930s.

After some trouble with jealous headliners, Tucker returned to vaudeville, doing material that "consisted of 'hot songs' filled with double entendres," which she felt were meant to be humorous rather than shocking because they had "a belly laugh in every line."[85] Even though Tucker was soon to become a star, the intimacy of the nightclub seemed to suit her because the "setting brought the entertainer and audience closer, and thus permitted personal qualities to operate." Also, according to *Variety*, she had the "forceful personality" that "was needed to overcome the very informality of the café."[86]

Tucker was able to take this kind of intimacy to a new level one night in 1915, when while out at The Tokio, a New York cabaret, with her husband, Frank Westphal, she was asked by owner Henry Fink to entertain the crowd as a favor. She found the audience so "appreciative of the unrehearsed performance" that she began to make the practice a regular part of her act. By staging such impromptu performances, Tucker gave audiences the "illusion that their presence sparked the performance, as they shared something truly intimate with the entertainer on that evening, as if they had been allowed to participate in the private hijinks of the celebrities' world."[87]

Even though Tucker would go on to make seven feature films between 1929 and 1944, she was always most comfortable before a live audience. Movies and radio were too restrictive because, as she once told an interviewer, while working in such media, "You can't do this, you can't do that. I couldn't even say 'hell or damn,' and nothing, honey, is more expressive than the way I say 'hell or damn.'" She continued to work nightclubs into the 1950s.[88]

Tucker died in 1966 at age seventy-nine, but not before leading a revolution in the entertainment world. The flaunting of her sexuality through jokes and bawdy songs such as "But He Only Stays Til Sunday" and "I Just Couldn't Make My Feelin's Behave," coupled with an attitude that declared that she expected her man to perform in the bedroom or else, forecast the sexually explicit comedy of the late twentieth century. She openly questioned societal values, mores and fairy tale ideas about marriage decades before Lenny Bruce shocked audiences by discussing the same subjects. She, like Bruce and Chris Rock years later, understood automatically that this particular kind of humor enabled audiences to bring "private desires into the public light" and that the best way to discuss sex was to get people to laugh about it and release their tension.[89]

In many ways, attitudes of the burlesque hall performer and Tucker's stage persona took on lives of their own. If the two institutions were built upon shocking patrons, prudes and America as a whole, then nightclubs and nightclub comedy were quick to pick up the mantle. During the fourteen years of Prohibition, Americans seemed to have little trouble violating liquor laws just as Tucker and the burlesque performers seemed to have little trouble violating mores. Ralph Blumenthal, for instance, writes in his history of New York's famous Stork Club, "If the rest of the country laughed at Prohibition, New York convulsed in hysterics. You couldn't find a drink—not unless you walked ten feet in any direction. If you owned a drugstore . . . you practically owned a wholesale liquor business."[90] Even Will Rogers quipped that "Prohibition is better than no liquor at all."[91]

One of the most important figures in the entertainment world during this time was Mary Louise Cecilia Guinan, who was more commonly known by her nickname, "Texas." A Waco native who had spent years in show business as a sharpshooter, an expert rider, Broadway and movie actress and vaudevillian, Guinan was very much at the center of New York's entertainment world—so much so that she redefined the role of the emcee when the situation demanded it. With liquor illegal, public drinking, by and large, had to be done in smaller venues than before, and the conditions were such that a good emcee could make or break a show. According to Erenberg, although the revue show the Folies Bergère

> had introduced the master of ceremonies as a continental invention as early as 1911, it did not catch on in the restaurant cabarets. The largest restaurants were too noisy to hear someone talking, and for that reason, both masters of ceremonies and verbal comedians were not strong presences in the early cafes. The advent of smaller clubs, however, meant that someone could talk and be heard, and during the 1920s some of the greatest stars were masters of ceremonies.[92]

No one seemed to be able to take advantage of the situation quite the way Guinan did. "Loud and raucous" and the owner of various clubs, Guinan was able to "attract celebrities and big spenders to every one of her numerous nightclubs" and "dominated her night-clubs" as she introduced the various acts with great liveliness, and "just when the revue threatened to eclipse audience participation, Texas activated the audience. She was a figure of intimacy, though not threatening."[93]

Although Prohibition was repealed in 1933, many of the hot spots that grew out of those ostensibly "dry" years also shaped American entertainment history in no small way. Not only did the Prohibition laws give organized crime a boost that would have been hard to obtain otherwise, but once liquor became legal again, the speakeasy was once again the cabaret or the nightclub with the master of ceremonies playing a much larger role. For stand-up comedians, this meant a lot more work in a time when burlesque shows and vaudeville were quickly becoming passé. In showrooms that featured different kinds of entertainment on different nights, comedians got work not just as headliners and warm-up acts, but also as emcees. According to Erenberg, the "successful master of ceremonies smoothed over the rough spots in the shows, kept the entertainment moving along at a fast clip, enhanced audience participation, and, most of all, kept alive a sense of enhanced audience sociability and friendliness."[94]

By the end of the next decade, when the United States emerged from World War II as both a military and economic powerhouse, the nightclubs became even more popular and it seemed that virtually every venue that featured entertainment had a working stand-up comedian to introduce the acts. According to Bushman, the top clubs were able to hire comedians who had established followings due to their work on the Borscht Belt and vaudeville.[95] By the middle 1950s, as the Beatnik revolt against Cold War values began to leach into other pockets of society—namely the so-called upscale urban night clubs or "chichi" rooms like Mr. Kelly's in Chicago, the hungry i[96] in San Francisco and The Bitter End in New York—nightclubs began to book edgier comics like Bruce, Sahl and Dick Gregory.

Also in the 1950s and 1960s, many of these comedians were able to cut their teeth in less formal and less lucrative venues called coffeehouses or "after-hours" clubs, such as the Gaslight and the Café Wha? in New York's Greenwich Village that had emerged as bohemian hangouts. In addition to comedians, the coffeehouses also featured jazz and folk musicians and singers and poets and sketch players. Here, comedians were wont to experiment, even though the gigs paid very little or nothing at all.[97] Berger reports that "Bill Cosby worked at the Gaslight and the Wha? and was so good that he once received a raise from $5.00 to $7.50 per set."[98]

If the nightclub phenomenon reached a pinnacle, it might have been with Hugh Hefner's Playboy Clubs, a chain of nightclubs that flourished around the world, but mainly in the United States, between the 1960s and 1991. The clubs were essentially upscale, exclusive nightclubs. For a $25 membership fee patrons were served drinks by Hefner's famous Playboy models and treated to some of the best entertainment the world had to offer. Not only did Hefner employ stand-up's biggest stars, comedians like Cosby, Woody Allen, Gregory and Bob Newhart, but he also featured plenty of up-and-comers such as Steve Martin and George Carlin.[99]

Despite the fact that stand-up comedy had been almost synonymous with nightclub entertainment since Prohibition, there were no dedicated comedy clubs until 1963, when Gerson "Bud" Friedman and his wife, Silver, opened the Improvisational Café in New York's Greenwich Village. Originally, Friedman had intended the room to be another after-hours hangout, but within two years, and quite organically, it had evolved into a venue where comedians gathered to work out their acts and audiences gathered to watch. Friedman estimates that in the fifteen years he operated what would come to be called the New York Improv, he introduced some 10,000 new acts, including Allen, Dick Cavett, Cosby and Rodney Dangerfield.[100] For the next twelve years, until comedian Sammy Shore, his wife Mitzi (parents of comedian Paulie Shore) and comedy writer Rudy DeLuca opened the Comedy Store in Los Angeles, the Improv would be the only comedy club in the world. By 1973, after divorcing Sammy, Mitzi bought out her partners and became sole owner of her club and began following her initial vision of having the Comedy Store as the centerpiece for an "art colony" of comedians.[101]

Like jazz, stand-up comedy is an expression of the city at night. In the early years of the twenty-first century it might seem only logical that comedians should work in bars, where the flowing of alcohol makes the jokes all the funnier. But that is only part of the story. Another dimension is that taverns, bars, nightclubs and cabarets have always been the profane answer to the church. Like houses of worship, these venues promote communion among those present by encouraging the sharing of food and (usually alcoholic) beverages. Thus, it seems quite fitting that the missing piece of the puzzle would be provided by the comedian. Like the cleric, minister, priest or prelate, the comedian stands on an elevated platform, faces all others in the room, presides over a meal and connects the audience members with spheres they could not approach in ordinary life.

Walkathons (1930s–1940s)

The Great Depression that hit the United States in 1929 brought with it more than a few trends that reflected a nation's desperation. In addition to contests that involved marathon hand-holding, peanut pushing, flagpole sitting and even kissing, there were the famed walkathons or dance marathons that would become the subject of the 1969 movie *They Shoot Horses, Don't They?* starring Jane Fonda. According to Frank M. Calabria, whose 1993 study *The Dance of the Sleepwalkers: The Dance Marathon Fad* remains the authoritative source on the matter, the shows were dancing endurance contests (the longest on record lasted more than nine months) in which contestants danced in teams and were required to stay in motion on the dance floor for forty-five minutes every hour. According to Calabria:

> The regimen walkathon teams followed was exact. At the sound of a police siren, on the hour, contestants were to be in a dance position ready

to start moving on the dance floor; after 45 minutes, a second siren sounded; contestants had two minutes to leave the dance floor. The next 11 minutes could be used to sleep or rest, attend to persona needs, or find some form of recreation. Two minutes before the hour, a third siren sounded calling couples back to the dance floor to being the next hourly stint. [102]

During the course of these affairs, contestants were given one hour early in the morning for bathing and four hours in every twenty-four to sleep in rest quarters. Other than that, the dancers ate, shaved and even slept as they danced.

The centerpieces of these early versions of the reality show were the emcees, entertainers whose job it was to keep "the attention of audiences with a continual round of chatter and comic asides."[103] In her master's thesis, Chelsea Dunlop writes that the emcee, who was virtually always a comedian, was

> Arguably the most important person employed by the show. . . . The emcee needed to be personable and entertaining. He kept the audience on their toes and got them emotionally engaged with the contestants who, in turn, reminded the audience about the larger struggles of Depression-era life "outside" that comprised the deeper over-riding theme of the show. The emcee kept track of the hours and motivated the contestants by repeating the common marathon phrase, "How long can they last?"[104]

Furthermore, the host's job, in no small measure, was to "sell every contestant to the audience and to attract a sponsor for each team in the show" or, in other words, to encourage the audience members to choose favorites and become emotionally involved. To do this, according to Calabria, the emcees learned to combine "corn" and "con" into what amounted to sales pitches for each team.[105]

At a time when families across the nation struggled and regularly missed meals, when the national unemployment rate exceeded twenty-five percent and as many as 14 million people were out of work, the walkathon, even though it was a "bastard, sub-basement form of show business never to achieve a high status among other forms of entertainment media like vaudeville, nightclubs and the movies, sources from which it borrowed . . . did play to large audiences and attracted thousands of contestants."[106] Not only was the entertainment cheap—admission was rarely more than twenty-five cents—but it was accessible as the contests continued virtually around the clock and spectators could enter at all hours. Besides that, at least on the West Coast, top stars like Bill "Bojangles" Robinson, Eddie Cantor and The Marx Brothers performed free of charge while stars like Mickey Rooney and Frankie Darrow offered their services as emcees.[107]

One of the most notable comedians to emerge from this environment was Red Skelton. According to biographer Arthur Marx, the young comedian had been "killing time in his rooming house in Kansas City" when he got word that a local walkathon promoter, Max McCaffrey, was looking for an emcee to replace the one who had just deserted him. After a sprint downtown, the future television star was at the city's Civic Auditorium discussing his credentials with McCaffrey. The promoter advised him that the walkathon customers were "becoming jaded" and were demanding entertainment other than the dancers, which is why he needed a comedian. McCaffrey advised Skelton that if the comedian "couldn't keep the audience constantly in stitches, or if the people walked out on him or fell asleep, the comic was automatically fired." Skelton summarily began a job in which he introduced contestants, asked "how long can they last?" and talked and joked for ten hours a day, seven days a week, without the help of a stage, microphone, curtain, spotlight, straight man or orchestra.[108]

Skelton was an immediate hit not only because

> his diamond-in-the-rough talent stuck out like a giant redwood in a forest of saplings, but because he literally knocked himself silly in order to please his audiences . . . all he had to fall back on were his enormous energy, a retentive memory that kept every joke or gag or routine he'd ever heard or seen before neatly catalogued in his brain, and a genius for comic inventiveness.[109]

From 5 p.m. until 3 a.m., seven days a week, Skelton kept up a running patter of jokes, sang songs, made faces, did imitations, took pratfalls, kissed ladies, crawled under seats, climbed chandeliers, sat on laps, ate neckties, broke plates, underdressed, doused himself with soft drinks yanked from customers' hands, walked on all fours, imitated drunks and rubes and "mean widdle boys," recited poetry, performed card tricks and even rode a tricycle around the edge of the balcony. Once he stole a mounted policeman's horse from the street and galloped around the auditorium on him, with the gendarme in hot pursuit.[110]

By the time World War II broke out in 1941, and despite "a dearth of good contestants" that included plenty of dance marathon teams,

the competitions had become too much the product of a commercia-
lized and corporate world, and the craze was all but dead. One fan
complained when she learned that in at least one competition the winner was picked by the show's management rather than by its panel of
judges. Another would-be contestant, meanwhile, protested that it had
all become too predictable and trite, saying, "My girl friend [sic] and I
have been trying to enter a walkathon for some time. But as we have
never been in one, we can't find a show willing to take a chance on two
amateurs. Why don't promoters give amateurs chance to break into the
endurance field?"[111]

Perhaps another contributing factor to the spectacles' demise was
the war itself. While, as Calabria argues, during the Depression, "in
place of patriotism there was hopelessness,"[112] with the bombing of
Pearl Harbor, the national climate demanded renewed patriotism and,
with it, renewed hope.

The Ed Sullivan Show (June 20, 1948–June 6, 1971)
Although minstrel shows, vaudeville and their R-rated counterpart, the
burlesque show, were largely supplanted by radio, motion pictures and
television during the post-war years, the vestiges have never died out
completely. The most notable descendant of these entertainment
forms is the television variety show, the most important and influential
of which was *The Ed Sullivan Show*. Called *The Toast of the Town* for its
first four years, the production was essentially the electronic age's answer to vaudeville, as it featured short acts, usually no more than five
minutes long, that showcased the talents of singers, dancers, musicians,
magicians and, of course, comedians.

Hosted and produced by Ed Sullivan, a former sportswriter who
continued through the last years of his life to write an entertainment
column for *The New York Daily News*, the show took full advantage of
its vaudeville-like format with one notable exception: while vaudeville
was largely segregated—Charley Case, who could pass for White, and
Bert Williams were among the very few African-Americans who could
make the cross-over[113]—Sullivan was a rabid anti-racist. Jerry Bowles,
in his book *A Thousand Sundays: A History of the Ed Sullivan Show*, reports that Sullivan

> once had a high Ford official thrown out of the theater when the man
> suggested that he stop booking so many black acts.
> When a dealer in Cleveland said to him, "We realize that you got to
> have niggers on your show, but do you have to put your arm around

them?" Sullivan had to be physically restrained from beating the man to a pulp. . . . Sullivan's appreciation of black talent went all the way back to his days on the New York *Graphic* when he once scouted New York for a place where the great black basketball teams of that day could play. . . . During the 1940s, he had tried to revive a black revue called *Harlem Cavalcade* without much success. His great good friend was Bill "Bojangles" Robinson. When "Bojangles" died, it was Sullivan who paid for the funeral.[114]

In a time when Jim Crow laws were still in effect and the Civil Rights movement was more than a decade away, Ed Sullivan's progressivism also had a direct financial benefit: it allowed him to draw from other pools of talent. Not only did the show feature former vaudevillians like Jimmy Durante, Buddy Hackett, Tucker, Skelton and Bob Hope, but it also introduced America to those who developed their skills in the Borscht Belt resorts and the Chitlin' Circuit.

The ostensible core American values of pluralism and sanctity of the individual were also, wittingly or not, core values of the *Ed Sullivan Show*. This, combined with the show's unprecedented popularity, resulted in a dramatic shift of the American consciousness. When he gave America Cosby, Sullivan introduced Americans to somebody just like them, with the same familial challenges and familiar characters like the frustrated parent and the bedeviling older brother, not to mention all the same ironies and dysfunctions. When he introduced Richard Pryor, he gave the nation a glimpse of life in a Peoria ghetto replete with a three-dimensional characterization of a wino who had served in World War I. When he showcased Jackie Mason, who appeared on the show fifty-six times, more than any other act with the exception of the comedy team of Wayne and Shuster,[115] he introduced a comedy act that was unabashedly Jewish.

While Bowles makes a good point when he tells us, "It is said that Sullivan did more to introduce the American heartland to culture than any other personality in the history of television,"[116] I would argue that such a statement sells the show a bit short. While Martin Luther King could only dream of a world in which a Black woman was welcomed into the home of a provincial White man or a Jew could tell his stories in the home of anti-Semitic Blacks, Ed Sullivan was able to make these things happen. During a time of turbulent transformation and realignment of political and social attitudes, during a time when most markets had three or, at most, four television networks, during a time when the majority of families across the country planned their Sunday evenings around his show, Sullivan changed American attitudes by booking comedians from all walks of life and exposing the nation to their stories and their points of view. By doing this, he provided America with a constant stream of miniature ethnographies. Through the magic of stand-up comedy and the widespread appeal of *The Ed Sullivan Show*, a great many Americans began to realize that the people whom they once believed threatened them were in fact thinking, feeling, breathing and vulnerable human beings with whom they had a great deal in common.

One can only imagine the hundreds of thousands of families across the continent reacting to the monologues of Cosby, Flip Wilson and Pryor, performers who never shied away from revealing vulnerability, honesty and passion. Dick Gregory tells of the process. After his first few television shows, he said, "I got letters from white folks sayin' they never heard a black person talk about their family."[117]

Indeed, Sullivan's genius involved, other than a keen eye for talent and his intrepid risk-taking, his ability to link the past to the future, to weave the strands of vaudeville, the Borscht Belt, burlesque and the Chitlin' Circuit into a new vision of America.

The Beats (Early 1950s–Early 1960s)

The nightmare that was World War I—once commonly referred to as "the war to end all wars"—paled in comparison to the horror of World War II. While some 40 million people, more or less half of them civilians, died in the earlier war, more than 72 million died in World War II, about two-thirds of them civilians—and some 200,000 were killed in the two U.S. attacks on the Japanese cities of Hiroshima and Nagasaki in August 1945. In the aftermath of such unfathomable carnage, the United States for the next twenty years or so attempted what might be considered a "return to normalcy." The country as a whole seemed to feel responsible for both ending history's most horrific period and for unleashing unimaginable destructive power. One response to this was to embrace the country's special role in world history, to see the United States as the "shining city on a hill" that had been forecast since the days of John Winthrop, an attitude that was embraced by the great majority of Americans. According to Andrea Shannon Prussing-Hollowell, those who participated in America's upward mobility during the post-war years "created suburbs, had babies, and participated in consumerism, hoping to establish a permanent, affluent, family-oriented society." Quoting from Douglas Brinkley's essay "The United

States in the Truman and Eisenhower Years," she undergirds the argument by pointing out that the those who saw themselves as the American mainstream during this time "are often remembered as the Greatest Generation, people who came of age in the 1940s, fought in World War II, and afterwards established 'the largest middle class in U.S. history with the niftiest conveniences.'"[118] It was between 1945 and 1965, after all, that the country tried to paint itself as a utopia. The country's self-portraits manifested in forms such as television shows like *Father Knows Best*, *Ozzie and Harriet* and *Leave It to Beaver*, which painted American life in the rosiest of colors. This dynamic, however, was perhaps most explicit in the characters played by actor James Stewart, a decorated U.S. Air Corps pilot in real life who provided dazzling portrayals of an idealized America. In movies such as *It's a Wonderful Life*, which was released just sixteen months after the Hiroshima bombing, and *The Spirit of St. Louis*, in which he played larger-than-life American aviator Charles Lindbergh, Stewart became the idealized American, the personification of an American who was humble, heroic and very much the boy next door.

There were those, however, who rejected the country's newfound status and values and who thus sought "alternatives to conformity they were expected to participate in,"[119] in no small measure because "they distrusted collectivity."[120] Among the most celebrated were the artists who eventually came to call themselves the Beatniks. The moniker was derived from the street term "beat," an expression which poet Allen Ginsberg explained meant, in street argot, "exhausted, at the bottom of the world, looking up or out, sleepless, wide-eyed, perceptive, rejected by society, on your own, streetwise"[121] with the added suffix "nik" which was culled from the name of the Russian satellite *Sputnik*, launched a few months earlier. The coinage was actually first presented by *San Francisco Chronicle* columnist Herb Caen, who in April 1958 wrote that *Look Magazine* was preparing a photo spread on the hipster scene in San Francisco's North Beach neighborhood and about "a party in a North Beach house for 50 Beatniks."[122] Novelist and poet Jack Kerouac, a charter member of the Beatniks, however, would sum up the phenomenon by writing how, shaped by their rejection of 1950s values and their embracing of bebop jazz,

> postwar youth emerged cool and beat, had picked up the gestures and the style; soon it was everywhere, the new look . . . the bop visions became common property of the commercial, popular culture world. . . . The ingestion of drugs became official (tranquilizers and the rest); and even the

clothes style of the beat hipsters carried over to the new rock 'n roll youth.[123]

In short, the Beatniks, who were also called "hipsters," were disillusioned with the country and its values and therefore rejected the newfound visions of the American utopia. According to Prussing-Hollowell, they "dwelled on the periphery because they engaged in activities that countered mainstream America's definition of 'growing up' as they indulged in recreational drug use, rejected marriage and often made their livings 'outside the legitimate marketplace, often in petty crime.'"[124] One of the main vehicles for the expression of this disillusionment was "jazz, particularly bebop," which had emerged in the early 1940s and emphasized creative expression and experimentation in a manner that was later "interpreted as a prototypical attitude not only towards the exploitative conditions of working in the entertainment business, but also towards the possibility of autonomous expression of black culture."[125]

Thus it was only a matter of time before the literary world of Ginsberg and Kerouac and the bebop world of jazz innovators such as Charlie Parker and Dizzy Gillespie began to dramatically impact the world of stand-up comedy. Much the way bebop rejected and even subtly mocked popular music or the way Beatnik literary works like Kerouac's novel *On the Road* tacitly criticized American suburbia by celebrating a bohemian lifestyle, comedian Lenny Bruce "began mocking everything traditional comedians left alone." According to Prussing-Hollowell, Bruce's rise to fame was powered by the way he

> developed his humor parallel to that of his audiences, who were typically members of the underground. Once he began mocking mainstream American beliefs, logic, and values, Bruce realized his audiences consisted of like-minded people who rejected mainstream standards and these people emerged as his primary audience, embracing him and his comedy.[126]

Thus Bruce soon began to emerge as the voice of "a wider discontent with the American society."[127]

By the way he and his contemporary Canadian-born comedian Mort Sahl chose to compromise their laughs-per-minute ratio in order to address headier, topical issues so as to shed light on social ills, Bruce asked his audiences—and by implication the rest of the country—to see beyond the cultivated illusions of *Father Knows Best* and *It's a Won-*

derful Life and to take a hard look at a United States that was far from perfect. For instance, just days after he was arrested in Philadelphia for drug possession in September 1961, Bruce introduced a bit entitled "To Come" at the San Francisco Jazz Workshop. Accompanying himself on drums, Bruce takes his audience into previously forbidden territory, the American bedroom, and reveals a side of *Ozzie and Harriet* most Americans would shudder to think about:

> *Toooooo*
> is a preposition, come is a verb.
> To is a preposition.
> *Commmmme*
> is a verb!
> To is a preposition.
> Come is a verb.
> To is a preposition.
> Come is verb intransitive . . . To come . . .
> Two words I've heard my whole adult life and as a kid when they thought I was sleeping . . .
> It's been like a big drum solo:
> . . . Did you come?
> Did you come good?
> Did you come good?
> Did you come? . . .
> I come better with you sweetheart than anyone in this whole goddam world . . .
> But . . . don't come in me. Don't come in me. Don't come in me mimimimi. Don't come in me.
> I can't come. Don't ask me.
> Because you don't love me, that's why you can't come.[128]

Unlike Henny Youngman, Bob Hope or Red Skelton, who worked with rather innocuous and mostly scripted material, Bruce embraced the improvisational style borrowed from bebop, saying once, "I know a lot of things I want to say; I'm just not sure exactly when I will say them," and seldom shied away from controversy. So provocative was Bruce, in fact, that he, along with Sahl, Jonathan Winters, and Don Adams (future star of the television show *Get Smart*), was among the comedians *Time* magazine labeled "The Sickniks," because "they joked about father and Freud, about mother and masochism, about sister and sadism . . .[and] of airline pilots' throwing out a few passengers to lighten the load, of a graduate school for dope addicts, of parents so loving that they always 'got upset if anyone else made me cry,'" not to mention that they "attacked motherhood, childhood, adulthood, sainthood."[129]

Not quite knowing what to make of the then-33-year-old comedian, *Time* wrote,

> Although audiences unquestionably laugh at Bruce, much of the time he merely shouts angrily and tastelessly at the way of the world (on religious leaders: 'They have missed the boat. 'Thou shall not kill.' they say, and then one of them walks comfortingly to the death chamber with [convicted kidnapper and rapist] Caryl Chessman. . . . His political routines recall [the Gershwins' satirical musical] *Of Thee I Sing* with some venom added.[130]

Despite such controversial subject matter and various arrests for obscenity violations and drug possession, Bruce's star did not shine quite as brightly as Sahl's, at least not in the early 1960s. After recording the first full-length comedy album, *Mort Sahl at Sunset*, in 1955 and being dubbed "the original sicknik" by *Time*, Sahl clearly was the leader of the New Wave of comedy or the sicknik pack. A year after the sickniks story ran, Sahl was featured on the magazine's cover and thus became the first stand-up comedian so honored.[131] The accompanying article entitled "The Third Campaign" (the Kennedy and Nixon presidential campaigns were the first two) discussed Sahl's comedy and influence. Years later, we can see how his work essentially forecast the age of the hippies. *Time* wrote that Sahl

> represents a new and growing feeling, described rather breathlessly by Historian Arthur Schlesinger Jr. as "a mounting restlessness and discontent, an impatience with clichés and platitudes, a resentment against the materialist notion that affluence is the answer to everything, a contempt for banality and corn—in short, a revolt against pomposity. Sahl's popularity is a sign of a yearning for youth, irreverence, trenchancy, satire, a clean break with the past."[132]

Like Bruce and Kerouac, Sahl also claimed jazz as among his chief inspirations. Not only was he at that time palling around San Francisco with saxophonist Paul Desmond, a West Coast/"cool jazz" icon and the composer of the Beatnik anthem "Take Five," but Sahl also felt that much of the beauty of comedy came through improvisation, which brought a certain intimacy to each show. He once told *Los Angeles Times* critic Charles Champlin that

> I never found you could write the act. You can't rehearse the audience's responses. You adjust to them every night. I come in with only an outline. You've got to have a spirit of adventure. I follow my instincts and the audience is my jury. If I try a joke and they like it, I extend it. The audience is bright, you have to believe that, and they'll know to find the nugget in the story. The audience will always find the joke.[133]

This approach would later be taken by Jerry Seinfeld, who during his interview with Larry Wilde said, "To me, really good comedy is a dialogue—it's not a monologue. Their laughs are as important as what I'm saying. Laughs contain thought, you know. There are different shapes and sizes and sounds and colors and each one says something."[134]

By the 1970s, the work of Bruce, Sahl and the other Beat comedians like Mike Nichols and Elaine May, Winters and Dick Gregory would become to stand-up comedy what the Beatles were to pop music. Not only would these routines open up a floodgate of more challenging styles and add a whole new vocabulary to the art form, but they would in essence become a dividing line. Even though Youngman and Skelton would still be revered, stand-up comedians would no longer shy away from the most serious of topics: George Carlin would build his career around criticizing American hypocrisy and consumerism, Bill Hicks would openly threaten to kill President Ronald Reagan, Kathy Griffin would dedicate her career to mocking Hollywood stars and Bill Maher would begin shows by saying, "President Bush must set a timetable for removing his head from his ass."[135] In other words, everything before Bruce and Sahl would seem old-fashioned and even trite while everything that followed would, in one way or another, pay them tribute.

The Boom (Early 1980s–1990s)

Like the Civil War, the success of the Pet Rock or the rise and disappearance of Christopher Cross from the American entertainment landscape, the sudden burst in the popularity in stand-up comedy in the 1980s eschews facile explanation. Did it have something to do with the mood of the country? The economy? Shifts in political attitudes? Social attitudes? The arrival of cable television? Free tickets to comedy clubs?

Although stand-up comedy, since the early years of the twentieth century, has had a somewhat committed following, a few post-war developments seem to have created the period that, during the Reagan years, comedians and bookers referred to as "The Boom." One factor, according to both Borns and Stebbins, was the comics' strike in 1979, which began after twenty-two Los Angeles-area comedians created an informal group called Comedians for Compensation after they estimated that Mitzi Shore's Comedy Store had an annual gross of $2.5 million. When the strike was resolved, comedians began to receive standard pay for their work. Although the compensation was modest, usually twenty-five dollars a set,[136] it was enough so that the comics could, with a week's worth of sets, devote themselves more fully to their crafts.[137] A secondary effect was that a great many entrepreneurs began to realize that comedy clubs had great money making potential.

Still another important factor was the advent of *Saturday Night Live*, a television variety show that catered to a hip, post-Beatles audience and showcased some of the most influential comedians of the era, Richard Pryor and Steven Wright among them. In the aftermath of the turbulent 1960s and the trauma that was the Vietnam War (which ended just months before the show launched), young Americans were ready to embrace a comedy/variety show that was aimed toward their sensibilities. With *The Ed Sullivan Show* off the air and *The Carol Burnett Show* geared more toward their parents than their peers, the high school and college crowd saw *Saturday Night Live* as representative of their tastes, values and attitudes. The show brought together several strands of entertainment history: from the Commedia dell'arte it culled the improvisational sketch, from vaudeville and the variety show it brought the musical number, from the Beatniks, the running commentary on the week's newsmakers and from the television sitcom short pre-recorded clips and parodies of commercials. Perhaps even more profoundly, at least as far as the history of stand-up comedy is concerned, it introduced America to the neo-Dadaist Steve Martin.

Martin's jokes and stage persona provided a sharp contrast to the political diatribes of George Carlin. With unbridled silliness that incorporated a fake Groucho Marx nose and glasses, a toy "arrow-through-the-head," balloon animals and signature lines such as "excuuuuuse *meeee*!" "I am a wild and crazy guy" and the declaration "I've got happy feet!" that sent him jittering about the stage, Martin brought a childlike energy to the stand-up world that had largely been missing since the Ed Wynn days. Within four years of his initial appearance on that show, Martin, a former writer for *The Smothers Brothers* show, would play to packed, 20,000-seat stadiums, release two major comedy albums, *Let's Get Small* in 1977 and *A Wild and Crazy Guy* the next year, and write a book of short stories called *Cruel Shoes*. He would also star in the hit movie *The Jerk* and release the novelty song "King Tut," which made it to the upper ranks of *Billboard* magazine's "Hot 100" popular songs. Martin had become the comedy act of the period.

Perhaps another factor was that, in times of national trials, stand-up comedy becomes not simply a form of entertainment, but a national palliative. The art form's first real peak in popularity, as evinced by the bookings on the vaudeville circuit, the Borscht Belt and the Chitlin' Circuit, did not come until the Depression years. The next jump came in during the early Cold War years, when the club comedian began to come into his own. A few years after that, it was the tension of the Vietnam War that sent audiences looking for comedians. In the 1980s stand-up provided a counterpoint to the nuclear fears that were growing due to the presumed hawkish jingoism of Ronald Reagan. Thus the term "The Boom" was not just a reference to the newfound interest in comedy, but also hinted at fears of nuclear annihilation.

By the mid-1980s, there would be some 260 comedy clubs scattered throughout the country and at least one in every major American metropolis,[138] so it was only a matter of time before the more lucrative and far-reaching medium of television got in on the deal. By November 1989, HBO had drawn up plans for a cable television channel devoted exclusively to comedy, a network that would eventually become Comedy Central and would offer an endless stream of stand-up.

If there is one comedian who benefited most from comedy's boom years, a single comedian who represents the resurgence of the art form, it is Jerry Seinfeld. In addition to being the centerpiece of what is arguably the most popular television show in history, Seinfeld, a calm, casual, boy-next-door observationalist, had the power to reveal to America what was going on just beneath the floor of our collective consciousness. While we laughed at Wynn, Skelton, Jonathan Winters and Robin Williams for their craziness, we laughed at Seinfeld because he legitimized our subjective experience—even though what was fleeting and insignificant to us was an obsession to him. He told us about those things we'd seen hundreds of times and hardly noticed, like a street sign that says, "Left Turn Okay" or the canary that flies into the mirror without thinking to avoid crashing into the "other canary." More a phenomenologist than an anthropologist, Seinfeld pointed out the comedy in the mundane and the common, the minutiae of everyday life and nudged us toward believing that if there is a divine plan to the universe, the comedic is built into the design.

But even with Seinfeld leading a great profusion of talent, the Boom could not last forever. Over the next few years, comedy clubs would struggle, go out of business or consolidate. Some blamed the rise of cable and later on, satellite television, while others blamed the club practice of giving away tickets, thereby diminishing the perceived worth of time spent in a comedy club. Still another explanation was that there was not enough tension in the air to support all the comedians who ached for the stage. Incidentally, in the weeks following the terrorist attacks of September 11, 2001, both comedy clubs and churches reported an immediate eighteen to twenty-percent jump in attendance. By the following February, the numbers for churchgoers had fallen dramatically (although not quite as far down as they were prior to September 11) while comedy club attendance stayed consistent until the end of the year. One club owner, who asked not to be identified, joked during this time, "If my numbers go down again, I'm jacking a damned plane."[139]

In the years to come, the stand-up business would experience yet another lull. While there is little doubt that America, during the George W. Bush years, certainly experienced its fair share of tensions, the country remains, jurisprudentially speaking, increasingly fragmented. In an age when it is not uncommon to find single households with four televisions, each tuned into to a different station, it seems to be increasingly difficult to get enough people to laugh at the same jokes.

The Glut (Mid-1990s–Present)

Signs that stand-up's bubble was about to burst came as early as 1987, when *Time* magazine warned of oversaturation of the market and club owners like Silver Friedman warned that the quality of acts was getting thin.[140] Since Seinfeld and the Boom, stand-up comedy has had to suffer a glut as virtually every mid-sized city—the Albuquerques, Tucsons, Odessas, Amarillos, Portlands and Omahas—have at least one comedy club and a variety of open-mike shows in bars and hotel lounges, each of which is teeming with self-professed devotees of the craft, some of whom actually have talent. Tryouts for the hit television show *Last Comic Standing*, for instance, commonly drew tens of thousands of aspiring comics who waited outside the headquarters for more than four days just to get three minutes of time in front of network cameras.

For the up-and-comer hoping to hit the big time, the competition was devastating. For the future of stand-up comedy and the American consciousness, however, it was, quite possibly, both healthy and hopeful. Before the Boom, and especially in the pre-Lenny Bruce days, comedy was predominantly Jewish and secondarily Black.[141] Before Paul Rodriguez burst upon the scene in the mid-1980s, virtually the only Latino comic anybody had heard of was Freddy Prinze, who committed suicide at the height of his fame in 1977, at age 22. Native American and foreign comics were virtually unheard of. There were a few female voices like Phyllis Diller and Joan Rivers, while Jean Carroll, despite her enormous influence, faded away and was all but forgotten, and Lily Tomlin, despite her obvious genius, was grossly underappreciated. Since the turn of the millennium, however, the world of stand-up comedy has begun to teem with various points of view, each with a new take on the old trials of, as Richard Pryor might say, getting through the day without "murdering a motherfucker." Not only are we now privy to the voices of suburban Joes like Jim Gaffigan and Brian Regan, products of the inner city like Dave Chappelle and Bernie Mac, but also comics like Kris Strobeck, who weaves born-again Christian messages into her routine; Charlie Hill, an Oneida-Mohawk-Cree who was raised both in Detroit and on the Oneida reservation in Wisconsin; a profusion of Latino comics like George Lopez, Alex Reymundo, Joey Medina, Jackie Guerra and Sandra Valls; comedians with disabilities like Alex Valdez, who is blind, or Josh Blue and Chris Fonseca, who have cerebral palsy, and Maysoon Zayid, who made her standard opening line "I'm a Palestinian Muslim virgin with cerebral palsy from New Jersey."[142] In 2005, half-Sicilian, half-Arab Dean Obeidallah joined forces with Iranian-American Maz Jobrani, Egyptian-American Ahmed Ahmed and Aron Kader, who is the product of a Mormon mother and Palestinian father, to launch *The Axis of Evil Comedy Tour*, which eventually became a Comedy Central special.

Besides that, comedy festivals abound for anybody with solid setups, punchlines, stage presence and delivery: San Antonio each year hosts The Latino Comedy Festival, while New York hosts an Arab-American comedy festival, Montreal's Just for Laughs holds the "Asian Sensation" festival; and Toronto and Los Angeles have lesbian-gay-bisexual transgendered comedy festivals. If the American invention of stand-up comedy is built around the American innovations of sanctity for the individual and freedom of speech, then it seems that what the literary form has to offer is nothing less than the perfect Jeffersonian mosaic, a place where everybody has a voice, everybody has a valid point-of-view and everybody, to one degree or another, is worth listening to.

Thus it seems that the real strength of stand-up is something the Marx Brothers understood instinctively and Richard Pryor figured out in the 1960s: sometimes it is much wiser to obliterate a stereotype by embracing it, better to become a parody of the fast-talking Jew, the conniving Italian, the slow-witted Irishman or the angry Black man than it is to correct the misperceptions by confronting them directly.

CHAPTER SIX

THE AMERICAN (COMEDIC) JEREMIAD

One of the longest, most colorful and most perplexing threads working its way through the fabric of American literature is the sermonic tradition known as the jeremiad. Rooted in the work and writings of such Old Testament prophets as Isaiah, Amos and Jeremiah (from whom the name is derived), the jeremiad serves as the individual preacher's assessment of how his congregation is—or more than likely—is not living up to its promises to God. For preachers of two and three millennia ago, this revolved around the covenants between Yahweh and the followers Abraham and Moses. To American Puritans such as Jonathan Edwards and Cotton Mather, it concerned their covenant with the God of Providence, He Who guided them on their "errand into the wilderness" and had delivered them to the shores of North America, to that New Eden where they were able to reinvent themselves as the New Adams and the New Eves. According to Sacvan Berkovitch, an expert on the American Puritans and long-time professor of American literature at Columbia University, the jeremiad can be considered "America's first distinctive literary genre."[1] In his seminal 1978 study *The American Jeremiad*, Bercovitz argues that while the traditional jeremiadic mode, namely that of the ancient Hebrews and the European Puritans, "was a lament over the ways of the world," the American version is different because its central message is one of hope and reassurance that the nation as a whole could do better. Berkovitch argues that the distinctiveness of the American jeremiad

> lies not in the vehemence of its complaint but in precisely the reverse. The essence of the sermon form that the first native-born American Puritans inherited from their fathers, and then "developed, amplified, and standardized," is its unshakable optimism. In explicit opposition to the traditional mode, it inverts the doctrine of vengeance into a promise of

ultimate success, affirming to the world, and despite the world, the inviolability of the colonial cause.[2]

Not surprisingly, it is a similar ideal that is of paramount importance when it comes to America, the conception of America and, perhaps most important for our purposes, American humor. Like the ancient Hebrews, the first people to call themselves Americans were also fully devoted to recreating some semblance of paradise on Earth, a task that was daunting and ambitious, to say the least. Walter Blair and Hamlin Hill, for instance, in their thorough study of American humor, point out that the earliest European explorers and colonists recorded how

> during endless summers [in the land anywhere in the area between the Artic Ocean and the Caribbean Sea] . . . wine, plants that cured all ailments, fruit, fish, fowl, and every sort of game were so plentiful that nobody had to stir to get them; stretch out a hand and, like love, they came a-tricklin' down. Indians were noble savages built like Renaissance nudes, easygoing about wealth, and with no sticky notions about personal property.[3]

Due in no small measure to the way the Puritans compared their stories with those found in the Mosaic books, America does indeed begin with a dream—a dream of prosperity and opportunity. Yet, like the one mentioned in the book of Genesis, the new Eden was also prone to spoilage and all too often that dream turned into a nightmare. In Jamestown in 1607, for instance, fifty-one of its one hundred and four men and boys were lost within the first six months due to starvation and disease. A few years later, half of those at the Plymouth settlement were dead, this also due to the ravages of the New England winter, malnutrition and disease.[4]

That valley between the mountain of dreams and sea of nightmares, however, was fertile ground for comedy. In his essay "The Great American Joke," Louis D. Rubin explores the matter:

> From colonial times onward, we have spent a great deal of time and effort criticizing ourselves, pointing out our shortcomings, exploring the incongruities and the contradictions within American society. As the novelist and poet Robert Penn Warren put it, "America was based on a big promise—a great big one: the Declaration of Independence. When you have to live with that in the house, that's quite a problem—particularly when you've got to make money and get ahead, open world markets, do

all the things you have to, raise your children and so forth. America is stuck with its self-definition put on paper in 1776, and that was just like putting a burr under the metaphysical saddle of America—you see, that saddle's going to jump now and then and it pricks." . . . if we look at Warren's remark, what we will notice is that it makes use of a central motif of America—the contrast, the incongruity between the ideal and the real, in which a common, vernacular metaphor is used to put a somewhat abstract statement involving values—self-definition, metaphysical—into a homely context. The state, in other words, makes its point through working an incongruity between two modes of language, the formal, literary language of traditional culture and learning, and the informal, vernacular of everyday life.[5]

To Rubin, this gap between the ideal and the real is nothing less than "the great American joke," which he argues arises "out of the gap between the cultural ideal and the everyday fact, with the ideal shown to be somewhat hollow and hypocritical, and the fact crude and disgusting."[6] Such contrasts have been explored by countless American writers—Frederick Douglass, Sandra Cisneros, F. Scott Fitzgerald, John Steinbeck and William Faulkner are among the most obvious—but perhaps no one has illustrated the contrast quite as ceremoniously or as poignantly as did Arthur Miller in his classic 1949 play, *Death of a Salesman*. The story of a traveling salesman named Willy Loman who despite thirty years of hard work struggles financially until the day he dies, this play has been widely regarded as a look at the underbelly of the American Dream. In the climactic confrontation with his son Biff, Willy tries not to listen as Biff tells him how, after waiting six hours inside an office to meet a prospective financier, he realized his life had been a lie, stole the man's pen and ran out the door. From there, argument escalates:

BIFF: . . . I ran down eleven flights with a pen in my hand today. And I suddenly stopped, do you hear me? And in the middle of that office building, do you hear this? I stopped in the middle of that office building and I saw—the sky. I saw the things that I love in this world. The work and the food and the time to sit and smoke. And I looked at the pen and said to myself, what the hell am I grabbing this for? Why am I trying to become what I don't want to be? What am I doing in an office, making a contemptuous, begging fool of myself . . . ?

WILLY: The door of your life is wide open!

BIFF: I'm a dime a dozen and so are you!

WILLY: I am not a dime a dozen! I am Willy Loman and you are Biff Loman!

BIFF: . . . . You were never anything but a hard-working drummer who landed in the ash can like all the rest of them! I'm one dollar an hour, Willy! . . . A buck an hour! Do you gather my meaning? I'm not bringing home any prizes. . . . I'm just what I am, that's all.[7]

Much of the power of this scene comes through comparisons between the real and the ideal, or more specifically, the ways in which the ideal has been corrupted. Obviously, Biff, to whom Willy has sold the dream that he is a "leader of men" and that "he has a greatness in him," is the voice of harsh reality, the unrelenting truth that the United States is a nation in which the great majority of its inhabitants struggle from paycheck to paycheck, just as the Lomans do, despite the rich promises of it being "the land of opportunity" and the New Eden, illusions Willy refuses to let go of.

This very issue came to the fore in a much different way fourteen years later, this time from a little-known minister named Martin Luther King Jr. When King delivered his now-famous "I Have a Dream" speech, the jeremiad propelled him to the forefront of the Civil Rights movement and cast him as nothing less than the American Moses. After leading a march of some 200,000 protesters to the steps of the Lincoln Memorial, King called his country to task and did so in pointedly American terms:

we've come to our nation's capital to cash a check. When the architects of our republic wrote the magnificent words of the Constitution and the Declaration of Independence, they were signing a promissory note to which every American was to fall heir. This note was a promise that all men, yes, black men as well as white men, would be guaranteed the "unalienable Rights" of "Life, Liberty and the pursuit of Happiness." It is obvious today that America has defaulted on this promissory note, insofar as her citizens of color are concerned. Instead of honoring this sacred obligation, America has given the Negro people a bad check, a check which has come back marked "insufficient funds."[8]

Despite fiery rhetoric recalling the diatribes of Ezekiel and Amos, electro-charged poetry and a passionate lament of failed promises—not to mention that it is being delivered by an ordained Baptist minister with a doctorate degree in theology—"I Have a Dream" diverges from the American jeremiadic convention in one important way: the speech does not concern human failures involving promises between Man and the God of Abraham, Isaac, Jacob, Moses and Jesus. Rather, it concerns that contract between Man and the God of Reason, the theistic God of Jefferson, the "God" and "Creator" referred to in the Declaration of Independence, He who endowed all people with the rights to "life, liberty and the pursuit of happiness." Appropriately enough, King concludes his speech by referring to an ideal that never would have been considered by the Old Testament prophets but that nevertheless remains paramount to the very concept of America:

> when we allow freedom to ring, when we let it ring from every village and every hamlet, from every state and every city, we will be able to speed up that day when *all* of God's children, black men and white men, Jews and Gentiles, Protestants and Catholics, will be able to join hands and sing in the words of the old Negro spiritual:
> *Free at last! Free at last!*
> *Thank God Almighty, we are free at last!*

Yet, while the great majority of senators, governors, congressman and presidents have historically been slow to embrace such a vision of America, comedians have, conversely, been all too ready to champion that utopian vision. By appearing on stage dressed as women, for example, Milton Berle and Flip Wilson implicitly challenged us to reconsider our notions of "male" and "female," just as Jackie Mason's unmollified Jewishness and Redd Foxx's stories about the ghetto asked the nation to reconsider what, exactly, was so scary about people from other ethnic groups. Like good food, a good novel or a good romantic love affair, good comedy challenges all those involved by continually asking us to consider possibilities we had never before dreamed of.

Lenny Bruce

King was not, however, the only public speaker taking up the jeremiadic mantle in the mounting turbulence of the 1960s. Just as the Civil Rights leader was gaining prominence on the national stage, coffee houses in San Francisco and New York's Greenwich Village were giving rise to a new brand of comedian, performers such as Lenny Bruce, Mort Sahl and Dick Gregory who, like King, broke with tradition in order to call attention to the country's failures. While those comics of earlier generations, the Red Skeltons, Henny Youngmans and Jack

Bennys, relied on street jokes, puns and inoffensive punchlines, the new breed of comic felt able, if not obligated, to discuss current political issues, even if it meant compromising the jokes-per-minute ratio. Consider, for example, this Lenny Bruce bit from 1962, one of the most provocative openers in the history of stand-up:

> By the way, are there any niggers here tonight?
> [Outraged whisper] "'What did he say?' 'Are there any *niggers* here tonight?' 'Jesus Christ, is that cruel. Does he have to get that low for laughs?. . .'"
> Are there any niggers here tonight? I know that one nigger who works here, I see him back there. Oh, there's two niggers, customers, and, ah, aha! Between those two niggers sits a kike—man, thank God for the kike! . . . The point? That the word's suppression gives it the power, the violence, the viciousness. If President Kennedy got on television and said, "Tonight I'd like to introduce the niggers in my cabinet," and he yelled "niggerniggerniggerniggerniggerniggernigger" at every nigger he saw, "boogeyboogeyboogeyboogeyboogey, niggerniggernigger. . . " 'til till nigger didn't mean anything anymore, till nigger lost its meaning—you'd never make any four-year-old nigger cry because [somebody called him a nigger in school].[10]

Despite its crassness, this tirade contains all the jeremiadic elements as it also grows out of a confidence in American pluralism. Its implicit message is, after all, that the country as a whole can and should overcome racism, a sin that has haunted it since the beginning. Delivered at various times and in various venues in the months before "I Have a Dream," Bruce, with these few seconds of monologue, pushes the cultural envelope and seeks to adjust the course America is on, to urge it closer to a pluralistic paradise that aligns easily with that referred to in both the Declaration of Independence and the closing lines of "I Have a Dream."

Mort Sahl

While Bruce has been dubbed "The Elvis of Stand-Up" and is repeatedly mentioned along with Richard Pryor and George Carlin as one of history's three most important stand-up comedians, he was not unique in the way he addressed American failings on the stage. Four years before Bruce's breakout performance in New York in 1958, another social commentator was making a name for himself among the beatnik hangouts on the West Coast. Dubbed with descriptors that recall jeremiadists from throughout the ages, labels like "A Voice Crying in the Wilderness," "the Will Rogers of the beat generation," "the nation's only employed philosopher," "the surrealist Montaigne," "and the "beat generation Cotton Mather,"[11] Sahl was the first of what would come to be called the "New Wave" or "sick" comics. When he burst upon the hipster scene in San Francisco in the early 1950s, Sahl began providing biting topical commentaries on everything from the Eisenhower administration to the beatniks themselves, offering observations such as "The beat generation is a coffeehouse full of people expectantly looking at their watches waiting for the beat generation to come."[12]

In addition to his subject matter, Sahl's style also allowed—if not demanded—the exploration of heavyweight issues. Since he started working Bay Area coffee houses in the early 1950s, he was known for his casual dress that almost always included a cashmere sweater and for the way he appeared on stage with a copy of that day's newspaper tucked under his arm. Furthermore, his conversational delivery, which was clearly influenced by the era's bebop jazz, would become the standard for every stand-up who came after him. In 1960, *Time* magazine noted that during his routines, Sahl

> takes off like a jazz musician on a flight of improvisation—or seeming improvisation. He does not tell jokes one by one, but carefully builds deceptively miscellaneous structures of jokes that are like verbal mobiles. He begins with the spine of a subject, then hooks thought onto thought, joke onto dangling joke, many of them totally unrelated to the main theme, till the whole structure spins but somehow balances. All the time he is building toward a final statement, which is too much part of the whole to be called a punch line, but puts that particular theme away forever.[13]

Furthermore, Sahl's material directly opposed the Bob Hope-style of the "older, machine-tooled and essentially safe topical joke,"[14] as he built his career on deft observations and biting wit in order to critique American values and political stances, both conservative and progressive. Like Bruce, Sahl implicitly acknowledged that original American vision by poking fun at Cold War values. His earliest routines directly challenged the nation's paranoia and hypocrisy that peaked with Sen. Joseph McCarthy's jingoistic tirades and the investigations of the House Un-American Activities Committee, both of which targeted suspected Communists in the early 1950s. Sahl railed against such witch-hunting with jokes like, "Have you seen the new Joe McCarthy jacket? It's like an Eisenhower jacket only it's got a an extra flap that fits over the mouth," "Joe McCarthy doesn't question what you say as much as your right to say it," "For a while, every time the Russians threw an American in jail, the Un-American Activities Committee would retaliate by throwing an American in jail, too" and "Maybe the Russians will steal all our secrets, then *they'll* be two years behind."[15] Similarly, when a critic of President Dwight Eisenhower's stand on civil rights commented that "if the President were really a man, he would take a little colored girl by the hand and lead her through that line of bigots into the high school," Sahl commented how, "That's easy to say if you are not involved. . . . But if you are in the Administration, you have a lot of problems of policy, like whether or not to use an overlapping grip."[16]

Although sometimes such jokes were not well-received—the "McCarthy jacket" joke, for instance, often elicited boos[17]—Sahl in two years went from sleeping in his Chevy and eating discarded hamburgers to becoming a comedy star,[18] recording the first full-length comedy album and earning thousands of dollars a week in a time when many headliners earned less than ten dollars a set. Such a dramatic rise is all the more remarkable when one considers that sometimes both his material and subject matter were downright frightening, such as this bit of riffing on the subject of nuclear fallout:

> The way I found the Mickey Mouse club was I was at home, see? and I was watching [Los Angeles Mayor Norris Poulson] on TV. He's our leader downtown. And he was talking about the smog. And he was talking about fallout within the smog, you know. We have a lot of fallout within the smog as you know. And he said that there's [nuclear] fallout within it, and coming from Nevada and that the government should do something about it. . . . . He said that the government should do something because the tests are in Nevada and it should be under interstate commerce or the Mann Act, someone suggested—to make it more interesting to people. So . . . Mayor Poulson said that somebody should do something about these tests, because it was double danger because of the acid and the smog. Our government didn't do anything about it, but Poulson said there's no telling what will happen if they keep testing these bombs every other day in Nevada, see? So, he kept talking about mutations and all that jazz. So I figured it was kind of like left wing propaganda. . . . I have that kind of attitude about the tests: I dig them because I think they're good for business, right? I feel the United States is going to go ahead with bomb tests in synagogues and schools. Anyway, so, any-

way, I dig the tests, and I've always had that position that, you know, I'm not planning a large family anyway.[19]

With diatribes such as this, Sahl revolutionized the art form in various ways. He not only "changed the image of the 'Jewish comic'— from the rowdy Borscht Belt *tummler* to brainy campus philosopher-wit,"[20] but as Woody Allen would later say, he "totally restructured comedy. He changed the rhythm of the jokes. He had different content, surely, but the revolution was in the way he laid the jokes down. His jokes were laid down with such guile."[21]

Unlike Will Rogers who a generation earlier had similarly called the country to task for its failings, Sahl made his mark by being a bitter and critical philosopher rather than by being a lovable good ol' boy. And by doing so he showed how the stand-up comedian, by virtue of his ability to lead us into uncomfortable territory, has the potential to be the country's social consciousness as well as a potent agent of change.

Dick Gregory

Even though Bruce and Sahl pulled no punches when they addressed social issues—and no subject was too hot handle, not the Cold War, dysfunctional families, sex or the Kennedy assassination—neither of them could address American racism as could their contemporary, Dick Gregory. Born in St. Louis in 1932, Gregory grew up poor and was often the target of discrimination. While in high school, he set a state track record, running the mile in four minutes and twenty-eight seconds, only to have the record disallowed because it happened at an all-Black track meet.[22]

Gregory began performing stand-up and impressions in special service shows while he was in the Army. After his discharge, he moved to Chicago where, at first, he played mostly the Black clubs for nominal pay.[23] His big break came in January 1960 when, while working in a car wash, he was asked to fill in for an ailing headliner, Professor Irwin Corey, at the flagship Playboy Club. A short time later, Gregory took to the stage and introduced himself to an audience that was expecting a White man:

Good evening ladies and gentleman. . . . I understand there are a good many Southerners in the room tonight. I know the South very well. I spent 20 years there one night. . . . The last time I was down South, I walked into a restaurant and this waitress come up to me and said, "We don't serve colored people here." "That's all right," I said. "I don't eat them. Bring the fried chicken instead."[24]

Within two years Gregory would become a Playboy Club regular, sign a record deal, would be written up in *Time* magazine and would become the first Black performer to successfully and permanently make the crossover into the White market. In a time when Blacks were precluded from spending money in Harlem's Cotton Club, Gregory's introduction into the arena was in itself a major socio-political statement.

According to African-American historian Mel Watkins, Gregory was "more of a candid satirist than an entertaining funny man," as well as someone whose act eradicated "all traces of the minstrel image."[25] Although not as collegiate as his contemporary and acquaintance Bill Cosby and prone to using slang and colloquialisms in his act, Gregory was nevertheless smooth and manicured as he perched himself on a bar stool and puffed on a cigarette, using it for punctuation the way George Burns or Groucho Marx might use a cigar. According to Nachman, Gregory was someone "Hugh Hefner could book without squirming, one who would further Hef's 'Playboy Philosophy' of being on the cutting edge of the social—not to mention satirical—revolution."[26] Gregory felt that part of his contribution was the way he introduced the nation to what he termed "healthy racial jokes."[27] Says Gregory, "When I hit in 1961, there wasn't a healthy racial joke in America. . . . They were all derogatory to one race or the other."[28]

Gregory's jokes ran along the lines of, "Would it be a helluva joke if all this were really burnt cork and you people were all being tolerant for nothin'?" "Lookin' for a house can be quite an experience. Especially when you go to into a white neighborhood, offer forty thousand dollars for a twenty-three-thousand dollar house and then get turned down 'cause you're lowering the property values"[29] or "In what other country would I have to attend the worst schools, live in the worst neighborhoods, eat in the worst restaurants and average five thousand dollars a week talking about it?"[30]

Gregory would eventually leave the world of stand-up just when he was becoming a national phenomenon. In the late 1960s he announced that he was abandoning his career in order to devote himself to social activism and campus lectures,[31] a transition that was not surprising considering that integration had become the core theme of his act. In a performance on the television show *ABC's Studio 67*, for instance, he delivered stand-up material from a stage set up like a jail cell, the clear implication being that he and others had just been arrested during a Civil Rights march.[32] It could be argued, then, that if Mark Twain, Martin Luther King, Lenny Bruce and Mort Sahl were some of the country's leading jeremiadists, Gregory took the matter one step further by becoming a living, breathing jeremiad.

George Carlin

If Bruce and Sahl voiced the attitudes, values and concerns of the beatniks, and Gregory personified the value shifts of the Civil Rights changes, George Carlin continued the tradition by making no bones about his connections with the counterculture. While Sahl distanced himself from the counterculture and Bruce and Gregory had little to say about such associations, Carlin dressed and wore his hair like the hippies and championed the values of that group that owed much of its existence to the Vietnam War. Consider, for instance, how with this sequence from the 1972 recording *Class Clown* that begins by looking at the plight of dethroned heavyweight champion Muhammad Ali, Carlin becomes the voice of the younger generation that is outraged and mystified by U.S. involvement in the Vietnam conflict:

> [*singing*] Muhammad Ali. Muhammad Ali. [*speaking*] It's a nice musical name. He's back at work again. He wasn't allowed to work for a while, Muhammad Ali . . . . For about three and a half years he wasn't allowed to work. Of course, he had a strange job: beating people up. But it's one you're entitled to. The government didn't see it that way. The government wanted him to change jobs. The government wanted to kill people. He said, "No, no. That's where I draw the line. I'll beat 'em up but I don't wanna kill them." The government said, "If you don't wanna kill them, we won't let you beat them up"—all because he didn't want to go to Vietnam. And now, of course we're leaving Vietnam—through Laos and Cambodia. That's gotta be the overland route. You gotta go through China and Russia to get out that way. What are we going to tell them? "We'll only be here for a short while looking for the Ho Chi Minh trail"?[33]

Due to his long career and the sheer force of his fame—he first began doing comedy in 1956, and between 1977 and 2008 had done fourteen HBO specials, released some twenty-two comedy albums and published five books—Carlin is perhaps the foremost and most prolific comedic jeremiadist, someone who has made a career of criticizing the American government, economic system and way of life.

One of his most incisive, observant, ingenious and biting critiques of American culture also comes from the *Class Clown* album, a piece entitled "Values (How Much Is That Dog Crap in the Window?)." The comedian begins the assessment by talking about the cultural shifts of the 1960s and 1970s, saying that "the whole revolution is about values—what you'll do for five dollars, what you'll do with five dollars." He then goes on to question American business ethics and to point out absurdities such as how, in the United States, it is normal for some people to go to work and order "three dozen vomit on the phone." Imitating a CEO he says, "Keep it in the black. Keep it in the black. Never mind the other guy. Never mind your soul. Keep it in the black." To illustrate, he examines items in the novelty stores or joke shops that were popular at the time, phenomena such as plastic false teeth, Whoopee Cushions, imitation vomit and imitation fried eggs. The bit climaxes with a discussion on "the ol' plaster-of-Paris dog crap"[34] as Carlin implicitly asks: What kind of country would produce such a thing? What kind of a person would sell such a thing? What kind of person would buy such a thing? And what does this say about American values? By nudging us so, he implicitly asks the nation as a whole to spend some time in difficult self-reflection.

By the early years of the twenty-first century, Carlin had lost much of his subtlety and criticisms have persisted that he is "too bitter" to be funny. Whether this is the case, up until his death in the summer of 2008, Carlin continued his jeremiads and ratcheted up his anger and vehemence a few notches. In the closing bit from his 2001 HBO special *Complaints and Grievances,* Carlin presents himself, in no uncertain terms, as nothing less than the early twenty-first century's answer to Moses as he takes on the most audacious of tasks, rewriting the Ten Commandments. In one of the most hubristic bits in the history of stand-up, he begins by declaring the first three commandments—"Thou shalt not have strange gods before Me," "Keep holy the Sabbath" and "Thou shalt not take the name of the Lord thy God in vain"—to be "pure bullshit" because they are full what he calls "spooky language," words such as "holy" and "Sabbath." But he does not stop there. The Fourth Commandment, "Honor thy father and mother," he dismisses as just another ploy, a way of convincing the common man to be obedient to authority figures and he declares that "respect should be earned." He then proceeds to collapse "Thou shalt not commit adultery" and "Thou shalt not covet thy neighbor's wife" into one dictum, since they deal with essentially the same core issue, lack of marital fidelity. Since "Thou shalt not bear false witness" and "Thou shalt not steal" both deal with the core value of honesty, he combines them as well.

The Eighth Commandment, "Thou shalt not covet thy neighbor's goods," Carlin says is "just plain fuckin' stupid" because it is the essence of "keeping up with the Joneses" and fuels the American economy. Commenting on the Fifth Commandment, Carlin gives the age-old argument that "religion has never really had a big problem with killing . . . . More people have been killed in the name of God than for any other reason" and says that all in all, most religious devotees see murder as being "negotiable."

When all is said and done, the comedian has boiled the list down to just two commandments: (1) "Thou shalt always be honest and faithful to the provider of thy nookie" and (2) "Thou shalt try *real* hard not to kill anyone, unless of course they pray to a different invisible man from the one you pray to." He concludes the sequence, and the performance, for that matter, by saying, "Two is all you need. Moses could have carried them down the hill in his fuckin' pocket. And if they had a list like that I wouldn't mind those folks in Alabama putting it up on the courthouse wall. As long as they included one additional commandment: 'Thou shalt keep thy religion to thyself.'"[35]

Despite criticism that Carlin in his later years had become too bitter, the comedian's diatribes clearly carried a message of hope and his routines can by and large be seen as corrective. In the "Ten Commandments" bit, for example, the implication is that the central messages of the Decalogue are something that the nation as a whole can easily agree upon. As in "Sinners at the Hands of an Angry God," the admonishing tone is laced with genuine hope.

Bill Hicks

Another of the most important heirs to Bruce, Carlin and Sahl was Bill Hicks, a Georgia-born, Texas-reared product of a Southern Baptist family. Like his contemporary Sam Kinison (who was an evangelical preacher as a child), Hicks went from practicing evangelical Christianity to steeping himself in physical pleasures and making discourses about his own hedonism a core part of his act. For his opening joke in the 1988 performance film *Comedy's Dirtiest Dozen*, for instance, Hicks comes out on stage, lights a cigarette and says, "They say cigarette addiction is harder to break than heroin addiction. So I'm O for two." In one of his most famous bits, "A Positive Drug Story," he says, "You never see positive drug stories on the news, do you? Isn't that weird, since most of the experiences I had on drugs were real fuckin' positive."[36]

Also in that concert film, Hicks launches into a tirade against then-President Ronald Reagan, saying, "John Lennon: murdered. John Kennedy: murdered. Why is it always good guys are murdered? . . . Mediocre hacks live on forever? Martin Luther King: murdered. Gandhi: murdered. Jesus: murdered. Reagan: shot, wounded, cancer eight times—that fucker still walks." Hicks then proceeds to commit a federal offense by offering to kill the president, saying: "My God, What's it gonna take? A syringe of AIDS shot in your eyeball? I'll do it. A Trident missile shot up your fascist, evil, mean-spirited, corporate puppet, devil-cocksucking ass? Where's the button?"[37]

After suggesting that Reagan may indeed be the antichrist mentioned in the Book of Revelation by saying "'Ronald': Six letters. 'Wilson': six letters. 'Reagan': six letters. Pretty frightening coincidence there, isn't it?" Hicks summarily dismisses the notion, saying "that would be too obvious and he's too stupid." He then brings out even more venom when he goes on a diatribe against Dick Clark, of *American Bandstand* fame, identifies him as the antichrist and acts out a story about how Clark, whom he refers to as "the Prince of Darkness," mates with pop singer John Davidson and Davidson consequently "begins to shit the brood." Hicks squats on the stage as though defecating and, as he does, announces the progeny of the two men he considers to be bastions of American mediocrity: "Geraldo Rivera . . . Kenny Rogers . . . Wham! . . . Oprah."[38]

What Hicks is railing against—this much he says explicitly—is mediocrity, and Clark's chief sin is "year after year, week after week, systematically lowering the standards of the earth, making mediocrity a goal." Consequently, Hicks' vision, a world where the Gandhis, John Lennons and Martin Luther Kings are allowed to live and shape society while the Dick Clarks and Kenny Rogers have very limited influences, is one that would meld neatly with those described by King and Bruce.

Chris Rock

In the two decades surrounding the turn of the millennia, one of the unique and most passionate voices rising above the din of a culture that is saturated with unoriginal comedic voices is that of Chris Rock, a performer who, while still in his teens, caught the attention of comic actor Eddie Murphy. In the years to come, Rock would go from lackluster performances such as those turned in for the 1987 HBO special *Uptown Comedy Express* and *Comedy's Dirtiest Dozen* a year later to being named one of history's top five stand-ups by Comedy Central, just behind Richard Pryor, Carlin, Bruce and Woody Allen. In performance films such as *Bigger and Blacker* from 1999, *Never Scared* from 2004, and perhaps especially *Bring the Pain* from 1996, a film that sealed his place in stand-up comedy history, the former cast member of *Saturday Night Live*, with his wit and courage, demonstrates that he is very much the heir to Carlin and Bruce. Consider, for instance, this bit from *Bring the Pain*, which is, in its own way, as provocative as Bruce's "Nigger" bit:

> Who's more racist, Black people or White people? Black people. You know why? 'cause we hate Black people too. It's like the civil war going on with Black people and there's two sides: There's Black people and there's niggers. And the niggers have got to go. Every time Black people want to have a good time, ignorant-assed niggers fuck it up.[39]

Upon his saying this, the kind of statement that usually spells comedic suicide, the mostly Black audience erupts into applause. Filmed in the Takoma Theater in Washington, D.C., a city that is important to the premise of the show not only because it is the nation's capital but also because, as Rock announces during his first few seconds on stage, it is "Chocolate Cit-tay" and site of the Million Man March, a rally to promote civic and familial responsibility among Black men, this performance explores sociological territory that in virtually all other cases would be forbidden. In a time when social commentators were wont to beat around abstract catch phrases like "the Black community" or "the Gay community," as if all Blacks and Gays had precisely the same attitudes, values and concerns, Rock looks right in the heart of American racism and announces that there is an ideal that transcends ethnicity, skin color and social status. As the bit continues, Rock says,

> You know what's the worst thing about niggers? Niggers always want credit for something they're supposed to do. For some shit they are supposed to do. A nigger will brag about shit that a normal man just does. A nigger will say stuff like, "I take care of my kids." You're supposed to, you dumb motherfucker. What are you talking about? [or] "I ain't never been to jail." What do you want, a cookie? You're not supposed to go to jail, you low-expectation motherfucker.[40]

While it is hard to take this bit without allowing for hyperbole—the epithet "nigger" suggests that certain people should be taken as slaves much the way the condemnation "faggot" suggests homosexuals should be burned at the stake, and it seems pretty clear that Rock is not advocating a return to slavery—it is important to note that Rock has designated himself as both the voice of the frustration endemic to inner-city blight and comedy's answer to the Million Man March. The strength of Rock's performance lies in no small measure in his unbridled anger, in the way in which he vocalizes the frustration of a nation that is not only built upon racism, but also cannot remain healthy without the responsible participation all its denizens.

Whoopi Goldberg

One of the most haunting versions of the comedic jeremiad comes at the beginning of Whoopi Goldberg's 1988 HBO show *Fontaine: Why Am I Straight?* Even though there may be some question as to whether this performance qualifies as pure stand-up since Goldberg, as in her other one-woman shows, relies on stage personas, the character on stage does address the audience directly and does provide the requisite set-ups, punchlines and act-outs. In this particular case she employs one personality, Fontaine, a Black androgynous junkie who holds a Ph.D. in comparative literature from Columbia University and has just been released from the Betty Ford drug rehabilitation clinic. Throughout the course of the performance, as Fontaine assesses the state of the country during the last of the Reagan years, the character keeps returning to the question "Why am I straight?" as if to say that there is no good reason to shoulder civic responsibility in a nation reeling from scandals in religious and political spheres perpetrated by people who are by all accounts not junkies. As someone who "just got straight," Fontaine looks at the madness of the nation with a fresh perspective and the implicit question is "What is the point of kicking drugs when those who are not high all the time are acting crazier than me?"

What is of particular interest here, however, is the opening scene of the performance proper. After Fontaine, during the introductory sequence, has been advised by Betty Ford, "When in doubt, sing the National Anthem," Fontaine slips into the back door of the Mayfair Theater in Santa Monica, California. Steeped in darkness, Fontaine declares, "I'm Stevie Wonder now," and recalls Ford's advice. Still in the pitch black theater, Fontaine begins singing: "Oh say can you motherfuckin' see, by the dawn's early motherfuckin' light? What so proudly we motherfuckin' hailed, at the twilight's last goddamned gleaming. . . ."[41]

Within seconds, the first glints of light appear as the comedian rises on a platform from beneath the stage floor. While some people have found this offensive, the statement is unmistakable social commentary. Androgynous, African-American, a junkie and holder of a "Ph.D. from Columbia that I can't do shit with,"[42] the character is a representation of someone who has been marginalized several times over. Once we get to know Fontaine, we not only understand that version of the national anthem, but we can even excuse it and perhaps even appreciate it. Fontaine has a different relationship with the country compared to those who usually sing the song in public arenas. Fontaine's is the voice of those who have fallen between the cracks of the American dream, if not those who have been run over by it. The darkness and the entry from beneath the stage are most revealing: Fontaine is providing for us the voice of the country's collective shadow, that which the country as a whole has forced by one means or another into a dark underworld because it is too ugly to bring out into the light. It is that which has been swept under the rug of history. And yet, as Carl Jung might argue, it is the shadow that cannot remain hidden forever.

This is yet another of the great openers in the history of stand-up comedy for a number of reasons. Not only does it strike at the heart of American jingoism and the American dream, but it also reveals much about the function of the American literary form. While literature, by and large, is the voice of the enlightened imagination, the higher human faculties, the ability for writers and poets to project themselves into other realities and entertain complex philosophical, dramatic and mystical questions, both the joke and stand-up comedy are arenas where the unpleasant, the animalistic and the visceral are allowed to take center stage. If the set-up line is the voice of decorum, propriety and acceptable behavior, then the punchline is the voice of the unacceptable, the immoderate and the taboo. Just like Fontaine, it is that stuff that rises out of the depths of the subconscious—if for no other reason than that it refuses to be contained. Consequently, stand-up comedy, which is first and foremost about jokes rather than plots, characters, themes or even wordplay, may very well be the closest thing literature has to a direct line to the subconscious.

These comedic jeremiadists consequently represent those voices that cannot be ignored, the collective statements of the frustrated masses who, for one reason or another, have been denied what they have been promised by the Declaration of Independence and U.S. Constitution. While each of the comedians mentioned above has a direct, in-your-face approach, it is important to note that there were also plenty of more subtle approaches to the same issues. Gregory, Bruce and Sahl changed attitudes about race in this country by attacking issues head-on while Bill Cosby, whose great gift was illustrating how all Americans shared virtually the same challenges, worked toward the same goals. With the help of vehicles such as *The Tonight Show*, *The Gary Moore Show* and especially *The Ed Sullivan Show*, Cosby was able to achieve at least one of King's dreams. Not only did he humanize the Black man to an America that has been historically xenophobic, but he, through the gift of the television and his repeated appearances on television variety shows, was the first Black man welcomed into virtually every living room in the nation. Despite his subtlety and his fundamentally happy disposition, Cosby too became a jeremiadic force as his very presence signaled a shift in American attitudes.

CHAPTER SEVEN

STEVEN WRIGHT AND THE POST-MODERN PICARESQUE

Of many comedians who were on their way to becoming legendary during the comedy boom of the 1980s—the Paula Poundstones, Jerry Seinfelds, Drew Careys and Garry Shandlings—perhaps none has been more enigmatic, influential and complex than Steven Wright, someone who has made mystery and reticence a powerful part of both his on- and offstage personas. And it is these very qualities that may well explain the comedian's sudden and dramatic rise to fame in the mid-1980s, as well as the respect and popularity he has maintained since then. A charter member of the Boston School of stand-ups, which also included Denis Leary, Poundstone, Bobcat Goldthwait and Lenny Clarke, Wright began doing comedy at age twenty-three and soon became a regular performer at both Boston's Comedy Connection and Ding Ho's Comedy Club and Chinese Restaurant in Cambridge, Massachusetts. In 1982, Peter Lasally, a producer with *The Tonight Show Starring Johnny Carson* who was in the area visiting prospective colleges for his child, saw Wright's act and booked him for a spot.[1] The invitation was so sudden that Wright had to scramble to "borrow a decent pair of pants."[2] Not only did Wright's act so impress Carson that he was asked to "do panel," which is comedianspeak for sitting down and chatting with the host after the performance proper, but he was also invited to return to the show the next week. Such compliments being bestowed upon an unknown is virtually unheard of in the world of stand-up.

Over the next few years Wright's presence would be felt in many pop culture sectors. Not only he would go on to make repeated appearances on the television show *Saturday Night Live* and be cast in movies such as *Desperately Seeking Susan*, Jim Jarmusch's *Coffee and Ciga-*

rettes, the Mike Meyers vehicle *So I Married an Ax Murderer* and to be heard as the voice of K-Billy DJ in Quentin Tarantino's cult classic *Reservoir Dogs*, but he would win an Academy Award for the short film *The Appointments of Dennis Jennings*, which he co-wrote and starred in, and his CD, *I Have Pony*, would be nominated for a Grammy Award in 1985. In the 2002 documentary *Comedian* about Jerry Seinfeld, producer Barry Katz identified Wright as "one of the most prolific, brilliant comedians of our generation," someone who gets on stage and says "thanks," does his act, and says "thanks" again, then exits and seldom talks about his work.[3]

Even though Wright's deadpan delivery is noteworthy, it is hardly unique—we saw something similar with Jackie Vernon back in the 1960s and 1970s, just as we did with Margaret Smith, who is of the same comic generation as Wright, and with Todd Barry a decade later. While Wright is certainly one of the most distinctive comedians to come out of the Boom, and is unquestionably an artist who lives out the credo that there is a joke in everything, the comedian just has to find it, Wright's inventiveness and unique point of view are only part of the picture. As any booker, club owner or headlining comedian can attest, there are plenty of performers with great talent who never get past the comedy club B-room circuit. Wright himself readily acknowledges this, saying that his success "was a fluke" and that his life easily could have been very different. He asks: "What if [Peter Lasally's] kid didn't want to go to college?"[4]

The comedian's work is difficult to classify. While jokes such as "Curiosity killed the cat, but for a long time, I was a suspect" or "I woke up this morning and everything in my apartment had been stolen and replaced with an exact replica" have the ring of paranoid ravings, other jokes express the point of view of the most innocent of children, jokes such as "What do batteries run on?" or "A policeman pulled me over for speeding and said, 'Don't you know the speed limit is fifty-five miles an hour?' I said, 'I know, but I wasn't going to be out that long.'" Sometimes, like his comedic descendant Mitch Hedberg, he becomes a Zen master who finds the curious and mysterious in the most unremarkable experiences, such as when he tells us, "I went to a restaurant that said 'breakfast anytime.' So I ordered French toast during the Renaissance," or, "I went to the cinema. It said 'Adults five dollars and children two-fifty.' I said, 'okay, give me two boys and a girl.'" Other times he seems possessed by the spirit of Harpo Marx as he plays both the trickster and the guileless mischief-maker with jokes such as "I met [my girlfriend] in Macy's. She was buying clothes and I was putting Slinkies on the escalators," or how, when asked if he has the correct time, he says, "Yes, but not now."[5]

While such jokes may be, in the words of Carson, "wonderfully inventive stuff,"[6] still another explanation for the Wright phenomenon might be the way in which he brings together two time-tested literary devices, the fool archetype and the picaresque story, in order to present to his audiences their own subconscious questions, fears and concerns. To put the matter another way, we can say that the nation's strong and sustained response to Wright's work may very well be the way in which audiences, whether they become aware of it, see him as a reflection of their own post-modern fears, anxieties and hopes illustrated through conventions with which they are both comfortable and familiar. When some three decades of his work are taken as a whole, Wright presents to us a new twist on the picaresque tale, a story that is long and complex as it leads the audience on a trek across America's psychological terrain, where all involved are forced to come face-to-face with their own post-modern fears, the most harrowing of which is the threat of nuclear annihilation.

The Picaresque

According to Frank Wadleigh Chandler, the picaresque is a style of literature that involves the story of a rogue who is "born of poor and dishonest parents, who are . . . [not] particularly pleased by his advent . . . he is innocent and learns by hard raps that he must take care of himself."[7] In such stories the protagonist relays his own account of his adventures, the majority of which involve his living on the fringe of society, where he schemes and scams, sometimes for mere survival, sometimes to get the best of someone and other times to get the best of society as a whole. In his study, Harry Sieber argues that even though the picaresque has come to be thought of as a story involving a hero who "takes a journey whose course plunges him into all sorts, conditions and classes of men,"[8] it also must include "a satire upon the conditions and persons of the time that gives it 'birth'."[9]

In Wright's work we see all of these criteria met organically. Even though his character reveals precious little about his biological parentage, little more than scattered bits like, "When I was little in my backyard we had a quicksand box. I was an only child. Eventually,"[10] and, "We moved around a lot because my father thought he was in the military,"[11] the ancestry of his art is very much the product of a lowly lineage.

First of all, Wright clearly is a descendant of the Tarot Fool, an image that is modeled upon the European court jester and was first used in a card game called *Tarocchi* in mid-fifteenth century Italy. Even in the decades before the card deck was used for divination purposes, the Fool card was the first in the deck and the earliest version of it shows a court jester-like character with feathers in his hair, a patched and belted coat, and rolled-up, calf-high hose and carrying a painted staff—all of which was originally depicted against a plain background. As new versions were produced by various hands, the image quickly evolved and the Fool increasingly began to be shown against a natural setting, one that usually included rolling hills, open meadows or riverbanks. Soon, other embellishments were added, such as the white rose of innocence, a white butterfly and a hobo's bindle that was said to be filled with mystery. Since then, one of the most popular images of the Fool has been a figure who looks very much like a medieval court jester and appears to be stepping off a cliff into an abyss,[12] a depiction that remains popular.

Just ten years after the signing of the Declaration of Independence, the image appeared west of the Atlantic in the character of the Jonathan in Royall Tyler's play *The Contrast*, a play that is widely acknowledged as one of the first stage plays to be written and produced in the United States. Considered "a clown, a country boy lost in the city, neither sophisticated nor intellectual and with no desire to be," the Jonathan has been regarded as one of the first attempts to portray the American character and whose function is to "mock old values and to define, to an extent, new ones."[13]

Consequently, it is hardly surprising that since the time of Columbus, who also came out of mid-fifteenth century Italy, the Fool has been a consistent American icon. Even a somber and serious piece like Jonathan Edwards' "Sinners at the Hands of an Angry God" is thick with Fool imagery. In this sermon, the Puritan minister says that "natural men" are very much like the tarot Fool in that they "are held in the hand of God" over an abyss which, in this case, is "the pit of hell."[14] The most elementary of Freudian interpretations unlocks the meaning of such an admonition, albeit presumably one quite different from that intended by Edwards. The deity in this scenario is the Oedipal father figure, the archetypal enemy, while Man is the child, the incipient consciousness, the impotent Fool. Throughout this sermon are repeated other references to man as being caught on the brink of an abyss, whether it is by means of divine whim or his own folly. The imagery reveals much about the circumstances of these first European-Americans whose quest it was to assert a Christian presence on the "howling wilderness," whose mission it was to conquer "Satan's wilderness world for Christ,"[15] or, in other words, to impose divine order on the chaos of nature. In many ways, Edwards is illustrating an important aspect of the American character in obverse. Whether the discussion involves the Minute Men taking on the British Army, Abraham Lincoln, Bill Clinton and Ronald Reagan rising from poverty to the White House, the frontiersman setting out to tame the expansive frontier or any one of thousands of American David and Goliath stories, the central myth remains: the father figure, whether it is British hegemony, a vast and wild continent or a seemingly invincible opponent, must be challenged. In much the same way, the American Jester challenges the great pit of chaos that yawns before him as he casts himself into the chasm in hopes of conquering it.

This dynamic is very much apparent in Wright's work, as he consistently reminds us that he has stepped off the *terra firma* of common experience into a vast psychological and experiential void. The opening joke of his 1985 HBO special says as much: he walks on stage, takes the microphone out of the mike stand, switches it on and says "Thanks," which gets a laugh (he is one of very few comedians, perhaps the only comedian, who can consistently get a laugh with the first word of his performance) and announces, "I got a postcard from my friend George, a satellite picture of the entire Earth. On the back he said, 'Wish you were here,'"[16] thus indicating he is in the greatest chasm of all, that of empty space. From there, as he ushers us into a psychological terrain where, in addition to exploring post-modern tensions, discussing his roguish antics and at times lapsing into paranoid ravings, he becomes the post-modern jester, trickster and Jonathan as he provides a running satire on the banalities of twentieth century life with jokes such as: "The first time I ever read the dictionary I thought it was a poem about everything" and "Why is the alphabet in that order? Is it because of that song? The guy who wrote that song wrote everything."[17]

The Roguish Nature

There is doubt about the roguish qualities of Wright's character. A little more than a minute into the performance proper of *A Steven Wright Special*, for instance, the comedian lets us know that he is as capable of scheming as classic rogues like the prototypical *picaro* Lazarillo de Tormes, Henry

Fielding's Tom Jones or Mark Twain's Huckleberry Finn. He says, "I was arrested today for scalping low numbers at the deli. I sold the number three for twenty-eight bucks."[18] Scheming and roguery become, in fact, one of a handful of recurring themes informing three decades of his performances. As with other American rascals such as Bugs Bunny or Melville's Confidence Man, he views everybody as fair game. In his 2006 Comedy Central show *When the Leaves Blow Away*, for instance, he describes how, as a child, he extorted his own grandmother:

> I was five and my grandmother said, "Steven, come over here."
> I said, "What do you mean?"
> She said, "You know, you're over there. Now come over here."
> She said, "Here's ten dollars and don't tell your mother that I'm giving this to you."
> I said, "It'll cost you more than that."[19]

Other times, again like a good *picaro*, he schemes for power rather than just money. In this sketch, also from the 1985 special, he tells of manipulating a particularly vulnerable woman. After visiting a bookstore and meeting a woman who was "a bilingual illiterate—she couldn't read in two different languages," he

> left the store and went down the street to my bus. My bus came and I got on. I started walking to the back, sat down beside this beautiful blonde Chinese girl. I said hello and she said hello. I said, "Isn't it an amazing day?"
> She said, "Yes it is. I guess."
> I said, "What do you mean 'you guess'?"
> She said, "Things haven't been going too well for me lately."
> I said, "Like what?"
> She said, "I can't tell you. I don't even know you."
> I said, "Yeah, but sometimes it's good to tell your problems to an absolute total stranger on a bus."
> She said, "Well, I've just come back from my analyst and he's still unable to help me."
> And I said, "What's the problem?"
> She paused and said, "I'm a nymphomaniac and I only get turned on by Jewish cowboys. By the way, my name's Diane."
> I said, "Hello Diane, I'm Bucky Goldstein."[20]

When the stories do not concern such outright chicanery, we are given glimpses into another picaresque dimension of his character, and that is his itinerant life. His acts are thick with suggestions that Wright has been leapfrogging from job to job, home to home and from town to town. In the HBO special, for instance, the comedian makes no fewer than seven references to distinctly different homes. In one bit he tells us that he lives "in a house on that is on the median strip of a highway. It's good. I like it. The only thing I don't like about it is that when I leave my driveway I have to be going sixty miles an hour." A minute or so after that, that he tells how he was "walking my dog around my building—on the ledge. A lot of people are afraid of heights, not me. I'm afraid of widths." Then he says, "My house is made out of balsa wood. When no one's home across the street except for little kids, I come out and I lift my house up over my head. Tell them to stay out of my yard or I'll throw it at 'em." In another instance he tells us that he lived "in a house that ran on static electricity. If we wanted to cook something we had to take off a sweater real quick. If we wanted to run a blender we had to rub balloons on our heads,"[21] and during his set in *Comic Relief III* he says, "I'm living on a one-way dead-end street. I don't know how I ever got there." His very next joke is, "I've been getting into astronomy, so I installed a skylight. The people who live above me are furious."[22] Apparently, it is also a mystery as to how they got there as well.

The following sequence has an unmistakable picaresque tone to it, one very much like that of Thomas Berger's *Little Big Man* or even Jack Kerouac's *On the Road* in that it combines the travelogue with unabashed rascality:

Last summer I drove cross-country with a friend of mine. We split the driving. We switched every half mile. The whole way across we had only one cassette to listen to. I can't remember what it was. We were in Salina, Utah, when we were arrested for not going through a green light. We pleaded "maybe." I asked the judge if he knew what time it was and he told me and I said, "No further questions."[23]

Of his working life, Wright tells us, "I used to be a proofreader for a skywriting company," "I was a narrator for bad mimes," "I used to work at the factory where they make hydrants, but you couldn't park anywhere near the place."[24] In this sequence from the 1985 special he portrays himself as both a pariah and a drifter, someone unfettered by the usual responsibilities that come with a normal adulthood:

I used to work at an organic health food store in Seattle, Washington. One day a man came in and asked, "If I melt dry ice can I swim without getting wet?"

I said, "I don't know. Let me ask Tony."

A few days later I got fired for eating cotton candy and drinking straight Bosco on the job. So I decided to leave the area since there was nothing keeping me there except this girl I was seeing. We had conflicting attitudes. I wasn't into meditation and she wasn't into being alive.

So I packed up my Salvador Dali print of two naked dental hygienists trying to make a circle on an Etch-A-Sketch, and started hitchhiking. Within five minutes one of those tractor-trailer rigs stopped and I went up to the cab and the driver said, "I don't have much room up here. Why don't you get into one of the cars in the back? And he was really into picking up hitchhikers because he picked up nineteen more. Then he went ninety miles an hour and we all got speeding tickets.[25]

Adding to the roguish qualities is the way in which the comedian seems to take delight in introducing chaos to random situations, such as when he broke into the home of his friend George and "went up to his dog and put little contact lenses on his eyes that had cats on them. The dog was flipping out all over the place. Then I took one out and he ran in circles."[26] In another instance he goes to "court for a parking ticket. I pleaded insanity. I said, 'Your honor, why would anybody in his right mind park in the passing lane?" Nobody—and apparently nothing—is immune to his rascality. To torment policemen he "had the photo on my license taken out of focus on purpose, so when the police do stop me they go, 'Here, you can go.'"[27] He teases people who telephone him by having as the outgoing message on his answering machine "a recording of a busy signal"[28] and he teases his houseplants by watering them with ice cubes. This propensity apparently began when he was a child. When his teacher asked what kind of an animal he would like to be he said "a bird" and she asked, "Why? So you could fly?" to which he responded, "'No. So my shit would be white.' The teacher started crying."[29] In this scene from *When the Leaves Blow Away* he tells us how he, like the Marx Brothers, Bugs Bunny, Charlie Chaplin's Little Tramp or the Sacha Baron Cohen alter ego Borat, he enjoys playing the trickster to the common man:

I went into a store and asked the woman if she had anything to put underneath the coasters. I told her my coasters were marking up my tables. The woman started crying. Then I went into another store and asked them if they had any maps that were not aerial views. That guy was weeping openly.[30]

Sometimes this rascality is self-directed, such as when he talks to himself "fluently in languages I'm unfamiliar with, just to screw with my subconscious."[31]

With jokes like these, the effects of which are underscored by his deadpan delivery, lethargic movements and stranger-in-a-strange-land stage presence, Wright becomes very much the classical trickster rogue, a character who has, as a chief function, the job of shocking us out of our comfort zones as he constructs miniature parodies of American life and reminds us that the universe may indeed be ordered but not necessarily in the way we like to think it is.

The Post-modern Frontier

As countless studies on the American character argue, ingrained in the American is the confrontation with the chaos of the frontier, whether that frontier is the New World, Westward expansion, outer space, or, as Leslie Fiedler argues, the world of madness. This tendency that began with Columbus and was later amplified by the Puritan errand into the wilderness is the subject of Fiedler's 1968 classic study of literary anthropology, *The Return of the Vanishing American*. Here, Fiedler argues that the final frontier is not that of space exploration, as Captain James Kirk declares at the beginning of each *Star Trek* episode, but rather the sphere in which Wright seems quite comfortable, that of madness. This world, Fiedler argues, is very much shaped by the ghosts of the continent's conquered tribes. He writes that "everyone who thinks of himself as being in some sense an American feels the stirrings in him of a second soul, the soul of the Red Man"[32] Fiedler concludes his study by discussing how the frontier of the American West serves as a metaphor for the unexplored terrain that is insanity:

> It is only a step from thinking of the West as madness to regarding madness as the true West, but it took the long years between the end of the fifteenth and the middle of the twentieth to learn to take that step. . . .We have come to accept the notion that there is still a territory unconquered and uninhabited by palefaces, the bearers of civilization, the cadres of imperialist reason; and we have been learning that into this territory certain psychotics, a handful of "schizophrenics," have moved on ahead of the rest of us—unrecognized Natty Bumppos or Huck Finns, interested not in claiming the New World for any Old God, King, or Country, but in becoming New Men . . . (How fascinating, then, that R.D. Laing, leading exponent among contemporary psychiatrists of the theory that some schizophrenics have "broken through" rather than "broken down,"

should, despite the fact that this is an Englishman, have turned to our world and its discovery in search of an analogy; he suggests that Columbus stumbling upon America and his first garbled accounts of it provide an illuminating parallel to the ventures of certain madmen into the regions of extended or altered consciousness . . . .)[33]

Fiedler looks to Ken Kesey, both as the author of *One Flew Over the Cuckoo's Nest* and the hero and LSD advocate of Tom Wolfe's *The Electric Kool-Aid Acid Test*, as an example of this kind of "New Man" since, through his use of hallucinogenic drugs, Kesey is able to temporarily experience schizophrenia. We can, however, these decades later see that all this has been taken even further by Wright, who can also be regarded as the Adlerian hero in that he seems to have "broken through" to the other side. Wright has hinted at this with jokes such as "I taped Xs over the mirrors so that I don't accidentally walk through them into another dimension" and "I like to skate on the other side of the ice."[34] At least one commentator has suggested that this has already happened and that the comedian has indeed explored realms of madness.[35] This much was not lost on Carson who, after Wright made his national debut, asked him, "Did they just let you out for the evening?" thus suggesting that he assumed Wright should be in a mental institution. Wright responded, "I have an hour left."[36] As the interview progressed—if you can call what transpired a progression or an interview—it became obvious that Wright was uncomfortable, as he was unable to put a sentence together for some time.

Elements of the insanity that Fiedler discusses can easily be spotted in plenty of Wright's bits. Just minutes into the performance proper of the HBO special, for instance, he tells us "I was on peyote when I took my ACTs. I got an 1800,"[37] thus suggesting the "second soul," that of the "Red Man," which Fiedler mentions is alive, well and influential as Wright's partaking in a Native American sacrament allows him to simultaneously increase his intelligence and make a foray into the realm of madness. Similar jokes, meanwhile, have the feel of schizophrenic ranting, such as when he says, rather casually: "I'm going to court next week. I've been selected for jury duty. It's kind of an insane case. Six thousand ants dressed up as rice and robbed a Chinese restaurant. I don't think they did it. I know a few of them and they wouldn't do a thing like that." Similarly, jokes such as "Why is it a penny for your thoughts but you put your two cents in? Somebody's making a penny,"[38] "I was five years old, watching T.V. [when I heard the commercial]: 'Only you can prevent forest fires.' Every night, [I was] out the window with a bucket of water,"[39] "The ice cream truck in my neighborhood plays 'Helter Skelter'"[40] reveal absurd dimensions of a profound paranoia. The same is true for this bit from *I Have a Pony*:

> I got up this morning, I couldn't find my socks, so I called information. I said, 'Hello, information?"
> She said, "Yes?"
> I said, "I can't find my socks."
> She said, "They're behind the couch."
> And they were."[41]

The following bit, meanwhile, takes on the quality of a schizophrenic delusion:

> A couple of nights I came home very late, it was the next night. I was having a little trouble getting into my apartment and I accidentally stuck in a car key, turned it, and the building started up. So I drove it around for a while. I went too fast and the police pulled me over and they said, "Where do you live?" and I said, "Right here." Then I parked it in the middle of a highway and ran out the door and yelled at all the cars to get the hell out of my driveway.
>
> Nobody who lives in the building noticed the building moved because everyone who lives in the building is absolutely insane. The man who lives above me designs synthetic hairballs for ceramic cats. The woman who lives beside me tried to rob a department store with a pricing gun. She walked in and said, "give me all the money in the vault or I'll mark down everything in the store."[42]

Perhaps the least-talked-about element of the picaresque is the way in which these stories provide a satire upon the societies out of which they arose. Just as *Lazarillo de Tormes* provides a running commentary on Spanish values and takes some hard swipes at the Catholic Church and *The Adventures of Huckleberry Finn* is almost always read as a commentary on American racism, hypocrisy and hubris, Wright's body of work could also be seen as a horrific mockery. With frequent references to 1960s and1970s pop culture icons such as the Beatles, *The Flintstones* and rock music, the comedian clearly aligns himself as a baby boomer and could be seen as a living, breathing satire of life in the nuclear age. At the very beginning of *A Steven Wright Special*, for instance, in a four-minute segment that precedes the performance proper, we see a shot of a small house on a deserted landscape. Whether it is just before sunrise or just after sunset is hard to determine, but the sky, and consequently everything in the scene, is tinged with red. As the camera moves closer a shaggy, mid-sized terrier-like dog appears, trots around a rickety fence and scratches on the house's screen door. The scene cuts to the interior, where Wright sleeps on a bare mattress on the floor. As the wind howls, an alarm clock, which says it is 12:30, sounds off and Wright switches it off, rises, puts on a shirt, falls back on the mattress and apparently goes back to sleep.

When he finally does get up, things get even more bizarre. To brush his teeth, he turns the spigot on the bathroom sink and water shoots out the shower head. He switches on the radio, which plays only thunder. He goes to his refrigerator and removes a package of Oreo cookies and a box labeled "Powdered Water." A few minutes later he walks out the door and tries to wave down a rickety old bus that happens to be passing. He ends up walking to what looks like a ghost town where he passes a primitive hand-lettered sign that reads, "Matinee Today/Steven Wright." The scene cuts to a green room (which is literally green), where Wright waits for his offstage introduction.

This introductory segment is thick with post-apocalyptic imagery. Not only do the reddish glow—especially when it appears a half hour after either midday or midnight—the landscape and the terrier cross recall L.Q. Jones's post-apocalyptic and darkly comic film from 1975, *A Boy and His Dog* (which was based on the Harlan Ellison novella), but the clock recalls the Doomsday Clock on *the Bulletin of Atomic Scientists*, which has traditionally been set at five minutes to midnight, the suggestion being that nuclear war is just a metaphorical "few minutes away." Since Wright's clock reads 12:30, the indication is that the apocalypse has already happened.

Furthermore, the scene's twisted logic tells us that we have entered a distinctly post-modern age, one that began with the bombing of Hiroshima. Wright has taken us—or perhaps we have followed him—into a post-modern frontier. Both Wright's physical presence and deadpan delivery reinforce the post-apocalyptic theme. The comedian is, in fact, making a profound political statement as he presents himself as a walking, joke-telling corpse, the last vestige of hippie idealism, and a reflection of what had become of the hippies and beatniks during the Reagan years. In a time when the world seemed closer to nuclear annihilation than it had been since the Cuban Missile Crisis, Wright has become a personification of Robert J. Lifton's concept of "psychic numbing," i.e. the idea that we must switch off part of our consciousness and consciences in order to function in a world constantly threatened by nuclear annihilation.[43]

Perhaps Wright's most revealing joke from the 1985 special involves his conversation with a strange woman in a bar. She asks him how he feels and he replies: "You know how when you're leaning back on a chair and you lean back too far and you're just about to fall and then at the last second you catch yourself? I feel like that all the time."[44] With this line, Wright takes us out of ourselves, shocking us with the strange logic so that we become unhinged and separated from both the world we live in and the entrapments of our egos. Consequently, this relieves us in two ways. We see ourselves in Wright as we identify with his fear: the world he lives in is cruel, illogical and, like the chair that teeters on its back legs, always precariously balanced. This reminds us of the world we live in, one that similarly teeters on the brink of nuclear annihilation and can, at any moment, be cast into oblivion. Yet, it is through his ability to reveal and examine these anxieties that he can begin to assuage them.

Loss of Self and Death Obsession

Two other unignorable themes of Wright's work are the loss of self and an obsession with death that rivals Woody Allen's. In his debut *Tonight Show* appearance, he told this joke that is brilliant in its simple elegance: "Today I was—no, that wasn't me,"[45] indicating that the comedian has only a tangential hold, at best, on who he is. Twenty-five years later, he addressed the same issue with this joke in *When the Leaves Blow Away*: "I need [a baby monitor] from my subconscious to my conscious so I can know what I am really thinking."[46] In the countless performances that occurred between these two instances, the matter was addressed with jokes such as "My mind was wandering. One time my mind went all the way to Venus and ordered a meal I couldn't pay for," "Four years ago I was—wait, that was yesterday," "Right now I'm having amnesia and déjà vu at the same time" and "I was walking through the forest, alone, when a tree fell right in front of me, and I didn't hear it."[47] In this sequence from *When the Leaves Blow Away*, the separation is so complex that it is hard to keep track of:

> So last night as I was downloading pornographic bootleg SpongeBobs, sent to me from a hairdresser I know in Argentina, I noticed I had no milk for tomorrow's coffee, so I looked at the car keys which had been strategically placed under the short leg of the kitchen table so that the soup wouldn't spill and I had to make a decision: do I walk to the store or do I drive and spill the soup? After half an hour on my hands and knees, I deli-

cately removed the car keys from under the table and the soup didn't spill, which pissed me off so much that I whipped it against the wall. Then I tried to wash it off with my machinegun squirt gun, which was full of another kind of soup and I kind of liked the pattern I made so I took photographs of it intending to do paintings of the photographs which I would sell them back to myself later since I am a private collector.[48]

Other jokes, meanwhile, take the loss of self to the next level and discuss his contemplations of suicide, jokes such as: "I have a paper cut from writing my suicide note. It's a start" and

The last time I tried to commit suicide was about an hour ago. I was down the street on the roof of this very tall building and I ran and I leaped off the edge and I accidentally did a triple back-flip and landed standing on my feet. Nobody saw this but two little kittens. One them said, "See? That's how you do that."[49]

And he is not only concerned with his own death. For the closing bit in *When the Leaves Blow Away* he strums his guitar and sings about the death of his friends:

Eddie was a friend of mine, he was killed playing checkers. You know that term "king me"? The other guy wasn't sure what he said.

Dennis was a friend of mine. He was killed breaking a wishbone. Nobody knows if it was an accident or suicide. Nobody knows what he was wishing for.

Like my daddy used to say, "If worse comes to worse we're screwed . . . he told me I was born eight and half months premature."

Paul was a friend of mine and he was killed playing tag. It wasn't really tag it was push. Near the Grand Canyon.[50]

Such jokes, which address the insecurity that each of us must endure if we are to continue living under such dangerous circumstances, have a dual effect on the audience. First of all, in the comedian we see ourselves—we see the personification of our own fears, self-alienation and psychic numbing as we identify with his fear, the precariousness that haunts him and the illogical and often cruel world in which he resides. Nevertheless, we turn to a personification of such fears for relief as we look to him to assuage those anxieties by reframing them so that they become the subjects of comedy rather than the subjects of abject horror. In the end, finally, he calms our fears by convincing us that it is him, and not us, who is skating on the other side of the ice.

CHAPTER EIGHT
RICHARD PRYOR, AMERICAN DANTE

Most stand-up comedians and stand-up comedy aficionados would probably agree that the 1982 performance film *Richard Pryor Live on the Sunset Strip* changed the art form forever. Widely regarded as history's most important and influential stand-up comedian,[1] Pryor, in this performance, sets a new standard in comedic honesty and intimacy in the way that he frankly and openly illustrates his plight with cocaine addiction and in the way that he renounces the use of the word "nigger," a slur that punctuated a great many of the routines of his early career. While the film is most famous for its climactic bits concerning conversations with a cocaine pipe[2] and a recounting of the famous "accident" that left him near death with third-degree burns over half his body,[3] the film as a whole can be taken as a commentary on American values and the pitfalls of the American dream. If a literary critic were to assess only its hellish nature and horrific scenes involving murder, a flaming body and conversations with a demon, the performance could easily be situated in the tradition of the great American horror tale, in line with the works of Hawthorne, Poe and Hemingway.

An even more demanding analysis might reveal that, by nature of its subject matter, its universal themes, the confessional quality, the deftness of the execution and the way in which it explores "the human heart in conflict with itself,"[4] *Live on the Sunset Strip* also belongs to the world of classical literature. When taken as a single unit, the twenty-eight bits included in the performance tell a story with a classic mythological structure, one that begins with a rebirth and ends with a dual baptism by fire and water, a story that follows closely the initiation-separation-return hero cycle Joseph Campbell describes in his seminal book *The Hero with a Thousand Faces*. Beyond that, it is an autobiographical story of a man who confronts a tragic flaw, celebrates an epiphany, is counseled by a wise grandfather, encounters spirit guides and confronts personifications of each of the Seven Deadly Sins. When all of this is taken together, *Live on the Sunset Strip* becomes a harrowing and vivid depiction of a journey through the chambers of a distinctly American version of Hell, where some of the nation's most nefarious sins must be accounted for. In this way, *Live on the Sunset Strip* provides late twentieth-century America with its own parallel to Dante Alighieri's epic poem from the fourteenth century, *Inferno*.

Perhaps it is fitting that Hell is a subject that unites two such different pieces of art, works ostensibly composed for very different purposes and audiences. Hell, after all, has never been far from the human imagination, as the belief in the karmic balance assures us that the universe contains at least a modicum of order. Virtually every society and mythological tradition—whether it is the Greeks' tradition with Hades and Tartarus, the Chinese and *Chi Yu*, the Hebrews and Sheol, the Christians and Gehenna or the Hindus and Buddhists with their *Narakas*—has supported one view of the underworld or another. Virtually all have more or less the same function: to punish people for their infractions against God and neighbor, and to thereby reassure the righteous that the wicked will be punished.

If Hell, however, is that place where souls are sent to account for sins and Pryor is exploring a distinctly American version of that Hell, then the question arises: For what sins will America be held accountable? While the most obvious answers to this question are slavery and the obliteration of Native peoples, other transgressions also warrant mention, such as consumption that is so excessive that it arguably threatens the very existence of the planet; the using and discarding of human beings, whether they be slaves, porn stars, movie stars or college athletes; and certainly the sins of drug abuse and drug addiction, two plagues that have haunted America throughout its history. There is no question that since the establishment of the first European colonies in the early seventeenth century, the nation has, in no small measure, been shaped by the proliferation of mood-altering substances such as tobacco, coffee, whiskey, fermented cider, beer, laudanum, marijuana, wine, Valium, sugar, Prozac and cocaine. It is no surprise, then, that the world that Pryor, a self-identified Black man and dope addict, the child of a pimp and a prostitute and a man who lived the rags-to-riches American dream, is the person ordained to lead his audience, and by extension America, on a trip through the underworld where all must confront a succession of demons who are direct results of the country's most heinous spiritual crimes.

For Dante, the horrors of Hell are explored through the story of a man who is very much like the poet, if not Dante himself, who in midlife finds himself wandering astray in a "dark wood" and then, with the help of the spirit of Virgil, the Roman poet from the first century B.C., journeys into the bowels of the Earth. There, the nine circles of Hell, each of which is deeper into the underworld than the previous one and contains more gruesome punishments, are divided into two regions: the first five circles, which lie outside the satanic metropolis called the City of Dis, and the last four, which are inside the city's walls. Although the poem is made up of thirty-four chapters or cantos, the narrative falls organically into eleven sections:

Prelude:	The Dark Wood
Circle 1:	Limbo
Circle 2:	Lust
Circle 3:	Gluttony
Circle 4:	Avarice
Circle 5:	Wrath
Circle 6:	Heresy
Circle 7:	Violence
Circle 8:	Fraud
Circle 9:	Treachery
Denouement:	Re-emergence

The story climaxes when Dante gazes upon the face of Satan and escapes into the upper world on the other side of the Earth.

Live on the Sunset Strip, meanwhile, also concerns a middle-aged man who finds himself in a dark wood and tours the underworld. Instead of one spirit guide, Pryor has four: a disembodied voice that speaks to him during his last hours in Africa, fellow comic actor Gene Wilder, National Football League Hall-of-Famer Jim Brown and a burn-unit nurse named Larry Murphy who cares for him after his holocaust. *Live on the Sunset Strip* also divides easily and organically into eleven chapters, which could easily be titled:

1. The Sunset Strip Montage
2. Sex

3. Lawyers
4. Marriage
5. Prison
6. Racism
7. The African Interlude
8. The Mafia
9. Mudbone
10. Cocaine
11. The Recovery

If, however, the chapters were named for their overriding themes, the progression would be:

1. Hubris
2. Lust
3. Envy
4. Wrath
5. Violence
6. Racism
7. The African Interlude
8. Avarice
9. Heresy
10. Gluttony
11. Rebirth

While nine of the chapters of the performance proper deal to varying degrees with Pryor's personal demons, the African Interlude, which comes exactly in the middle of the show—thirty-eight minutes into a seventy-seven-minute performance—stands out in terms of tone and setting. Inspired by the comedian's 1979 trip to Africa, the bit stands out for a number of other reasons. Although it has its punch lines, it is uncharacteristically serious and repentant and, with the exception of a few lines in the cocaine sequence, is the only story in the performance that is concerned primarily with events that happen out-of-doors. If the African Interlude were excised from its position in the middle and placed at the beginning of the performance, the two works would align like this:

	Dante	Pryor
Prelude	Dark Wood	Dark Wood
Circle 1	Limbo	Hubris
Circle 2	Lust	Lust
Circle 3	Gluttony	Envy
Circle 4	Avarice	Wrath
Circle 5	Wrath	Violence
Circle 6	Heresy	Racism
Circle 7	Violence	Avarice
Circle 8	Fraud	Fraud
Circle 9	Treachery	Addiction
Denouement	Re-emergence	Re-emergence

Each would then begin in a natural setting and involve confrontations with animals and a visit by a spirit guide and involve a guided journey through nine horrific realms, the last four of which are the most gruesome and contain the most haunting and disturbing images. Each would then address the deadly sins of lust, avarice, wrath and gluttony; climax with an encounter with a demon; and conclude with a symbolic resurrection. While nothing in any of Pryor's biographies suggests that the comedian was familiar with or interested in Dante's poetry, the poet and the comedian seem to have sipped from the same inspirational waters. Just as Dante did for the world at the beginning of the Renaissance, Pryor provides for twentieth-century America a literary and spiritual assessment of the times.

I. The Dark Wood

Though *Inferno* includes hills, rivers and canyons existing within the inner circles of Hell proper, the bulk of the narrative takes place within an enclosed space, that is, the world beneath the Earth's crust. Only two scenes—the very first and the very last—are set outside this realm. Consisting of the initial three cantos, the prelude tells of how the protagonist finds himself wandering "astray" in the "dark wood" and as he makes his way to a mountain in the distance he soon encounters three animals—a leopard (which represents lust), a lion (which represents pride) and a she-wolf (which represents anger)—who scare him off his path. Soon, Dante is approached by the "shadow" of Virgil, who says he has been sent by Beatrice, Dante's true love who resides in Heaven.

Presently, Virgil ushers him into the underworld to begin the journey.[5] Similarly, *Live on the Sunset Strip*'s African Interlude also takes place in a "dark wood," specifically the African jungle, which Pryor describes as "the real jungle. Not that shit Tarzan live [sic] in."[6] In his autobiography, *Pryor Convictions and Other Life Sentences*, the comedian tells of the chain of events that led him and his soon-to-be-wife Jennifer Lee on the trip to Africa, the excursion that formed the foundation for that bit. The process was set in motion a few months earlier with the death of his maternal grandmother, Marie Carter, whom he called "Mama." Pryor recalls the defining moment, a time when he too went off the straight and narrow:

> I was awash in depression that crashed over me after Mama's death. I truly felt as if I was flailing underwater, stuck in a surreal nightmare. . . . The flow of hookers and my frequent all-night sometimes week-long disappearances into the squalid home of a strung-out female drug dealer . . . told [his girlfriend, Jennifer] I was in trouble. . . . Any doubt I was on a path to self-destruction was erased the day I emerged from the bath with half my mustache shaved off, dressed in a red jogging suit, silver shoes, and a top hat, and announced that I was going out.
> "Oh, really," she said. "Where ya goin'?"
> "Shuffling off to Buffalo," I grinned madly.
> After that, she checked my ass into a hospital. It was clear the egg had cracked.[7]

While working with a psychiatrist at the hospital shortly thereafter, Pryor began to understand the impact Mama's death had on him. It was the psychiatrist who suggested the Africa trip. As with Dante, the venture into the Dark Wood is initiated by the loss of female love. Just as Beatrice's love is lost with her death and then returns with the message from Virgil, Mama Bryant's love is lost and then resurrected in the person of Jennifer. Pryor also tells of stare-downs with animals, specifically a lion. Says Pryor, "You see a lion in the jungle, that's what they look like: lions. He'll be in the bush going . . . " [rolling his shoulders, looking like a lion ready to pounce and then speaks as if he is the lion:] 'Yeah, get your ass out the car. And bring that camera with you. 'Cause we gonna eat all that shit.'"

Also in the opening canto, Dante describes how Virgil magically appears to him saying, "a shape was offered to my vision wan/as if from a long silence it had kept."[8] Pryor also tells of his other-worldly encounter with a long-silenced spirit, one that he refers to merely as "a voice." He says:

One thing I got out of it was magic that I'd like to share with you. I was leaving. I was sitting in a hotel and a voice said to me: "Look around, and what do you see?"

And I said, "I see all colors of people doing everything."

And the voice said, "Do you see any niggers?"

And I said, "No."

And it said, "you know why? 'cause there aren't any."

And it hit me like a shot, man. I started crying. I was sitting there and I said, "I've been here three weeks and I haven't said it. I haven't even thought it. And it made me say, "Oh my god, I been wrong. I been wrong. I got to regroup my shit. I ain't never gonna call another black man "nigger" 'cause that word is dead, you know. 'Cause we never was no niggers. That's a word that is used to describe our own wretchedness.

Each of these epics is launched from the same platform, the archetypal setting that is the deep woods, a symbol of challenge and depression. Both also rely heavily on images of wild animals to build dramatic tension and each invokes a spirit from another realm as a guide. Thus, the two pieces appear to align not just in tone, subject matter and narrative structure, but also in terms of the images and metaphors the artists invoke in order to tell their respective stories.

II. The Vestibule: The Sunset Strip

For Dante, the first circle of Hell is not a place of severe punishment. Rather, it is the Circle of Limbo, that place in the afterlife that has been reserved for the righteous unbaptized, those benevolent souls who did not have the benefit of Christ's salvation. Here, the poet commits what at first glance seems like an act of supreme hubris, positioning himself alongside the legendary poets Horace, Ovid, Lucan, Homer and Virgil. Even though Dante scholar and translator Michael Palma argues that Dante saw his talents as "God-given, not a personal attainment worthy of boast,"[9] it appears, seven centuries after the fact, that the poet's ranking himself with these other masters is quite justified, since his poetry is unquestionably among history's most memorable. In *Live on the Sunset Strip*, a clear parallel to this comes in the opening montage. As the credits roll up the screen, the audience is given a miniature tour of the most famous landmarks along the mile-and-a-half stretch of Hollywood's Sunset Boulevard known as The Sunset Strip. Included are images of Schwab's drug store, which has been called "one of Hollywood's most enduring legends, where Charles Chaplin made his own sodas and starlets awaited discovery,"[10] where in November 1940, F.

Scott Fitzgerald suffered a "coronary episode" that eventually killed him,[11] where sitting in his car in the glow of the neon, Harold Arlen is believed to have penned the music to "Over the Rainbow."[12] Also shown are the façade of the Roxy theater, a favorite hangout of Bruce Springsteen, Neil Young and Prince; The Rainbow Bar, where Joe DiMaggio had his first date with Marilyn Monroe; and the Chateau Marmont, where John Belushi died of a drug overdose. When the credits end and the camera fixes itself upon the individual letters of the sign of the Hollywood Palladium, where the performance takes place, it has been established unequivocally that just as Dante is worthy of hobnobbing with the legends of his particular craft, Pryor belongs in the land of legends of American show business.

III. Lust

In the few seconds leading into the performance proper of *Live on the Sunset Strip*, the screen is filled with a cartoonish image depicting Pryor as sixty feet tall and standing on Sunset Boulevard while cars whiz by his feet. His mouth is open as if he is screaming and he holds his foot and stares down at a crumpled Volkswagen Beetle, the implicit story being that the car has just crashed into his foot. The image is fitting as it depicts the comedian as a vulnerable giant. As the camera pans down to the showroom entryway, Pryor struts out from the shadows, his attire unmistakably diabolical: he wears a red designer suit, black shirt and tie and gold boots. Once on the stage, where he is virtually steeped in the colors red and black, he launches into a "preacher routine," a gimmick popularized by Lenny Bruce. In a voice mocking an evangelical preacher, he says, "We are gathered here today to make sure everybody eats. If not each other, [then] food." With this initial utterance, the comedian establishes that he and the audience are in a realm that is the obverse of the holy, a place where a profane cleric uses the metaphorical bread to satisfy corporeal, rather than spiritual, appetites.

Once the laughter dies down, Pryor continues with the theme into the first full-blown bit of the evening, saying, "I was gonna talk about something that's very serious, and I hope that no one gets offended. I wanna talk about fucking." The climax of the particular chunk comes a few minutes later when the narrative moves from the general to the personal. Pryor says, "One time I got some Playboy Bunny pussy. I thought I was in the big time. Going home with a *Playboy Bunny*. . . . Her apartment was *bad*. It was one of those apartments where [I thought], 'If I don't get the pussy I'm gonna fuck this couch.'" He tells of how the woman indicated that she got aroused when he talked in a child's voice. Pryor says, "And she started taking off her clothes. The more clothes she took off, the younger I got. When she got down to her panties I was talking about [baby noises]. She gave birth to me about nine-thirty."

This circle aligns closely with Dante's second circle of Hell proper, the realm where the lustful are punished. The central metaphor of Dante's discussion is also a passionate and lustful woman who, like the Playboy model who bares her body for purposes of nourishing male fantasies, puts male needs above her own. For Dante, this comes in the character of his contemporary Francesca da Rimini, a woman who, after committing adultery with her husband's brother, sacrificed herself for the sake of her lover.

For both artists, the introduction to Hell involves the realm of lust and carnal appetites. Early in their respective pieces, the two artists acknowledge the power of sexual incontinence, that which compromised—if not crippled—the careers of the Mark Antonys and Bill Clintons of history.

IV. Envy

While Dante's third circle is reserved for the gluttonous, Pryor's is reserved for avaricious and manipulative lawyers. While the two discussions are ostensibly different, they share a strong thematic link. Dante personifies gluttony through the character of Ciacco, a Florentine whose name means "the hog" and who, in essence, is a parasite. The Ciaccos of Pryor's world, the parasites who feed off of him, are unmistakably the lawyers he wrangles with during those months surrounding the filming of *Live on the Sunset Strip*. Furthermore, Ciacco's description of his (and Dante's) home city of Florence as "a city stuffed so tight/with envy that the sacks have overflowed" and "a city of glutto-ny"[13] can certainly apply to Pryor's home of Los Angeles, a city that consumes people and dreams, is rife with parasites and can also be described as being "stuffed with envy." These parallels become clear as Pryor tells of his troubles with lawyers, saying: "I got a lawyer. First week the motherfucker brought me a bill for forty thousand dollars. I said, 'Motherfucker, I just met you.'" He continues the diatribe, first by mocking the stereotypical aloofness and stoic demeanor of lawyers and then by examining the perils of misdirected allegiance. He tells of the trouble he encountered when he chose a lawyer because he was Black: "There's a guy I'm suing. [He] was my brother. 'Right on.' [applause from the audience] The motherfucker took me hook, line and sinker. On dry land."

In their illustrations of these parallel realms, Dante and Pryor address very much the same disease, albeit in different guises. For Dante, the gluttonous are those who consume food and beverage with either no ability or no concern for moderation. For Pryor it is those who take living, breathing people like Britney Spears, Michael Jordan, Anna Nicole Smith and Elvis Presley and turn them into products and franchises. For both these artists, the third circle is an indictment of those people who choose parasitic consumption over symbiotic relationships.

V. Wrath

As Dante and Virgil venture into the Fifth Circle of Hell, which borders the marsh that is part of the River Styx, they encounter two sets of souls. The first includes the wrathful, who crouch on the riverbank punching, kicking and biting each other, while the second contains the sullen, those who have been condemned to gurgle in the mud for eternity. Presently, the poets are accosted by Furies, spirits of vengeance, who summon Medusa, the mythological woman with snakes for hair, who can literally turn men to stone. Dante turns his eyes away and Virgil leads him away to the gate of the City of Dis, which marks the region of Lower Hell.

This also has a close parallel in the fourth chapter of *Live on the Sunset Strip*, when Pryor discusses his marriage, saying, "My wife is white and the first two years we went together she thought her name was White Honky Bitch." If the mud mentioned by Dante symbolizes, as mud so often does in stories and poems, a lack of clarity and a lack of communication, then Pryor's take on his wife indicates that she is trying to clear the emotional waters. In this bit Pryor tells us how his wife constantly coaxes him to "express yourself. Darling, express your feelings, emotions. Try to talk. Try not to be so physical. Learn how to speak. Try to talk. Darling, what is the problem?" to which Pryor answers, in a voice that that is simultaneously restrained and teeming with anger: "Bitch, I'm gonna kill you."

If Medusa as she appears in *Inferno* represents the threat of turning men to stone, Jennifer goes a step further, as she is directly involved in her husband's becoming so consumed with rage that he "can't even talk." Says Pryor, "The madder I get, the quieter I get. My voice just goes down. . . 'specially. . ." At this point, Pryor acts out an argument—a chunk that draws huge laughs—in which he pummels his wife with silent screams, ending the tirade with an unmistakable silent "Fuck you." Or to put the matter another way, the comedian's wrath has left him emotionally and linguistically petrified.

V. Violence

Dante's Seventh Circle of Hell is reserved for those souls who committed violent acts against their neighbors, themselves and God, many of whom have been plunged into a river of boiling blood as punishment. In many ways, Pryor addresses the world of violence much more directly and honestly than does the poet. While Dante is merely guided through this realm, the whole time staying aloof and only occasionally looking upon the prisoners, Pryor enters the Arizona State Penitentiary, the setting of his 1980 film *Stir Crazy*. Pryor recalls conversations and how co-star Gene Wilder serves as a guide. Pryor says, "Gene Wilder loved to jump in the middle of the killers and start talking: 'Hi guys, how you doin' . . . .'"

It is during these conversations Pryor learns to appreciate the hellish quality of prison life. He says, "Six weeks I was up there. I talked to the brothers. I was up there and I talked to them. . . . [Up until then] I thought Black people killed people by accident." The conversations, he indicates, summarily changed this perception. This much is clear when he shudders, rolls his eyes and says of the experience, "Thank God we got penitentiaries."

He goes on to discuss how the conversations took on increasingly more mortifying and increasingly more surreal, otherworldly and hellish qualities and how the prison became a realm filled with characters unmistakably like many of those found in Dante's poem:

> I ask [one of them], "Why did you kill everybody in the house?" He goes, "They was home." I mean . . . these motherfuckers was murderers. I met one motherfucker, his name was Jaybo, motherfucker lift weights—he was in charge of it. Jaybo, muscles everymotherfuckin'where. He was doing a sentence: triple life. How in the fuck do you do triple life? I mean, I mean if he die and come back, he got to go to the penitentiary. Right? They'll say, "Fuck kindergarten, get your little ol' ass back in the penitentiary, motherfucker. You know what you did last time you was here."

This is all the more harrowing when we consider that Pryor was not the product of a sheltered suburban upbringing but was raised in the inner city, in a world filled with prostitutes, pimps, burglars and other street thugs. Furthermore, Pryor recounts in his autobiography how he, while a child, was exposed to numerous horrors. Not only did he fall in "with some bad guys" who abandoned him during a robbery,[14] but he was sodomized by a neighbor,[15] served ninety days in jail in Pittsburgh for beating a woman[16] and spent time in jail after being caught with marijuana while he was crossing the U.S.-Mexican border at Tijuana.[17] Nevertheless, much the way Dante's tour of Hell leaves the poet reeling and sometimes so weak he must be carried, Pryor's tour shakes him to his core as he is forced to look squarely into the face of the horrible, unimaginable and—at least to bourgeois America—very much hidden.

VI. Heresy

The sixth circle in *Inferno* is the realm of heretics, which for Dante means those who follow their own opinions rather than that of the Church. As Virgil guides Dante along a secret path, the two are accosted by spirits of these heretics who speak to them from tombs that are currently open but will be sealed after the final judgment. Pryor's sixth circle, meanwhile, climaxes with a discussion of racism. Again, even if the parallelism is less than exact, the two discussions nevertheless broach similar themes, albeit from different angles.

If *Live on the Sunset Strip* is a tour of a distinctly American version of Hell, and a heretic is, by definition, someone who opposes the authority of God, then a heretic in this case is someone who challenges He who inspired the founding principles of the nation, namely the God of Reason. This is the "Creator" whom Thomas Jefferson declares endowed each human with "certain inalienable rights, that among these are the right to Life, Liberty and the Pursuit of Happiness." Certainly, in a country founded upon the ideas of such individual rights and pluralism, in a country that celebrates the birthday of Civil Rights leader Martin Luther King, those who embrace and perpetrate racism are not only directly attacking the gospel of the God of Reason, but they are also challenging His authority. Pryor addresses the matter directly, saying,

> Racism is a bitch. I mean, White people, you gotta know. It fucks you up, but what it does to Black people is a bitch. . . . It's hard enough being a human being. It's really fuckin' hard enough just to be that. Just to go through everyday life without murdering a motherfucker is hard enough. Just to walk through life, decent as a person. But having another element added to it when you're Black. [You White] Motherfuckers got that little

edge on us. It's enough to make you crazy. If you're in another argument with another man, he may be White, but it's man-on-man for a minute and the shit get rough, he end up calling you "nigger." You gotta go, "oh, shit. Fuck. Now I ain't no man no more . . . now I got to argue with that shit. Fuck, throw my balance all off. But it's an ugly thing. I hope some-day they give it up, because it don't work.

These last two sentences serve as a short aside that contains neither set-up nor punch line but nevertheless accomplishes two things in terms of the performance. First of all, it tells us that the comedian has undergone some emotional and political maturation since the days of the albums *That Nigger's Crazy* and *Was It Something I Said?* This is sig-nificant for Pryor who has no small investment in his use of the slur. According to one commentator, Pryor's use of the word "'nigger' was the masterstroke. It aced him out of the mainstream, plus it made it quite clear where his racial allegiance lay. Everyone knows that White people aren't allowed to say that word."[18] Secondly, it foreshadows an even longer and more poignant aside that will come a few minutes lat-er, at the end of the African interlude. With this attack on racism and his newfound cultural sensitivity, Pryor becomes the living embodi-ment of the changes in the American cultural landscape during the second half of the twentieth century. In the years between the Civil Rights demonstrations and Martin Luther King's birthday's becoming a national holiday, he illustrates for his audience that the perpetuation of racism amounts to nothing less than an attack on the American ideal, that to call another person "nigger" is not only to deny that per-son's humanity but also to deny the power of the One who inspired the invention of the United States.

VII. Avarice

If Pryor's visit to the penitentiary underscores the Hellish nature of *Live on the Sunset Strip*, his bit on working for the Mafia reinforces the point. In this sequence, Pryor discusses how early in his career he worked at a Mafia nightclub in Youngstown, Ohio, and how one night he was informed by one the strippers that he might not be paid. Pryor says that, at nineteen, he took a starter's pistol into the office and threatened the club owner, "doin' my best Black shit, you know. 'Cause usually that shit scare Whitey to death." The owner responds by laughing so hard that he can hardly speak. In the most uncanny parallel to *Inferno*, this scene presents an almost perfect analogy to Dante's Fourth Circle, which is reserved for misers and spendthrifts. Overseen by Plutus, who personifies the "wealth of the Earth"[19] and who speaks unintelligibly to Dante and Virgil, this circle of avarice holds within it various souls who have been condemned to rolling great weights for all eternity. Misers push the weights one way while the spendthrifts push them the other. When the weights collide the misers scream out, "Why throw it away?" and the spendthrifts yell back, "Why pinch it?"[20]

Just as Dante and Virgil are assailed with Plutus' garbled and unintelligible utterances, Pryor's threat to the club owner is met with waves of laughter and gibberish that is meant to sound like Italian from a character who is unmistakably a manifestation of Plutus. Pryor tells how, after the initial laughing fit, the owner utters what, to Pryor, was "shit you don't understand." Throughout the bit the owner says things like, "he's got a pair of gagoozies on him, huh?" At one point the owner grabs Pryor's face and lets loose with another string of gibberish that is meant to sound affectionate and then offers him some Italian food, saying, "Hey, you want a little cozimadomi? Hey Paolo, fix him a little midimozaguli. And put some struzzi on it."

Also, the Mafia boss tells of arguments between camps who, like Dante's spendthrifts and misers, are poisoned by the same disease but exhibit different symptoms. In one of the bits that Pryor felt was the most successful of an otherwise disappointing performance,[21] he recounts how the club owner can barely contain himself as he recounts the of killing a colleague as casually as anybody else might relay a vacation story:

> So we take this jerk-off out bowling, drive him around, get him a few drinks. "Say, let's get some broads." Little motel where it's set up. Remember that, Johnny? So we take him around, gets kinda stoned, drops his glass, I say 'now.' I pop him with the fuckin' ice pick, right? I'm poppin' this cocksucker, blood squirtin' every whicha way. I'm stabbing and he's, 'Oh God, don't kill me.' 'Oh fuck you, you guinea cocksucker.' And the fuckin' ice pick breaks. I'm standing there with a fuckin' piece of wood in my hand. I say, 'Johnny Salami, whatta I do?' He says, 'Wait 'til it melts.' [more laughter]"

The horror of this scene is unmistakable as it signals to the audience that the relatively light discussions on lawyers and sex are over and that Pryor is heading deeper and deeper into increasingly more terrifying realms, much the way Dante does when he passes the walls of the City of Dis. Pryor also adds another dimension to all of this when he discusses the way in which the club owners "let everybody go but kept me as a pet." Such a situation echoes the history of an America that is built on hegemony, especially one in which Europeans have taken Africans as chattel and, at best, allowed Native Americans restricted use of their own homeland.

Even though the conversations at the penitentiary hint at equally disturbing scenes, the blood and gore are only suggested and are never presented directly in the performance as they are in the Mafia bit. In one of the segment's closing lines, Pryor describes what happens when greed takes possession of the soul:

> One time I was in a room with one of these motherfuckers and I don't know how to describe it. You ever seen a face just turn to stone? . . . A stone thing came over his face and a chill went through my fuckin' body. I said, "This motherfucker's dead. I'm looking at a dead man that walks around." 'Cause it was just stone. There wasn't no compromise in it.

Now it is clear that Pryor is into the deeper realms of the American Hell, where the gods of capitalism demand obedience and sacrifice and, in some cases, the surrender of one's soul.

VIII. Fraud

The penultimate circle of Dante's Hell is reserved for the souls of those who have committed great acts of fraud, such as hypocrisy, manipulation and the buying and selling of ecclesiastical favors. Like the other circles in the City of Dis, this one is also divided into sub-realms, which in this case are called *bolge*, or "pits," each of which is devoted to a special class of fraud. The fourth pit, for example, is dedicated to diviners and magicians, the fifth to lenders who charge exorbitant interest rates, and the ninth to those who sow discord. Of primary concern here, however, at least as far as *Live on the Sunset Strip* is concerned, are the first, which contains flatterers, the second, which contains seducers, and the ninth, which houses fraudulent counselors. In their respective pits the seducers are damned to run from one edge to another, only to be whipped back into place by an overseer, while the flatterers are forced to wallow in excrement for all eternity. Finally, the pit of fraudulent counselors contains spirits who have been reduced to flames, one of whom is Ulysses, the soldier who led the Greek siege of Troy via the great manipulation that was the Trojan Horse plot.

These very same issues come to the fore during the eighth circle of Pryor's movie, an eight-minute sequence that Pryor delivers in the guise of his most famous character, Mudbone, who is "a belligerent old curmudgeon, brimming over with nuts-and-bolts wisdom about life" and who is more than likely based on Pryor's maternal grandfather, Thomas "Pops" Bryant.[22] Mudbone is a complex character. While sometimes he is a doting grandfather, at other times he is a manipulative lech. Sometimes he is the voice of ancient wisdom and still other times he is the personification of Pryor's super-ego and self-castigation. Furthermore, he is also a character of mythological proportions. Not only does his moniker echo the name of the biblical Adam, a name that means "made of mud," and who, like Mudbone, is associated with a seduction near an apple tree, but like the characters of fairy tales or science fiction fantasies who lived "once upon a time" or "long, long ago in a galaxy far, far away," Mudbone hails from another dimension, which he says was "*waaay* back," a time so far removed from our own that "they didn't have a year for it. They just called it Hard Times." Mudbone sounds like the storyteller of an ancient tribe when he says things like, "It was dark all the time. I think the sun came out on Wednesday. And if you didn't have your ass up early, you missed it."

Throughout the course of his monologue, Mudbone lets us know in no uncertain terms that he is a seducer, a flatterer and fraudulent counselor, and that if he were living in Dante's Hell, the Eighth Circle would undoubtedly be his home. Within his first few sentences, Mudbone begins his flattering, when he says of Pryor: "I remember the motherfucker. He could make a motherfucker laugh at a funeral on Sunday, Christmas day." Within a few minutes, Mudbone is recalling his seduction of Lucinda Belle Mae, about how "one Wednesday" Mudbone happened to be out and "the sun hit me right in the face. So I grabbed a bunch of it and rubbed it all over myself." He and Lucinda then had to "tip away" in order to "go up and do a little kissing up in the apple orchard. . . . We get up there and I make her put a little [sun] on her face, and she relaxed. She relaxed and I started rubbing all over her."

The bit concludes with a long speech that has the air and presentation of genuine wisdom, but is actually just a collection of respun clichés:

> So what I'm saying. What the point I'm trying to make is, that there is no point to be made. That's all there is. There ain't no point to it. . . . . Don't take this shit serious. You better have some fun, and plenty of it. 'Cause when the shit over and you ask for a recharge, it's too late. So all I can say is keep some sunshine on your face.

With this last speech, which Pryor has established as "the last time Mudbone will be seen anywhere. This is Mudbone's last show," the character shows that he is even more adept at the art of the fraudulent counsel than he is at seducing or flattering. It seems that Pryor has in fact taken the advice to heart. Pryor makes it quite clear over the course of the performance that he has consistently followed Mudbone's advice willy-nilly. His Playboy Bunny, sex and marriage bits, as well as his frequent passing references to infidelity, show that he continually gives in to his bodily urges, much the way Mudbone might advise him to.

Perhaps even more telling, however, are Mudbone's references to the comedian's suicide attempt of eighteen months earlier. Although he appears to be addressing the audience, Mudbone could very well be scolding Pryor directly about his holocaust when he says, "You didn't ask to come to this [life] and you sure can't choose how to leave. 'Cause you don't know when you're gonna go." It is the sign-off, however, the last suggestion to "keep some sunshine on your face," that is particularly haunting. It was, after all, Pryor's pouring the stuff of sunshine, to wit, fire, all over his body that took him to the brink of death.

Mudbone's appearance in the context of this performance indicates that he may in fact be more than a mere fictional character, since virtually every action, choice and failure Pryor discusses in the show suggests that he has been following the old man's advice all along.

IX. Treachery

When, in *Inferno*, Dante and Virgil finally reach the ninth and final circle of Hell, they encounter a being of consummate evil who is referred to as Satan, Lucifer or Dis—the implication being that no single name can adequately describe the beast. Upon seeing this, Virgil declares, "Behold Dis! Here behold the place where you/must summon courage and be fortified."[23] At this, Dante says that he "did not live and yet . . . did not die," but has been "deprived of both states."[24] The beast, frozen in ice up to his chest, has three heads and three mouths, one red, one yellow and one black. In the black mouth he tortures Brutus and in the yellow he tortures Cassius, the two men who betrayed Julius Caesar. In the black mouth he chews the living head of Judas Iscariot, who betrayed Jesus. Upon seeing this, Virgil takes Dante on his back and leads him down Satan's body back to the surface of the Earth.

Matters of betrayal, entrapment, karma and consummate evil, along with the need to summon deeper levels of courage, also make up the emotional centerpiece of *Live on the Sunset Strip*. Throughout the course of his career, Pryor has been known for the ingenious way in which he gives voices to those entities who otherwise would have no voice, such as animals, inanimate objects such as cars, Mother Nature and even, as he does in the earlier film, *Richard Pryor Live in Concert*, a heart attack. In what is probably the most talked-about sequence in stand-up comedy history, Pryor employs this genius to give a voice to the beast that is cocaine addiction, something he refers to as "a monster" and tells how the disease was consuming him. He says that at one time he had been stuck in his room for eight weeks and hadn't even bothered to bathe, saying, "Funk is my shadow. . . . I'm talking about a year later, Jack. I'm drawn up, fucked up and out of my mind."

He then proceeds to lead the audience into increasingly deeper levels of his own personal Hell as he tells of the beast that has betrayed him and is consuming him. In the decade before the crack epidemic began devastating American cities, Pryor illustrates the stranglehold of this new kind of cocaine consumption, saying, "[T]his pipe used to tell me when to go to bed. The pipe would say, 'Time to get up. Time for some smoke, Rich. Come on, now. We're not going to do anything today. Fuck all your appointments. Me and you is just gonna hang out in this room together.'"

Soon, the pipe advises him to turn against his friends:

I'd get mad and frustrated. People didn't understand me. [The] Pipe [would] say, "Come on in the room with me. I gotcha covered. I know how you feel, Rich. I understand. Just light me up, hold me for a couple of days and we'll talk it over . . . ." I understand, Rich. They don't know. It's your life. Why, they don't have a right to fuck with you. Where were they when you needed them? Come on in here with me, because I love ya."

Then the pipe starts saying shit like, "You let me get a little low yesterday. I don't like that. Now don't let me get low again or I'm gonna hurt ya." . . . I did it so bad that dope dealers tried not to sell me none . . . when a dope dealer says, "Nah, I'm not gonna give you no more of that shit. I'm sorry, brother. I can't see you do it to yourself." Now dope dealers don't usually give a fuck about nothin' usually people think. These dudes refused to sell me cocaine. . . . Now, I ain't never heard of dope dealers doin' that. I mean, you can sooner get free food in a Chinese restaurant.

The parallelism with *Inferno* also reaches a climax at this point. Not only does the pipe represent Pryor's imprisonment, but it also betrays him with the constant reassurance that it cares deeply for him when it says things like, "I understand," and "I love ya." Yet, rather than sounding like an inner-city thug or the street corner pusher, the voice has the calm and cool confidence and sophistication of an insurance salesman or corporate executive. The most emotional the pipe gets is when it scolds Pryor for letting it get "a little low yesterday." Even when the threat is direct, such as when it says, "I'm gonna have to hurt ya," the tone is only stern, never angry or frantic. Judging by its voice, the demon seems not to be associated with those who are usually thought to be connected with cocaine trafficking, such as Latin American drug lords or urban gang-bangers, but rather with corporate, bourgeois America. These are subconscious messages that surround the average American with suggestions that he consume at all costs. This is the voice of an America that, since the first European explorers discovered tobacco, has built itself upon addictions, whether it is the addiction to nicotine, whisky, beer, prescription drugs, television, high-fat diets or, as President George W. Bush referenced in his 2006 State of the Union address, an addiction to oil. This is the same subtle voice of American capitalism and consumerism that sells scotch by hiding skull-and-crossbones images in magazine ads and intersperses anti-depressant commercials between news reports on terrorist attacks.

Pryor then relays an anecdote which, despite the more tragic outcome, closely parallels the way in which Virgil takes Dante on his back and carries him to safety. He tells of how his "ol' lady called Jim Brown up" to help her get Pryor to a hospital. The former NFL star visits Pryor, demands that Pryor do something about his dire state and manages to respect the comedian's dignity the whole time. Pryor tells how he fills his pipe, lights it and continues smoking as Brown enters the room, something that Brown initially ignores. Pryor responds to this by pointing at the pipe and holding it out in front of the NFL Hall-of-Famer and, finally, as he gets more frustrated, by taking long, exaggerated puffs. This is the most tragic moment of the whole show as the motions become, despite the audience's roaring with laughter, a tacit but desperate plea for help, an illustration of how, while he is at the lowest point in his life, Pryor, much like Dante in the last circle, is caught between life and death and is so incapacitated that he can only plead for help through a succession of impotent and inert gestures.

Presently, the calm Brown asks Pryor over and over again, "Whatcha gonna do? About that shit? . . . You gonna get well, or you gonna end our friendship? Whatcha gonna do?" After a brief consultation with the pipe, Pryor responds with, "Jim, I am a man," to which Brown replies, "There ain't no doubt about that. But whatcha gonna do?" the implicit message being that Pryor could surrender to help without compromising his dignity. Despite his best efforts, Brown is ultimately unable to get Pryor to the hospital although, after the suicide attempt, he is "in the hospital with me, every day, when I was getting well. . . . Jim would be there with me, giving me strength."

The climax of the scene and the entire performance comes when Pryor speaks candidly about his holocaust, telling about how he was "standing there on fire" and looking at his flaming hand and thinking, "that's a pretty blue. You know what? That looks like . . . *fire!*" In light of the previous silent pleas, this final conflagration can only be interpreted as another plea for help, one that could not go unheeded.

XI. The Denouement

The final scene of *Inferno*, which is made up of the last fifty-four lines of the poem, shows how the two poets escape from Hell using the hair on Satan's legs as a ladder and eventually climb out the opposite end of the Earth. It is only the last line, "and we came out again to see the stars," that reveals Dante has returned to the Earth's surface. Dante quotes Virgil as saying of their journey from the terrestrial interior that "the road is hard and we have far to go,"[25] a description that could easily apply to Pryor's recuperation. For Pryor, however, the denouement is much more protracted and includes other, more effective mythological elements, namely his final baptism by water. Pryor tells of his stay in the hospital, discussing the heroism of a burn-unit nurse named Larry Murphy who "used to come in [and say,] 'We're gonna wash you, Rich. We're gonna wash you down and you're gonna feel great. We're gonna wash ya, wash ya. We're gonna put you in the tub." Pryor responds, "Yeah, when you gonna wash me, motherfucker?" Murphy tells him, "We're gonna wash you in a couple of days, Rich."

Finally, when Pryor does get in the tub, he experiences unimaginable pain because of the extensive damage to his skin. Once again, he is incapacitated, so much so that he is hardly able to speak. He whines and whimpers: "I don't want you to wash me no motherfuckin' more. And if you do I'll bite you, motherfucker. . . . I don't care if I die." When he finally breaks the scene and returns to the present, Pryor says of his caretakers, "but they were wonderful." With this, it becomes clear that Murphy was the last of the four guides, the person who took over from Brown, the last person to guide him back to health, to a place Dante might have referred to as "the bright world."[26]

Conclusion

One of the magical things about art is its multidimensionality. Mark Twain's masterpiece *The Adventures of Huckleberry Finn*, for instance, isn't merely treating its readers to a wonderfully amusing story and poetic descriptions of the Mississippi River, but also to a political, cultural, economic and historical mosaic concerning the years surrounding the American Civil War. This is because the imaginative spores that blow around all sectors of a society quite often—and perhaps most often—find places to thrive in the soil of the artistic imagination. Sometimes, however, it is not only the beautiful that an artist brings to light, but rather the tragic and the horrific. The 1990s MTV phenomenon that was the *Beavis and Butt-head* cartoon, for instance, certainly held within it warnings about the Columbine High School shootings of April 20, 1999, when high school students Dylan Klebold and Eric Harris killed thirteen students and a teacher before killing themselves. Klebold and Harris had more than a little in common with the pariahs of Mike Judge's cartoon. Beavis, Butt-head, Klebold and Harris all came from White suburbia and high schools where they were ostracized and tormented by the other "popular students,"[27] and somewhere along the line each of these teenagers lost the capacity for empathy and love. In an April 1994 episode of the cartoon entitled "Water Safety," Butt-head is believed to have drowned. When Mr. Buzzcut, the boys' gym teacher, asks Beavis if he cares that the only friend he has in the world is dead, Beavis replies, "Uh, no."[28] This lack of empathy and understanding was shared by the Columbine killers who, according to a report in the on-line magazine *Salon*, "had little concern for the welfare of their friends and the siblings of their friends . . . [T]hey mention nonchalantly that some of their friends might die and casually point out that their families would be devastated but justified it by saying, 'War is war.'"[29] Also, after blowing a classmate's head off, one of them reportedly said, "Look at this black kid's brain. Awesome, man!"[30]

What makes *Live on the Sunset Strip* so disturbing, then, is that the implicit agenda draws attention to pathologies that are lying beneath the country's bourgeois surface, pointing a finger at American failings much the way Dante did for fourteenth-century Europe. While it might be easy enough to decry America's sins as growing out of a permissive moral climate that tolerates abortion, homosexuality, illicit drug use, divorce and broken families, Pryor's indictment provides insight that is far more penetrating, far more horrific and, ultimately, far more valuable. Each of the sins Pryor discusses and illustrates—lust, envy, wrath, violence, racism, avarice, fraudulent counsel and drug addiction—are all produced at the same factory: the objectification of human beings. Whether it is his reducing a Playboy Bunny to a semen receptacle, a lawyer reducing him to a money machine, a sociopath killing people "because they was home," a Mafia boss keeping him "as a pet" or the demon of cocaine addiction urging him to destroy his mind and body, the great cord connecting virtually all the bits of the performance is that in virtually every scenario the Buberesque "I-Thou" relationship is abandoned in favor of the easier and more lucrative "I-it" relationship.

There are, however, three different instances in *Live on the Sunset Strip* in which the "I-Thou" relationship takes center stage. They are, in order of importance, Pryor's cocaine dealers' refusal to sell him cocaine; Jim Brown's devotion to Pryor during his breakdown and convalescence; and, finally, Pryor's sudden change of heart when he decides that "I ain't never gonna call another Black man 'nigger'. . . . we [are] men and women."

There is no question that *Live on the Sunset Strip* is a jeremiad and an assessment of the current threats to the great Jeffersonian experiment called America. Perhaps, however, Pryor is the only person of the last century able to venture into the depths of this particular Hell, encounter the devil and reveal the pearls of wisdom he stumbled upon in the process.

CONCLUSION
THE COMEDIC FRONTIER

Early in this volume I conclude that whether or not stand-up comedy is literature, it does everything literature is supposed to do. I did this knowing full well that such an endeavor runs a great risk for reasons that most eighth graders know intuitively: explaining a joke often does not enhance its appreciation so much as it exorcises its most delightful devils. No less a commentator than Susan Sontag has put the point much more subtly, warning that any attempt to explain humor is either grossly reductionist or so broad it is meaningless. Such wisdom would easily render my investigation hollow if stand-up comedy were merely about the laughs.

But it is much more than that.

First of all, stand-up comedy is a young art form just as it is a distinctly American one, the nationality of the comedian and the location of the performance venue notwithstanding. It is an art form which, at its very core, is about pluralism and individualism and thus could have been born only in the United States. It is the singular person standing against the crowd, exercising the right to free speech and sinking or swimming (or killing or bombing, as it were) on unique merits. It is individuals adopting unique points of view and telling individual stories directly to their communities. It is Lenny Bruce discussing his court appearances, Gabriel Iglesias discussing his weight problem and Richard Pryor illustrating the terror of addiction in the most open, honest and horrifying ways. It is Rodney Dangerfield recreating the cuckold, a stock comic character, in modern American terms and Phyllis Diller casting herself as a crone who is as bitter as her fairy tale counterpart but yet, somehow, quite lovable.

Furthermore, stand-up's history is simultaneously jubilant and tortured. It is the Chris Rocks, Joey Bishops and George Lopezes lifting themselves from poverty to stardom just as it is the Lenny Bruces, Richard Pryors and Freddie Prinzes succumbing to their tragic flaws. Like America herself, it has a history plagued with racism, homophobia, anti-Semitism and drugs, drugs and more drugs: Pryor was a notorious cocaine addict, Bob Newhart a notorious chain-smoker and Bill Maher an unabashed marijuana user; Jerry Lewis spent decades fighting addiction to the painkiller Percodan and Jonathan Winters' alcoholism certainly played a part in his nervous breakdown. Tobacco, whiskey, beer, LSD and modern pharmaceuticals like Paxil, Valium and Viagra are an integral part of American history, so it only follows that drugs are an essential part of stand-up's history.

And stand-up is an art form that invites innovation. Gallagher and Carrot Top fill their stages with props and inventions. Steve Martin closed one of his shows by leading his audience down the street and having everyone pile into an empty swimming pool; as part of one act, Andy Kaufman invited patrons of the Improv onstage to feel the cyst on his neck; Henry Rollins tells jokes as he mixes political rants and social commentary into hybrid performance art; and Ellen Degeneres once employed interpretive dance to illustrate how she came out as a lesbian. Searching for novel ways to tell jokes is as much a part of being a comedian as memorizing a set list.

Yet, in the early years of the twenty-first century, it appears that stand-up comedy is in a slump. Clubs struggle and close and cable networks and one-night shows teem with countless mediocre comedians telling more or less the same jokes. This does not, however, mean that stand-up is dead or ailing. Not only does enthusiasm for the truly great ones—the Rickleses, the Degenereses, the Poundstones, the Cosbys, the Wrights and Chappelles—remain high, but the art form continues to evolve and impact other arenas.

Consider, for example, the White House Correspondents' Dinner on April 29, 2006, when comedian Stephen Colbert was the featured speaker. Colbert appeared as the caricature of a right-wing news pundit that he plays on his Comedy Central show, *The Colbert Report*, and proceeded to take pot shots at President George W. Bush. With the president sitting just a few feet away, Colbert discussed the president's failures in ways that clearly made Bush uncomfortable, a situation recalling the way the medieval court jester would ridicule the king to his face. Feigning admiration for the president, the comedian advised the crowd, "Don't pay attention to the approval ratings that say that sixty-eight percent of Americans disapprove of the job this man is doing. I ask you this, does that not also logically mean that sixty-eight percent approve of the job he's not doing?" A short while later, he addressed the president's arrogance, saying that he admires Bush because the president "believes the same thing Wednesday that he believed on Monday, no matter what happened Tuesday. Events can change. This man's beliefs never will."[1]

That night, Colbert's stage was the White House Correspondents' Dinner podium and his audience included, in addition to the president and First Lady Laura Bush, national media bigwigs like political satirist Christopher Buckley, Hearst columnist Helen Thomas, filmmaker Ken Burns and CBS newsman Bob Schieffer—not to mention notables like the Rev. Jesse Jackson, Supreme Court Justice Antonin Scalia and Sen. John McCain. While this was certainly not conventional direct-address comedy, the performance had all the hallmarks of high-powered stand-up: the comedian spoke directly to the audience, employed the set-up/punchline format, openly discussed taboo matters and kept the laughs going.

Another example of the power of stand-up comes by way of the work of British comedian Sacha Baron Cohen. In his 2006 mocumentary film *Borat: Cultural Learnings for Make Benefit Glorious Nation of Kazakhstan*, Cohen poses as Borat Sagdiyev, a Kazakh television personality who travels to America in his quest to win the romantic affections of former *Playboy* Playmate and sex symbol Pamela Anderson. Along the way, he interviews and makes fun of Americans—or perhaps more accurately, he puts the Americans he encounters in positions where they make fools of themselves. In one scene, for instance, Borat speaks at a rodeo in Salem, Virginia. There he makes pro-U.S. announcements including, "We support your war of terror"—a statement for which he gets thunderous applause—and then launches into a fake version of Kazakhstan's national anthem, which he sings to the tune of "The Star Spangled Banner." Lyrics like "Kazakhstan greatest country in the world/All other countries are run by little girls/Kazakhstan number one exporter of potassium/Other countries have inferior potassium" quickly elicit boos from the crowd and Borat and his crew are summarily run off the grounds. In another sequence, he tells a group of feminists that it has been proven that women "have a smaller brain than man," that one government scientist has proven that the female brain is "size of squirrel's."[2] Borat presses on, and soon the women walk out of the interview.

While *Borat* certainly is not stand-up comedy, the movie is a clear corollary of the comedic contributions of innovators like Mark Twain,

Charley Case, Steve Martin and Andy Kaufman. Borat has not only obliterated the fourth wall but has invaded other people's spaces altogether. He has allowed the actions and attitudes of self-serious Americans to serve as the set-ups so that his own antics can become the punchlines.

But isn't this just another chapter in a grand tradition?

Tricksters, jokesters and fools, after all, fulfill a basic human need. This is why almost as soon as humans discovered language and the art of storytelling, we were telling amusing stories of mischievous spirits like Loki, Coyote and Mercury who crept out of nowhere, introduced chaos to order, and then skittered back into hiding. The modern stand-up comedian's job is, in no small measure, to continue the practice. When, for instance, Emo Philips says, "There's nothing I like better than sitting in front of a roaring fire with a copy of *War and Peace*. You know a big fat book like that will feed a fire for hours,"[3] he assaults us with his logic. First, the set-up line seduces us, allowing us to believe the world Philips refers to is the same as ours. Then, he delivers the punchline and we realize that we are in a different reality altogether. The implicit message is that the cosmos may indeed be ordered, but not necessarily in the ways that we like to believe it is. The jokester reminds us that reality is made up of infinite possibilities and that indulging in silliness, if only for a few minutes, is sometimes the best response to a universe we cannot understand.

A STAND-UP COMEDY TIMELINE

1840: Vaudeville begins when Boylston Hall in Boston opens its summer season.

January 17, 1856: While attending a meeting of printers celebrating Benjamin Franklin's 150th birthday in Keokuk, Iowa, a 20-year-old Samuel Langhorne Clemens (who would come to be known as Mark Twain) delivers an after-dinner speech. This launches Twain's career as a humorous lecturer.

Oct. 2, 1866: Mark Twain begins his first lecture tour. Over the next 43 years, lecturing will be a major part of his life. His last lecture is on June 9, 1909, ten months before his death.

1880s–1890s: Charley Case, a vaudevillian, begins performing humorous monologues directly to the audience using no costume or props. Stand-up comedy is born.

1890s: New York's Sullivan and Ulster counties, in the southern Catskill Mountains, begin a transformation from a region of egg and dairy farms to an area of vacation resorts catering chiefly to Jews from New York City. The Borscht Belt is born.

1890–1920: Burlesque is in its heyday.

1895: Beatrice Hereford begins performing comic monologues in London.

1909: The Theater Owners Booking Association, a Black vaudeville circuit, is established.

1909: While touring on the Orpheum vaudeville circuit, Will Rogers, a world-class horseman, simplifies his act. He decides to forgo horses and a roping troupe in lieu of a solo act that involves rope tricks and humorous patter.

1910–1925: Vaudeville is in its heyday.

1911: Cabaret-style entertainment becomes more popular and available in New York City.

1915: Will Rogers joins *The Midnight Frolic*, a show held on the roof of the New Amsterdam Theatre, a highbrow New York City nightclub.

1916: Charley Case dies in New York City.

1917: Marcel Duchamp enters an inverted urinal in a New York art show and dubs it *Fountain*. Dada, an "anti-art" art movement, is officially under way.

Jan. 16, 1920: Prohibition begins in the United States, forcing liquor establishments to become smaller and less visible. Crowds are smaller, entertainment is simplified and venues are more intimate. Consequently, emcees take on more important roles as entertainers.

1933: Prohibition is repealed.

Aug. 15, 1935: Will Rogers dies in an airplane crash.

1930–1955: The Borscht Belt is in its heyday.

June 20, 1948: *The Toast of the Town*, a television show with a vaudeville format, begins with Ed Sullivan, a columnist for *The New York Daily News*, as host and producer. Four years later the show's name is changed to *The Ed Sullivan Show*. It runs until June 6, 1971.

1951: Former concert violinist Enrico Banducci buys the hungry i, an 83-seat basement club in San Francisco's North Beach. Within four years the club becomes a beatnik hangout and the epicenter of the "New Wave" stand-up comedy movement.

Sept. 27, 1954: *The Tonight Show* begins with Steve Allen as host.

1955: *Mort Sahl at Sunset*, the first stand-up comedy album is recorded.

July 29, 1957: Jack Paar begins hosting *The Tonight Show*.

Jan. 1958: Lenny Bruce begins to gain national recognition while working at Ann's 440 in San Francisco.

July 13, 1959: A *Time* magazine article entitled "The Sickniks" announces the New Wave of stand-up comedy.

Feb. 29, 1960: *Playboy* publisher Hugh Hefner opens the flagship Playboy Club in Chicago.

Jan. 13, 1961: Dick Gregory headlines at the Playboy Club, becoming the first Black stand-up comic to permanently cross over to a previously all-White venue.

March 1961: *Playboy* magazine publishes "The *Playboy* Panel: Hip Comics and the New Humor," a discussion on New Wave humor. Panelists include Lenny Bruce, Mort Sahl, Jonathan Winters, Steve Allen, Bill Dana and cartoonist Jules Fieffer.

April 12, 1961: The comedy album *The Button-Down Mind of Bob Newhart* wins the Grammy Award for Album of the Year. Newhart wins Best New Artist.

Sept. 1961: Lenny Bruce premieres "To Come" at the San Francisco Jazz Festival.

Oct. 4, 1961: Lenny Bruce is arrested and charged with obscenity after using the word "cocksucker" on stage.

Oct. 1, 1962: Johnny Carson begins hosting *The Tonight Show.*

1963: Bud Friedman opens the Improvisational Café, later to be called The Improv, in New York's Greenwich Village. It is the first dedicated comedy club.

1963: Hugh Hefner commissions Lenny Bruce to write his autobiography, which is eventually titled *How to Talk Dirty and Influence People.* The book is serialized in *Playboy* magazine from Oct. 1963 to March 1964.

April 1964: Lenny Bruce is arrested for obscenity at the Café Au Go-Go in New York City.

Oct. 18, 1964: Ed Sullivan accuses Jackie Mason of giving him the finger on national television.

1966: The term "stand-up comedian" is added to *The Oxford English Dictionary* and *Webster's Ninth New Collegiate Dictionary.*

Aug. 3, 1966: Lenny Bruce is found dead in the bathroom of his home in Hollywood Hills, California.

Sept. 17, 1970–June 27, 1974: *The Flip Wilson Show* becomes the first successful nationally televised show to be hosted by a Black entertainer.

April 1972: Mitzi and Sammy Shore and Rudy DeLuca open The Comedy Store on the Sunset Strip in Los Angeles. It is the second dedicated comedy club.

1973: Mitzi and Sammy Shore divorce. Mitzi takes ownership of The Comedy Store and establishes an art colony of comedians.

May 1974: Richard Pryor's *That Nigger's Crazy* is released. The album wins a Grammy Award for best comedy album.

Oct. 11, 1975: NBC's *Saturday Night Live* debuts.

Oct. 23, 1976: Steven Martin hosts *Saturday Night Live* and generates renewed national interest in the art form.

March 1979: After estimating that The Comedy Store earned $2.5 million a year, twenty-two Los Angeles comedians form the group Comedians for Compensation, essentially a union, and begin a comedians' strike. Within eight weeks, the group has 150 members. As a result of negotiations, performers in major clubs are paid at least $25 a set and are able to work full time as professional comedians. The Boom begins.

June 9, 1980: In a fit of cocaine-induced psychosis, Richard Pryor attempts suicide by dousing himself with liquor and setting himself on fire.

1981–1989: The Boom Years: stand-up comedy is in its heyday.

Feb. 3, 1982: *An Evening at the Improv*, a dedicated stand-up comedy show, begins broadcasting from the Los Angeles club. The series lasts six years.

Aug. 6, 1982: Steven Wright makes his first national television appearance on *The Tonight Show Starring Johnny Carson*.

Dec. 1982: Richard Pryor returns to performing with *Richard Pryor Live on the Sunset Strip*.

March 29, 1986: Whoopi Goldberg, Robin Williams and Billy Crystal host *Comic Relief*, a stand-up comedy show produced by HBO, to raise money for the homeless. Performers include Henny Youngman, Garry Shandling and Paul Rodriguez.

Nov. 1989: TimeWarner launches Comedy Central, the first dedicated comedy television network.

May 25, 1992: Jay Leno begins hosting *The Tonight Show*.

Dec. 23, 2003: New York Governor George Pataki grants Lenny Bruce a posthumous pardon for his 1964 obscenity conviction.

Dec. 10, 2005: Richard Pryor dies of cardiac arrest in Encino, California.

April 29, 2006: Stephen Colbert roasts President George W. Bush during the White House Correspondents' Dinner.

June 22, 2008: George Carlin dies.

A STAND-UP COMEDY GLOSSARY

abject, the: literary critic Julia Kristeva's term for those materials and those aspects of oneself that a person cannot be entirely rid of because they are neither subject nor object—materials such as blood, urine, feces and the corpse. Usually, humans react to the abject with horror.

act out: to assume a persona or project another situation for the sake of comic effect.

ad-lib: to make up a joke or jokes spontaneously while on stage.

beat: a pause in delivery that enhances a punchline.

Beatniks: a countercultural movement in the 1950s that rejected Cold War values.

behavioral jokes: jokes that rely on physical, rather than verbal, connectors and punchlines.

bit: a section of a stand-up comedy routine that addresses a single topic.

blue material: jokes that employ profane language and reference bodily functions and sexual acts.

bomb: to perform an unsuccessful or ineffective comedy show.

Boom, The: the late 1980s and early 1990s, a period when stand-up comedy was at its peak of popularity.

Borscht Belt: also called the "Jewish Vaudeville": a string of resorts in Sullivan County, New York, known for employing stand-up comedians.

burlesque: a type of theatrical production that began in the mid-nineteenth century and involved parody, bawdy humor and, often, striptease acts.

callback: a joke that references a joke told previously in the show or routine.

Chautauqua: an adult education program that began in New York State in the late nineteenth century and often included comic lectures, dramatic readings and musical performances.

closer: the final joke of a comedy performance, one that should get a big laugh.

Commedia dell'arte: a theater troupe that began in Renaissance Italy and specialized in comedic improvisation. It is the direct forerunner of modern sketch comedy troupes such as Chicago's Second City.

connector: the centerpiece of a joke. A word, idea or image that suggests one thing in the set-up line and is revealed to mean something else in the punchline.

Dada: a cultural and artistic movement that began in Switzerland in the early part of the twentieth century as a reaction to World War I and emphasized the illogical and the absurd over the traditional.

decoy assumption: the misdirecting assumption in a joke's setup that creates the first story and is shattered by the reinterpretation.

defamiliarization: taking ordinary objects and occurrences and casting them in a different contexts so that they appear strange.

ego: according to Freud, one of the three divisions of the subconscious. The ego mediates the tension between the id and super-ego and represents what may be called reason and common sense.

first story: the scenario imagined in the mind of the audience as a result of a set-up line.

Glut, The: the last decades of the twentieth century and the first decades of the twenty-first, when the stand-up comedy market is flooded with talent, much of which is second-rate.

hack: overused and trite material.

headliner: the last comedian to perform in a given show; the show's main attraction.

heckler: an audience member who yells and interrupts the comedian during a show.

id: according to Freud, one of the three divisions of the subconscious. It is driven by bodily appetites and seeks instant gratification. See *ego* and *super-ego*.

improvisation: the spontaneous creation of jokes and scenarios while on stage.

Incongruity Theory: a theory that explains laughter as resulting from experiences, scenarios and occurrences that do not fit ordinary, expected patterns.

joke: a device, usually verbal, for creating laughter.

material: jokes that are composed and constructed specifically to be delivered during a stand-up performance.

Medicine Show: a traveling show from the late nineteenth and early twentieth centuries in which the main objective was to sell elixirs. The performances featured "spielers," or hucksters who engaged in banter with the audience and delivered humorous speeches in order to sell inert concoctions.

Minstrel Show: an early form of American entertainment that featured White people in blackface singing, dancing, telling jokes and performing skit comedy.

mix: putting two incongruous situations together in a single comedy bit.

monologist: a comedian who tells long and complex stories.

Victorian Music Hall: a type of variety entertainment that began in London in the mid-nineteenth century and featured singing, dancing and comic songs and skits.

New Wave: a new type of comedy that began in the mid-1950s and involved comedians such as Mort Sahl, Lenny Bruce and Dick Gregory compromising their laughs-per-minute ratios in order to address topical issues.

one-liner: a joke that consists of only one or two short sentences.

opener: the first joke of a stand-up comedy routine.

premise: the central concept upon which a joke or bit is based.

punch or punchline: the funny part of the joke; follows the set-up.

reinterpretation: an unexpected interpretation of the connector; resulting from the punchline and an essential part of the second story.

Relief Theory: a theory that explains laughter as the venting of nervous energy.

riffing: the ad-libbing of jokes during banter with the audience.

second story: the scenario imagined in the mind of the audience as a result of a punchline.

segue: material designed to lead the audience from one bit to the next.

sequence: a series of jokes in which one joke depends upon or builds upon the next.

setup: the first and unfunny part of the joke that contains a decoy assumption and a connector.

shtick: a Yiddish word meaning a "comic scene" or "piece of business"; also the comedian's signature joke.

sight gag: a non-verbal joke; one that is meant to be seen.

signature line/catch phrase: a repeated phrase which becomes identified with a particular comedian, such as Rodney Dangerfield's "I don't get no respect."

stand-up comedy: an American literary form that involves one person, usually uncostumed, on stage for the explicit purpose of telling jokes so as to elicit laughter from an audience.

stump speech: a part of the standard minstrel show ; a speech filled with puns and malapropisms and delivered to the audience in Black dialect.

super-ego: according to Freud, one of the three divisions of the subconscious. It represents the internalized voice of the parents and serves essentially the same function as the conscience.

Superiority Theory: a theory that explains laughter as resulting from one person's feelings of superiority over others.

tag: an additional punchline that does not require a new setup.

Theater Owners Booking Association: also called "Black Vaudeville" or "The Chitlin' Circuit"; a entertainment circuit that, in the 1920s and 1930s, catered to African-American audiences and employed almost exclusively African-American performers.

timing: the use of rhythm and tempo to enhance a joke or emphasize a punchline.

toomler: a comedian working in one of the Borscht Belt hotels who was supposed to keep the guests laughing throughout the day—at the poolside, in the dining room and during bridge games, for example—before doing a formal act at night.

topical jokes: jokes about current events, usually concerning politicians and political events.

trickster: a mythological being who plays tricks on normal people and violates ordinary rules of behavior.

vaudeville: a type of variety entertainment in the United States that featured multiple acts among which could be dancers, singers, jugglers, acrobats, sketch comedians and monologists. Vaudeville lasted from the middle nineteenth century until the 1930s.

walkathons: dance marathon competitions in the 1930s that often lasted for weeks at a time and employed emcees who told jokes, bantered with the audience and clowned around in order to keep the audience engaged in the competitions.

NOTES

Chapter One

[1] Eagleton, Terry. *Literary Theory: An Introduction.* Minneapolis: University of Minnesota Press. 1989, 2.

[2] Ibid., 7-8.

[3] Ibid., 9.

[4] Tolstoy, Sir Leo. "What Is Art?" *Criticism: Major Statements.* 3rd ed. Eds. Charles Kaplan and William Anderson. New York: St. Martin's. 1991, 406-409, *passim.*

[5] Pirsig, Robert. *Zen and the Art of Motorcycle Maintenance: An Inquiry into Values.* New York: Bantam. 1980, 316.

[6] Freud, Sigmund. *The Interpretation of Dreams.* New York: The Modern Library. 1978, 161.

[7] Gadamer, Hans-Georg. *Truth and Method.* New York: Crossroads. 1989, 132.

[8] King, Stephen. "Why We Crave Horror Movies." *The Bedford Guide for College Writers with Reader, Research Manual and Handbook.* Eds. X.J. Kennedy, Dorothy M. Kennedy and Sylvia A. Holladay. Boston: Bedford/St. Martin's. 1999, 595. Orig. published in *Playboy,* Dec. 1981.

[9] Kesey, Ken. *Sometimes a Great Notion.* New York: Penguin. 1977, 286.

[10] Twain, Mark. *The Adventures of Huckleberry Finn: An Authoritative Text.* Ed. Thomas Cooley. New York: Norton. 1999, 170.

[11] Hemingway, Ernest. *The Old Man and the Sea.* New York: Scribner. 1995, 122.

[12] Baker, Carlos. *Hemingway: The Writer as Artist.* Princeton: Princeton UP. 1990, 292.

[13] Ibid., 294.

[14] Hemingway, 87.

[15] Ibid., 51, 67, 74.

[16] Ibid., 58-59, 61.

[17] Ibid., 107.

[18] This group of early Christians believed that the experience of *gnosis,* the intuitive and esoteric process of knowing one's true self, resulted in spiritual transformation. For an extended discussion of *gnosis,* see Elaine Pagels, *The Gnostic Gospels* (New York: Vintage Books. 1979). For the Buddhists, "Enlightenment" involves seeing through the false and into the root of human suffering, which eradicates personal emotional difficulties. For an extended discussion of Buddhist enlightenment see Young-Eisendrath, Polly; Muramoto, Shoji. *Awakening and Insight : Zen Buddhism and Psychotherapy* (New York: Taylor and Francis. 2002), 161.

[19] Hemingway, 63.

[20] Ibid., 66.

[21] Ibid., 121.

[22] cummings, e.e. "l(a." *Complete Poems: 1904-1962.* Ed. George J. Firmage. New York: W.W. Norton. 1991, 673.

[23] Faulkner, William. *As I Lay Dying.* New York: Vintage. 1990, 4.

[24] García Márquez, Gabriel. *One Hundred Years of Solitude*. New York: Avon. 1971, 11.

[25] Fitzgerald, F. Scott. *The Great Gatsby*. New York: Scribner. 1995, 117.

[26] Atwood, Margaret. *Cat's Eye*. New York: Bantam. 1989, 202-203.

[27] Newhart, Bob. "Introducing Tobacco to Civilization." *Something Like This . . . The Bob Newhart Anthology*. Rhino/Wea, 2001.

[28] Koziski, Stephanie. "The Stand-up Comedian as Anthropologist: Intentional Culture Critic." *The Journal of Popular Culture* 18:2 (Fall 1984), 57.

[29] Ibid.

[30] Morreall, John. *Taking Laughter Seriously*. Albany: SUNY UP. 1983, 22.

[31] Ibid., 108-109.

[32] Youngman, Henny. *Henny Youngman's 500 All-Time Greatest One-Liners*. New York: Pinnacle Books. 1981, 71.

Chapter Two

[1] Jones, Howard Mumford. *O Strange New World: American Culture, the Formative Years*. New York: Viking. 1964, 33.

[2] Columbus, Christopher. From "Letter to Luis de Santagel Regarding the First Voyage." *The Norton Anthology of American Literature*, 5th ed. vol. 1. Ed. Nina Baym. 1998, 12-13.

[3] Qtd. in Samuel B. Girgus. "The New Covenant: The Jews and the Myth of America." *The American Self: Myth, Ideology and Popular Culture*. Albuquerque: U of New Mexico Press. 1981, 106.

[4] Hawthorne, Nathaniel. *The Scarlet Letter and Other Writings: Authoritative Texts*. Ed. Leland S. Person. New York: Norton. 2005, 40.

[5] Emerson, Ralph Waldo. "Self Reliance." *Emerson's Essays*. New York: Thomas Y. Crowell. 1951, 35.

[6] Hawthorne, 38.

[7] Ibid., 56.

[8] Vanden Heuvel, Jean Stein. "William Faulkner Interview." William Faulkner. *The Sound and the Fury: An Authoritative Text*. Ed. David Minter. New York: Norton. 1994, 233.

[9] Faulkner, William. *The Sound and the Fury: An Authoritative Text*. Ed. David Minter. New York: Norton. 1994, 29.

[10] Boyer, Paul. *By the Bomb's Early Light*. New York: Pantheon. 1985, 109.

[11] Ibid., 126-127, 156.

[12] Heller, Joseph. *Catch-22*. New York: Simon and Schuster. 1994, 189-190.

[13] Rosenberg, Debra, and Karen Breslau. "Winning the 'Values' Vote." *Newsweek*. Nov. 15, 2004. Accessed online June 6, 2007. <http://www.newsweek.com/id/55717>.

[14] Campbell, Joseph, with Bill Moyers. *The Power of Myth*. New York: Doubleday. 1988, 151.

[15] Ibid., 25.

[16] Curry, Richard O., and Lawrence B. Goodheart. "Individualism in a Trans-National Context." *American Chameleon: Individualism in a Trans-National Context*. Eds. Richard O. Curry and Lawrence B. Goodheart. Kent, OH: Kent State UP. 1991, 1.

[17] Ibid., 2.

[18] Ibid., 2-9, *passim*.

[19] Curry, Richard O., and Karl E. Valois. "Individual Ethos in American Society." *American Chameleon: Individualism in a Trans-National Context.* Eds. Richard O. Curry and Lawrence B. Goodheart. Kent, OH: Kent State UP. 1991, 36.

[20] Thoreau, Henry David. *Walden and Civil Disobedience.* Boston: Houghton Mifflin. 2000, 43.

[21] Ibid., 101.

[22] Kesey, Ken. *Sometimes a Great Notion.* New York: Penguin. 1977, 2.

[23] Ibid., 9.

[24] Porter, Gilbert. M. *The Art of Grit: Ken Kesey's Fiction.* Columbia: U of Missouri Press. 1982, 37.

[25] Fitzgerald, F. Scott. *The Great Gatsby.* New York: Scribner. 1995, 104.

[26] O'Connor, Flannery. "A Good Man Is Hard to Find." *Flannery O'Connor: The Complete Stories.* New York: Farrar, Straus and Giroux. 1971, 119-120.

[27] Ibid., 122.

[28] Ibid., 126.

[29] Ibid., 131.

[30] Ibid., 132.

[31] Ibid., 133.

[32] Ibid., 130-132.

[33] Ibid., 128.

[34] "Mapping: Tasting," *This American Life.* Chicago Public Radio. Orig. broadcast Sept. 4, 1998.

[35] Qtd. in Luther S. Luedtke, "The Search for American Character." *Making America: The Society and Culture of the United States.* Ed. Luther S. Luedtke. Chapel Hill: U of North Carolina Press. 1992, 3.

[36] See 2 Sam. 18:33, The New Oxford Annotated Bible with the Apocrypha, RSV. New York: Oxford UP, 1994.

[37] Faulkner, William. *Absalom, Absalom!* New York: Vintage. 1990, 285.

[38] Twain, Mark. *The Tragedy of Pudd'nHead Wilson and Other Tales.* New York: Oxford UP. 1998, 12.

[39] Lahiri, Jhumpa. *The Namesake.* New York: Houghton Mifflin. 2003, 26.

[40] Ibid., 141.

[41] Ibid., 136.

[42] Ibid., 137.

[43] Ibid., 170.

[44] Ibid., 144.

[45] Ibid., 177.

[46] Ibid., 177-178.

[47] Ibid.

[48] Ibid., 182.

[49] Ibid., 257.

[50] Ibid., 282.

[51] Ibid., 290-291.

[52] See Leslie Fiedler. *The Return of the Vanishing American.* New York: Stein and Day. 1969, 184-187.

[53] Hemingway, Ernest. *The Green Hills of Africa.* New York: Scribner's. 1935, 22.

[54] Twain, Mark. *The Adventures of Huckleberry Finn: An Authoritative Text.* Ed. Thomas Cooley. New York: Norton. 1999, 296.

[55] Lewis, Pierce. "America's Natural Landscapes." *American Chameleon: Individualism in a Trans-National Context.* Eds. Richard O. Curry and Lawrence B. Goodheart. Kent, OH: Kent State UP. 1991, 41.

[56] "Paul Bunyan" cartoon short, Disney Studios, 1958.

[57] Blair, Walter, and Hamlin Hill. *America's Humor from Poor Richard to Doonesbury.* New York: Oxford UP. 1978, 391.

[58] Untemeyer, Louis. Qtd. in Daniel Hoffman, *Paul Bunyan: The Last of the Frontier Demigods.* East Lansing: Michigan State UP. 1999, 159. Accessed online March 22, 2007. <http://www.netlibrary.com/Reader/>.

[59] Ibid.

[60] Wolfe, 7.

[61] Kesey, 101.

[62] Ibid., 111.

[63] Ibid., 327.

[64] Although *On the Road* was written in 1951, it was not published until 1957.

[65] Kerouac, Jack. *On the Road.* New York: Penguin Classics. 1991, 55.

[66] Ibid., 18-19.

[67] See Genesis 1:26.

[68] See Paula Gunn Allen. *The Sacred Hoop: Recovering the Feminine in American Indian Traditions.* Boston: Beacon Press. 1986, 216-217, and Elizabeth Jameson, *Writing the Range: Race, Class, and Culture in the Women's West.* Norman, OK: U of Oklahoma Press. 1997, 125. Accessed online Dec. 1, 2007. <http://www.netlibrary.com/Reader/>.

[69] George Carlin, "Childhood Cliches." *Classic Gold.* New York: Atlantic Studios. 1992.

[70] Emerson, 31.

[71] Rock, Chris. *Bring the Pain.* Dir. Kieth Truesdell, perf. Chris Rock. Dreamworks, 1996.

[72] Bruce, Lenny. *How to Talk Dirty and Influence People (with a New Introduction by Eric Bogosian).* New York: Fireside Books. 1992, 104. This is also discussed at length in *Ladies and Gentlemen—Lenny Bruce!!* by Albert Goldman from the journalism of Lawrence Schiller. New York: Penguin. 1971, 377-386, 391-393.

[73] Carlin, "Seven Words You Can Never Say on Television." *Classic Gold.*

[74] *Bring the Pain.*

[75] I discuss this matter much more in depth in Chapter Six.

[76] *Bring the Pain.*

[77] Ibid.

[78] Qtd. in *The Hutchinson Dictionary of Quotations.* Abingdon: Oxon Helicon Publishing Limited. 2005, 381.

[79] Dangerfield, Rodney. "It's Not Easy Being Me." *The Ultimate No Respect Collection,* Disc 2.

[80] Ibid.

[81] Wilde, Larry. *Great Comedians Talk about Comedy.* Mechanicsburg, PA: Executive Books. 2000, 333-334.

Chapter Three

[1] Kinison, Sam, in *Rodney Dangerfield: The Ultimate No Respect Collection*. R2 Entertainment, 2004. Disc 2. Perf. Sam Kinison, Jerry Seinfeld, Rodney Dangerfield, Rosanne Barr.

[2] Martin, Rod. *The Psychology of Humor: An Integrative Approach*. Burlington, MA: Academic Press. 2006, 31.

[3] Morreall, John. *Taking Laughter Seriously*. Albany: SUNY UP. 1983, 4.

[4] Ibid., 6.

[5] Ibid., 5-6.

[6] Ibid., 16.

[7] Oring, Eliot. *Jokes and Their Relations*. Lexington: University of Kentucky Press. 1992, 1-2.

[8] Morreall, 38-42.

[9] For a more extensive discussion on this see Sigmund Freud, *Civilization and Its Discontents*. New York: W.W. Norton. 1961.

[10] Pinette, John. "Around the World in 80 Buffets." Youtube. Accessed March 7, 2008. <http://www.youtube.com/watch?v=XUosUk6X9gE>.

[11] Quoted in Morreall, 7.

[12] Philips, Emo. *Emo Philips Live at the Hasty Pudding Theater*. Perf. Emo Philips. Dir. Cynthia L. Sears. HBO Home Video, 1988.

[13] Dangerfield, Rodney. *Rodney Dangerfield: The Ultimate No Respect Collection*. R2 Entertainment, 2004. Perf. Sam Kinison, Jerry Seinfeld, Rodney Dangerfield, Rosanne Barr. Disc 3.

[14] Novosad, John "Hippieman," in performance.

[15] *Emo Philips Live at the Hasty Pudding Theater*.

[16] Qtd. in Nancy Walker, *What's So Funny? Humor in American Culture*. Wilmington, DE: Scholarly Resources, Inc. 1998, 11.

[17] See John Ayto, *The Arcade Dictionary of Word Origins*. New York: Arcade. 1990, 289.

[18] Limon, John. *Stand-Up Comedy in Theory or Abjection in America*. Chapel Hill: Duke University Press. 2000, 4.

[19] For an extended discussion on this, see Sigmund Freud's essay "Infantile Sexuality" from *Three Essays on the Theory of Sexuality* (New York: Avon. 1962), 82. Here Freud argues that the child treats feces as "part of the infant's own body and represents his first 'gift': by producing them he can express his active compliance with his environment and by withholding them, his disobedience."

[20] Provine, Robert. *Laughter: A Scientific Investigation*. New York: Viking. 2000, 95.

[21] See Provine 3, 46-47, 190 and Morreall 114-117.

[22] Carlin, George. "Cute Little Farts." *Classic Gold*. New York: Atlantic Studios. 1992. Disc 2.

[23] Dawson, Jim. *Who Cut the Cheese? A Cultural History of the Fart*. Berkeley: Ten Speed Press. 1999, 7.

[24] For an extensive discussion on this see William Willeford, *The Fool and His Scepter: A Study in Clowns and Jesters and their Audience*. Evanston: Northwestern UP. 1969, 10-11.

[25] For an extensive discussion, see Dawson, 17-26.

[26] Qtd. in Dawson, 3.

[27] York, Dwight, in performance.

[28] Regan, Brian. "String Theory." Youtube. Accessed March 7, 2008. <http://www.youtube.com/watch?v=iHI-foSNccA>.

[29] Hicks, Bill. *Bill Hicks—Totally.* Perf. Bill Hicks. Channel 4 DVD. 2006.

[30] See Lao Tzu, *The Tao Te Ching*, verses 1 and 57.

[31] See Matthew 27:46.

[32] Ong, Walter J., S.J. "The Writer's Audience Is Always a Fiction." *Publications of the Modern Language Association of America* 90:1 (1975), 10-11.

[33] Limon, 27.

[34] Nachman, Gerald. *Seriously Funny: The Rebel Comedians of the 1950s and 1960s.* New York: Back Stage Books. 2004, 88.

Chapter Four

[1] See William Willeford, *The Fool and His Scepter: A Study in Clowns and Jesters and their Audience.* Evanston: Northwestern UP. 1969, 18-19.

[2] Henderson, Joseph L. "Ancient Myths and Modern Man." *Man and His Symbols.* Ed. Carl G. Jung. New York: Dell. 1968, 103-104.

[3] Jung. Carl G. *Archetypes and the Collective Unconscious.* Princeton, NJ: Princeton UP. 1981, 264.

[4] Rosenberg, Ellen. "Native American Trickster Tales and Cycles." *Fools and Jesters in Literature, Art, and History: A Bio-Bibliographical Sourcebook.* Ed. Vicki K. Janik. Westport, CT: Greenwood Press. 1998, 156.

[5] Callahan, Tim. "Devil, Trickster and Fool." *Mythlore* 17:4 (1991) 29.

[6] Philips, Emo. *Emo Philips Live at the Hasty Pudding Theater.* Dir. Perf. Emo Philips. HBO Home Video. 1988.

[7] Philips, Emo. *Emo Philips: 1983 (part 2 of 2).* Accessed on youtube.com, March 19. 2008. <http://www.youtube.com/watch?v=CqETaGrSwrc&feature=related>.

[8] Koziski, Stephanie. "The Stand-up Comedian as Anthropologist: Intentional Culture Critic." *The Journal of Popular Culture* 18:2 (Fall 1984) 57.

[9] Willeford, 14.

[10] Hoffman, Daniel. *Poe Poe Poe Poe Poe Poe Poe.* Garden City, NY: Anchor. 1973, 220.

[11] White, C. Todd. "The Anthropology of Fools." *Fools and Jesters in Literature, Art, and History: A Bio-Bibliographical Sourcebook.* Ed. Vicki K. Janik. Westport, CT: Greenwood Press. 1998, 34.

[12] White, 34.

[13] For a discussion on this see John Ayto, *The Arcade Dictionary of Word Origins.* New York: Arcade. 1990, 119.

[14] Janik, Del Ivan. "The American Circus Clown." *Fools and Jesters in Literature, Art, and History: A Bio-Bibliographical Sourcebook.* Ed. Vicki K. Janik. Westport, CT: Greenwood Press. 1998, 136.

[15] Ibid., 138.

[16] For examples of this see, for instance, chapter one, "Lazaro Tells of his Life and His Parents" in the anonymous picaresque tale *The Life of Lazarillo de Tormes, his Fortunes and Misfortunes as Told by Himself* and Edgar Allan Poe's short story "Lionizing."

[17] Rourke, Constance. *American Humor: A Study of the National Character.* New York: New York Review of Books. 2004, 25.

[18] Jenkins, Ron. *Subversive Laughter: The Liberating Power of Comedy.* New York: The Free Press. 1994, 171-172.

[19] See, for instance, Ronald Lande Smith, *The Stars of Stand-up Comedy.* New York: Garland. 1986.

[20] Forti-Lewis, Angelica. "Commedia dell'Arte." *Fools and Jesters in Literature, Art, and History: A Bio-Bibliographical Sourcebook.* Ed. Vicki K. Janik. Westport, CT: Greenwood Press. 1998, 146.

[21] Bushman, 24-25.

[22] Ibid., 24.

[23] Brunvand, Jan Harold. *American Folklore: An Encyclopedia.* New York: Garland. 1998. Accessed online Dec. 17, 2007. <http://www.netlibrary.com/Reader/>, 488.

[24] Jenkins, 183; see also Blyden Jackson, "The Minstrel Mode" in *The Comic Imagination in American Literature.* Rahwey, NJ: Rutgers UP. 1973, 152.

[25] Jackson, 153.

[26] Brunvand, 488.

[27] Tapia, John. E. *Circuit Chautauqua: From Rural Education to Popular Entertainment in Early Twentieth Century America.* Jefferson, NC: McFarland and Co. 1997, 14.

[28] Ibid., 15.

[29] Ibid., 25.

[30] Ibid., 47.

[31] Cherny, Robert W. *A Righteous Cause: The Life of William Jennings Bryan.* Norman: U of Oklahoma Press. 1994. Accessed online Dec. 17, 2007. <http://www.netlibrary.com/Reader/>, 93.

[32] Ibid., 95.

[33] Ibid., 172.

[34] Tapia, 60.

[35] Cherny, 96.

[36] Tapia, 67-68.

[37] Anderson, Ann. *Snake Oil, Hustlers and Hambones: The American Medicine Show.* Jefferson, NC: McFarland and Company. 2004, 13.

[38] Ibid., 4.

[39] Ibid., 32.

[40] Stratton, Owen Tully. *Medicine Man.* Ed. Owen S. Stratton. Norman: U of Oklahoma Press. 1989, 35.

[41] Ibid., 31.

[42] Ibid., 34.

[43] Ibid., 35.

[44] Ibid., 45.

[45] Ibid., 120.

[46] Marx, Arthur. *Red Skelton.* New York: E. Dutton. 1979, 9-10.

[47] Baily, Peter. *Popular Culture and Performance in the Victorian City.* Cambridge, UK: Press Syndicate, Cambridge UP 2003, 81; Kift, Dagmar. *The Victorian Music Hall: Culture, Class and Conflict.* Trans. Roy Kift. Cambridge, UK: Press Syndicate, Cambridge UP. 1996, 17.

[48] Kift, 17-18.

[49] Bailey, 81.

[50] Brandreth, Gyles. *The Funniest Man on Earth: The Story of Dan Leno*. London: Hamish Hamilton. 1977, 2.

[51] Ibid., 74.

[52] Ibid., 48.

[53] Ibid., 50.

[54] Ibid., 50-51.

[55] Ibid.

[56] Ibid., 45.

[57] Obituary. "Dan Leno." *The Times* (London). Nov. 1, 1904.

[58] Osbourne, John. *The Entertainer*. London: Faber and Faber. 1957, 7.

[59] Rasmussen, Kent. *Mark Twain A to Z: The Essential Reference to his Life and Writings*. New York: Oxford UP. 1995, 277.

[60] Stebbins, Robert A. *The Laugh-Makers: Stand-up Comedy as Art, Business and Life-Style*. Montreal: McGill-Queen's UP. 1990, 7.

[61] Bushman, 24.

[62] Twain, Mark. *Roughing It*. New York: Oxford UP. 1996, 559.

[63] Ibid., 561-563.

[64] Twain, Mark. *Life on the Mississippi*. New York: Oxford UP. 1996, 586.

[65] Rasmussen, 277.

[66] "Adventure Marked Life of Humorist" [Will Rogers Obituary]. *The New York Times*. Aug. 19, 1935.

[67] See *The Story of Will Rogers*. Dir. Michael Curtiz, Narrated by Bob Hope. Shanachie Entertainment, 1961.

[68] Ketchum, Richard M. *Will Rogers: His Life and Times*. New York: McGraw-Hill. 1973, 95. See also Rogers' *New York Times* obituary, "Adventure Marked Life of Humorist," published Aug. 19, 1935, two days after Rogers' death. A *Time* magazine report of the incident published in the July 19, 1926, issue, however, says of the incident that "a berserk steer . . . went mad and jumped the paling that divided the ring from the spectators . . . a young cowboy dashed to the spot, swung his rope and, with a deft flick of the wrist, saved the life of a little girl. That young cowboy was not William Penn Adair Rogers. But a reporter liked the name."

[69] Ketchum, 124-125.

[70] Rogers, Will and Arthur Frank Wertheim. *Will Rogers at the Ziegfeld Follies*. Norman: U of Oklahoma Press. 1992, 7.

[71] Blair, Walter, and Hamlin Hill. *America's Humor from Poor Richard to Doonesbury*. New York: Oxford UP. 1978, 522.

[72] *A Will Rogers Treasury: Reflections and Observations*. Compiled by Bryan B. Sterling and Frances N. Sterling. New York: Crown. 1982, 2.

[73] Ketchum, 336-337.

[74] Ibid., 353.

[75] *Will Rogers Treasury*, 3.

[76] Ketchum, 150.

[77] Robinson, Peter McClelland. *The Dance of the Comedians: The People, the President and the Performance of Political Stand-up Comedy in America*. Diss. Miami University, Miami, Ohio. 2006, 100.

[78] Dudden, Arthur Power. "The Record of Political Humor." *American Quarterly* 37:1 (Spring 1985), 58.

[79] Ibid.

[80] Ibid.

[81] Ketchum, 392-392.

[82] Stebbins, 7.

[83] Ibid.

Chapter Five

[1] See Linda Martin and Kerry Segrave. *Women in Comedy.* Secaucus, NJ: Citadel Press,1986, 30, and David Bushman, "The Stand-up Comedian on Television." *Stand-Up Comedians on Television.* Ed. Larry Gelbart. The Museum of Television and Radio. New York: Harry N. Abrams. 1996, 24-25.

[2] *Vaudeville.* American Masters. New York: WNET, KCTS/9 Television and Palmer/Fenster, Inc. 1999.

[3] See Frank Cullen, Florence Hackman and Donald McNeilly. *Vaudeville, Old and New: An Encyclopedia of Variety Performers in America,* Vol. 1. New York: Routledge. 2007, xiv.

[4] Bushman, 24-25.

[5] Cullen, xv; *Vaudeville.*

[6] Ibid.

[7] Ibid., xxii; *Vaudeville.*

[8] Cullen xxii.

[9] Rasmussen, Kent. *Mark Twain A to Z: The Essential Reference to his Life and Writings.* New York: Oxford UP. 1995, 278.

[10] Stebbins, Robert A. *The Laugh-Makers: Stand-up Comedy as Art, Business and Life-Style.* Montreal: McGill-Queen's UP. 1990, 7-8.

[11] Martin and Segrave, 30; Bushman, 29.

[12] Gilbert, Douglas. American *Vaudeville: Its Life and Times.* New York: Dover Books. 1963, 176.

[13] Cullen, 203.

[14] Gilbert, 176.

[15] Ibid., 177.

[16] Ibid.

[17] Cullen, 204.

[18] Ibid., 80-81.

[19] Ibid., 178.

[20] Ibid., 184, 185.

[21] Green, Stanley. *The Great Clowns of Broadway.* New York: Oxford UP. 1984, 177.

[22] Allen, Robert Clyde. *Horrible Prettiness: Burlesque and American Culture.* Chapel Hill: U of North Carolina Press. Dec. 18, 2007, <http://www.netlibrary.com/Reader/>. 1991, 26.

[23] Ibid., 10.

[24] Ibid., 12.

[25] Ibid., 136.

[26] Ibid., XII.

27 Marx, 22.

28 Allen, 29.

29 *It's Burlesque!* A&E Home Video. Dir. Angie Brown. Orig. release date Aug. 20, 2001.

30 Qtd. in Allen, 129.

31 Ibid., p. 129.

32 Limon, John. *Stand-Up Comedy in Theory or Abjection in America.* Chapel Hill: Duke UP. 2000, 105.

33 Nachman, Gerald. *Seriously Funny: The Rebel Comedians of the 1950s and 1960s.* New York: Back Stage Books. 2004, 400-401.

34 Arnason, H.H. *The History of Modern Art: Painting, Sculpture, Architecture, Photography* (Fourth Edition). Upper Saddle River, NJ: Prentice Hall. 1998, 274.

35 Ibid.

36 Ibid., 575-6.

37 Trachtman, Paul. "Dada." *Smithsonian* 37:2. May 2006, 70.

38 Seldes, Gilbert. *The Seven Lively Arts.* 1924. New York: Sagamore. 1957, 162-164. While some sources spell Case's first name as "Charlie" it seems clear that the comedian preferred the less conventional "Charley."

39 Hartman, J.F. *Monologues, Epigrams, Epitaphs and Parodies.* New York: George Sully and Co. 1910, 29.

40 Ibid., 30.

41 Wright, Steven. *When the Leaves Blow Away.* Perf. Steven Wright. Dir. Michael Drumm. Image Entertainment. 2007.

42 Hedberg, Mitch. *Mitch All Together.* Comedy Central Records, 2003.

43 While some distinguish between the Chitlin' Circuit as a Black burlesque, a small-time venue circuit, and The Theater Owners Booking Association circuit, others do not. See Smith 135 and Elsie A. Williams, "Moms Mabley and Afro-American Comic Performance" in *Women's Comic Visions.* Ed. June Sochen. Detroit: Wayne State University Press. 1991, 158.

44 Bushman, 25.

45 Smith, 134.

46 Ibid., 135.

47 Martin and Segrave, 288.

48 Harris, Trudier. "Moms Mabley: A Study in Humor, Role Playing and Violation of Taboo." *The Southern Review,* 24:4 (Autumn 1988), 767; Martin and Segrave, 289.

49 Harris, 766.

50 Williams, 162.

51 Harris, 770.

52 Martin and Segrave, 290.

53 Williams, 167.

54 Ibid., 164.

55 Ibid., 165.

56 Brown, Phil. *In the Catskills: A Century of the Jewish Experience in "The Mountains."* New York: Columbia UP. 2002, 7.

[57] Lavender, Abraham, and Clarence Steinberg. "Jewish Farmers in the Catskills." *In the Catskills: A Century of the Jewish Experience in "The Mountains."* Ed. Phil Brown. New York: Columbia UP. 2002, 24.

[58] Ibid., 22.

[59] Ibid.

[60] Brown, Phil. "Sleeping in My Parents' Hotel." *In the Catskills: A Century of the Jewish Experience in "The Mountains."* Ed. Phil Brown. New York: Columbia UP. 2002, 12.

[61] Stebbins, 8.

[62] Adams, Joey, with Henry Tobias. "Comics, Singers, and Tummlers." *In the Catskills: A Century of the Jewish Experience in "The Mountains."* Ed. Phil Brown. New York: Columbia UP. 2002, 228.

[63] Bushman, 27.

[64] Brown, 221.

[65] Wadler, Joyce. "The Fine Art of Mountain Tummling." *In the Catskills: A Century of the Jewish Experience in "The Mountains."* Ed. Phil Brown. New York: Columbia UP. 2002.

[66] Adams, 232.

[67] Wadler, 250.

[68] Adams, 226.

[69] Ibid., 228.

[70] Ibid., 226.

[71] Ibid.

[72] Bushman, 28.

[73] "Analyzing Jewish Comics." *Time.* Orig. pub. Oct. 2, 1978. Accessed online Jan. 30, 2008. <http://www.time.com/time/magazine/article/0,9171,948701,00.html>.

[74] See Exodus 3:8.

[75] See Perry Miller. *Errand into the Wilderness.* Cambridge: Harvard UP. 1956.

[76] Berger, 88.

[77] Mason, Jackie. "The Real Me." *Breaking It Up! The Best Routines of the Stand-up Comics.* New York: Bantam Books. 1975, 52-54. Another version of this routine appears in the DVD *Jackie Mason: The World According to Me.* West Long Branch, NJ: White Star. 2003.

[78] Erenberg, Lewis A. *Steppin' Out: New York Nightlife and the Transformation of Culture, 1890-1930.* Chicago: U of Chicago Press. 1981, 119.

[79] Ibid., 129.

[80] Ibid., 75.

[81] Ibid., 76.

[82] Ibid., 134.

[83] Martin and Segrave, 75.

[84] Ibid., 76.

[85] Ibid.

[86] Erenberg, 180.

[87] Ibid., 184.

[88] Martin and Segrave, 78-79.

[89] Erenberg, 197.

[90] Blumenthal, Ralph. *Stork Club: America's Most Famous Nightclub and the Lost World of Café Society*. New York: Little, Brown and Co. 2000, 87.

[91] Ibid., 96.

[92] Erenberg, 246-247.

[93] Ibid., 247.

[94] Ibid.

[95] Bushman, 28.

[96] Although some sources spell the name with capital letters, the name of Enrico Banducci's San Francisco club has traditionally been spelled with lower-case letters. The name has various interpretations such as "hungry id" or "hungry intellectual." See Goldman, 226.

[97] Stebbins, 10.

[98] Berger, Phil. *The Last Laugh: The World of Stand-up Comics*. New York: Cooper Square Press. 2000, 133.

[99] See the documentary *The Bunny Years: Inside the Playboy Empire*. Dir. Anne Pick. A&E Home Video. 2000.

[100] Borns, Betsy. *Comic Lives*. New York: Fireside. 1987, 31; Stebbins, 10-11.

[101] Borns, 32.

[102] Calabria, Frank M. *The Dance of the Sleepwalkers: The Dance Marathon Fad*. Bowling Green, OH: Bowling Green State U Popular Press. 1993, 21.

[103] Ibid., 24.

[104] Dunlop, Chelsea. *American Dance Marathons, 1928-1934, and the Social Drama and Ritual Process*. Master's Thesis, Florida State University. 2006, 39.

[105] Calabria, 25.

[106] Ibid., 18.

[107] Ibid., 21.

[108] Marx, Arthur. *Red Skelton*. New York: Dutton. 1979, 27.

[109] Ibid., 27.

[110] Ibid., 28.

[111] Ibid., 51.

[112] Ibid., 18.

[113] Bushman, 25.

[114] Bowles, Jerry. *A Thousand Sundays: The History of the Ed Sullivan Show*. New York: G. P. Putnam's Sons. 1980, 44.

[115] Ibid., 147.

[116] Ibid., 111.

[117] Nachman, 492.

[118] Prussing-Hollowell, Andrea Shannon. *Stand-up Comedy as Artistic Expression: Lenny Bruce, the 1950s, and American Humor*. Master's Thesis, Georgia State University. 2007, 18.

[119] Ibid.

[120] Holmes, John Clellon, "This Is the Beat Generation." *Beat Down to Your Soul: What Was the Beat Generation?* Ed. Anne Charters, New York: Penguin Books. 2001, 223-224 (qtd. in Prussing-Hollowell, 18).

[121] Qtd. in Anne Charters, "Introduction." *The Portable Beat Reader*, ed. Anne Charters. New York: Penguin Books. 1992, XVIII.

[122] Charters, XXII.

[123] Qtd. in Charters, XXI.

[124] Prussing-Hollowell, 21.

[125] Ross, Andrew, *No Respect: Intellectuals and Popular Culture*. New York: Routledge. 1989, 78 (qtd. in Prussing-Hollowell, 20).

[126] Prussing-Hollowell, 17.

[127] Ibid.

[128] Bruce, Lenny. *The Essential Lenny Bruce: His Original Unexpurgated Satirical Routines*. London: Panther. Ed. John Cohen. 1975, 142-143. Other versions of this bit are also found in the stage play *Lenny* by Julian Barry (New York: Grove Press, 1971), 89-90, and the 1974 movie *Lenny*, based on Barry's play, starring Dustin Hoffman and directed by Bob Fosse.

[129] "The Sickniks." *Time*. Orig. pub. July 13, 1959. Accessed online Nov. 20, 2007. <http://www.time.com/time/magazine/article/0,9171,869153-1,00.html>.

[130] Ibid.

[131] Nachman, 53.

[132] "The Third Campaign." *Time*. Orig. pub. Aug. 15, 1960. Accessed online Oct. 8, 2007. <http://www.time.com/time/magazine/article/0,9171,939769,00.html>.

[133] Qtd. in Nachman, 64.

[134] Wilde, Larry. *The Great Comedians Talk about Comedy*. Mechanicsburg, PA: Executive Books. 2000, 336.

[135] Maher, Bill. *The Decider*. HBO Home Video. 2007.

[136] Borns, 35.

[137] Stebbins, 12.

[138] Zoglin, Richard. "Stand-Up Comedy on a Roll." *Time*. Orig. pub. Aug. 24, 1987. Accessed online, Nov. 23, 2007. <http://www.time.com/time/magazine/article/0,9171,965297,00.html>.

[139] Personal interview conducted by Eddie Tafoya, Jan. 19, 2002.

[140] Ibid.

[141] "Analyzing Jewish Comics." *Time*. Orig. pub. Oct. 2, 1978. Accessed online Jan. 19, 2008. <http://www.time.com/time/magazine/article/0,9171,948701,00.html>.

[142] Debruge, Peter. "Raucous Rainbow of Ethnic Comics." *Variety* 403:8, July 17-23, 2006. Wilson Select Plus. NM Highlands University Lib., Las Vegas, NM. Accessed online Oct. 9, 2007. <http://newfirstsearch.oclc.org/WebZ/FTFETCH?sessionid=fsapp3-58593-fade24vk-jpy6hg:entitypagenum=9:0:rule=100:fetchtype=fulltext:dbname=WilsonSelectPlus_FT:recno=25:resultset=4:ftformat=PDF:format=BI:isbillable=TRUE:numrecs=1:isdirectarticle=FALSE:entityemailfullrecno=25:entityemailfullresultset=4:entityemailftfrom=WilsonSelectPlus_FT:>.

Chapter Six

[1] Berkovitz, Sacvan. *The American Jeremiad*. Madison: University of Wisconsin Press. 1978, 6.

[2] Ibid., 6-7.

[3] Blair, Walter and Hamlin Hill. *America's Humor from Poor Richard to Doonesbury*. New York: Oxford UP. 1978, 3.

[4] Ibid., 4-5.

⁵ Rubin, Louis. D. Jr. "The Great American Joke" in *What's So Funny? Humor in American Culture*. Ed. Nancy Walker. Wilmington, DE: American Visions: Readings in American Culture. 1998, 109.

⁶ Ibid., 12.

⁷ Miller, Arthur. *Death of a Salesman: Text and Criticism*. Ed. Gerald Weales. New York: Penguin. 1996, 132-133.

⁸ King, Martin Luther, Jr. "I Have a Dream." *The Rinehart Reader*. Eds. Jean Wyrick and Beverly Slaughter. New York: Holt, Rinehart and Winston. 1989, 507-508.

⁹ Ibid., 510.

¹⁰ Bruce, Lenny. *The Essential Lenny Bruce: His Original Unexpurgated Satirical Routines*. London: Panther. Ed. John Cohen. 1975, 83-84. Another rendition of this bit also appears in Julian Barry's stage play *Lenny* (New York: Grove. 1971, 50-51) and in the 1974 movie of the same name starring Dustin Hoffman, directed by Bob Fosse and written by Barry.

¹¹ Nachman, Gerald. *Seriously Funny: The Rebel Comedians of the 1950s and 1960s*. New York: Back Stage Books. 2004, 51.

¹² Ibid.

¹³ "The Third Campaign." *Time*. Orig. pub. Aug. 15, 1960. Accessed online Oct. 8, 2007. <http://www.time.com/time/magazine/article/0,9171,939769,00.html>.

¹⁴ Ibid.

¹⁵ Qtd. in Nachman, 61.

¹⁶ "The Third Campaign."

¹⁷ Ibid.

¹⁸ Ibid.

¹⁹ Qtd. in "Mort Sahl." *Comedy College*. Minnesota Public Radio. Accessed online Jan. 2, 2007. <http://comedycollege.publicradio.org/archive/sahl_mort.shtml>.

²⁰ Nachman, 68.

²¹ Ibid.

²² Ibid., 95.

²³ Smith, Ronald Lande. *The Stars of Stand-up Comedy: A Biographical Encyclopedia*. New York: Garland. 1986, 94-95.

²⁴ Smith, 94.

²⁵ Nachman, 484.

²⁶ Ibid., 485-486

²⁷ Ibid., 484.

²⁸ Ibid.

²⁹ Ibid., 487.

³⁰ Smith, 96.

³¹ Ibid.

³² "A Time for Laughter: A Look at Negro Humor in America." *ABC's Stage 67*. Originally broadcast April 6, 1967.

³³ Carlin, George. "Muhammad Ali—America the Beautiful." *Classic Gold*. New York: Atlantic Studios. 1992.

³⁴ Ibid.

³⁵ Carlin, George. *Complaints and Grievances*. Perf. George Carlin, Dir. Rocco Urbisci. MPI Home Video. 2004.

[36] *Comedy's Dirtiest Dozen.* Perf. Bill Hicks, Chris Rock, John Fox, Tim Allen, et al. Dir. Lenny Wong. D3K Studios. 2000.

[37] Ibid.

[38] Ibid.

[39] Rock, Chris. *Bring the Pain.* Perf. Chris Rock. Dir. Kieth Truesdell. Dreamworks. 2002.

[40] Ibid.

[41] *Fontaine . . . Why Am I Straight?* Perf. Whoopi Goldberg. Dir. Steven J. Santos. HBO Home Video. 1988.

[42] Although Goldberg does not make this statement in *Fontaine . . . Why Am I Straight?* the character does announce it during his segment of *Whoopi Goldberg: Live on Broadway.* Lions Gate/Vestron, 1991.

Chapter Seven

[1] "Steven Wright." Current Biography Yearbook, Vol. 64. New York: H.W. Wilson. 2003, 590-591. See also *When Stand-Up Stood Out.* Perf. Steven Wright, Lenny Clarke, Paula Poundstone, et al. Dir. Fran Solomita. ThinkFilm, 2005; and Kristin McMurran, "TV Comic Steven Wright Sets Off, Worriedly, on a Steep Ascent." *People,* March 13, 1989. Accessed online May 15, 2001, elibrary. <wwws.elibrary.com/id/192/getdoc.cgi?id+1959>.

[2] Ibid.

[3] *Comedian.* Perf. Jerry Seinfeld, Robert Klein, Jay Leno. Dir. Christian Charles. Miramax. 2002.

[4] *When Stand-Up Stood Out.*

[5] *A Steven Wright Special.* Perf. Steven Wright. Dir. Walter Miller. HBO Films. 1985.

[6] *The Best of the Tonight Show: Stand-Up Comedians.* Perf. Johnny Carson, Rosanne Barr, Steven Wright. Carson Entertainment. 2005.

[7] Qtd. in Seiber, Harry. *The Picaresque.* Norwich, U.K.: Fletcher & Son. 1977, 2.

[8] Seiber, Harry. *The Picaresque.* Norwich, U.K.: Fletcher & Son. 1977, 3.

[9] Ibid., 1.

[10] Wright, Steven. *I Have a Pony.* Wea International, 1998.

[11] Wright, Steven. *When the Leaves Blow Away.* Perf. Steven Wright. Image Entertainment. 2007.

[12] Conford, David. "The Tarot Fool." *Fools and Jesters in Literature, Art, and History: A Bio-Bibliographical Sourcebook.* Ed. Vicki K. Janik. Westport, CT: Greenwood Press. 1998, 455.

[13] Hrkach, Jack. "The Yankee." *Fools and Jesters in Literature, Art, and History: A Bio-Bibliographical Sourcebook.* Ed. Vicki K. Janik. Westport, CT: Greenwood Press. 1998, 500-502.

[14] Edwards, Jonathan. *Basic Writings.* Ed. Ola Elizabeth Winslow. New York: Signet Classics. 1966, 156.

[15] Berkovitz, Sacvan. *The American Jeremiad.* Madison: University of Wisconsin Press. 1978, 12.

[16] *ASWS.*

[17] Ibid.

[18] Ibid.

[19] *WTLBA.*
[20] *ASWS.*
[21] Ibid.
[22] *Comic Relief III.* Perf. Billy Crystal, Whoopi Goldberg. Rhino. 1998.
[23] *ASWS.*
[24] Ibid., *IHAP.*
[25] *ASWS, IHAP.*
[26] *Comic Relief.*
[27] *ASWS.*
[28] *IHAP.*
[29] *WTLBA.*
[30] Ibid.
[31] Ibid.
[32] Fiedler, Leslie. *The Return of the Vanishing American.* New York: Stein and Day. 1969, 12.
[33] Ibid., 186.
[34] *ASWS.*
[35] Biography, 591.
[36] Carson.
[37] *ASWS.*
[38] Ibid.
[39] *Comic Relief.*
[40] *ASWS.*
[41] *IHAP.*
[42] Ibid.
[43] For extensive discussions on this subject see Robert J. Lifton's *Death in Life: Survivors of Hiroshima* (New York: Random House, 1968) and "Psychological Effects of the Atomic Bombings," in *Last Aid: The Medical Dimensions of Nuclear War*, edited by Eric Chivian et al. (San Francisco: W. H. Freeman, 1982), 67.
[44] *ASWS.*
[45] Carson.
[46] *WTLBA.*
[47] *ASWS.*
[48] *WTLBA*
[49] *ASWS.*
[50] *WTLBA.*

Chapter Eight

[1] A five-part miniseries aired on Comedy Central in April 2004 designated Pryor history's top stand-up comedian, followed by George Carlin, Lenny Bruce and Woody Allen, while in a 1997 HBO special, *George Carlin: 40 Years in Comedy*, host Jon Stewart introduced Carlin as belonging to the "holy trinity" of stand-up comedy, the other two members being Bruce and Pryor. Comedian Chris Rock has famously claimed that Pryor was "the greatest comedian of all time." An Oct. 30, 2002, *Time* interview with Jerry Seinfeld declares that Pryor was "perhaps the greatest artist of all stand-ups," even though Seinfeld himself says that, "People say that Pryor at his peak was

the best there ever was . . . but Bill Cosby is just as good." In a May 2005 interview, also in *Time*, Pryor is referred to as Dave Chappelle's "idol." Whoopi Goldberg, Professor Irwin Corey and Steve Martin, among others, have also made similar acknowledgments. An informal survey of some 200 comedians with whom I have worked with in one also ranked Pryor solidly as history's most important stand-up comedian.

2 In *Richard Pryor Live on the Sunset Strip*, Pryor never uses the term "crack," but refers to the process of "free-basing." The chief difference between the two is that the free-basing that was popular in the 1970s and 1980s involved using volatile solvents like ether and ammonia to produce smokable rocks of cocaine while the crack method uses water and baking soda. Both, however, are forms of free-basing. In the course of the performance, Pryor mentions the use of ether in connection with the free-basing process.

3 Although Pryor and his publicists in the days after the incident said that the holocaust resulted from an accidental explosion during the free-basing process, Williams and Williams and Pryor himself, in their respective biographies, report that the burning was actually a suicide attempt in which Pryor poured high-proof liquor over his body and lit himself. Pryor pokes fun at the publicist's lie in the *Live on the Sunset Strip* when he talks about the incident saying that "I mixed the lowfat milk with the pasteurized milk, stuck in a cookie, and the shit blew up." Thanks to Anna Riggs-Eader for this observation.

4 In his Nobel Prize acceptance speech delivered in Stockholm, Sweden, on Dec. 10, 1950, William Faulkner noted that "the problems of the human heart in conflict with itself . . . alone can make good writing because only that is worth writing about, worth the agony and the sweat."

5 This and all subsequent references are from Dante Alighieri. *Inferno: A New Verse Translation by Michael Palma*. Trans. Michael Palma. New York: Norton, 2003. See Canto I.

6 This and all other references to Pryor's work are from *Richard Pryor Live on the Sunset Strip*. Perf. Richard Pryor. Dir. Joe Layton. Columbia Pictures. 1982, except where noted.

7 Pryor, Richard, with Todd Gold. *Pryor Convictions and Other Life Sentences*. London: Revolver Books. 2006, 185.

8 Canto I: 62-63.

9 *Inferno* 46, fn.

10 "Schwab's, Hollywood Drugstore, Shut." *The New York Times* archives. Orig. pub. Oct. 25, 1983. Accessed April 16, 2007. <http:query.nytimes.com.gst/fullpage. html?res=9500E3DCI133B936A15753CIA965948260>.

11 Bruccoli, Matthew Joseph. *Some Sort of Epic Grandeur: The Life of F. Scott Fitzgerald*, 2nd rev. ed. Columbia: University of South Carolina Press. 2002, 485.

12 Violanti, Anthony. "The Rainbow Journey of Harold Arlen." *The Buffalo News* archives. Originally published Feb. 6, 2005. Accessed May 2, 2007. <http:// www.buffalo news.com/195/story/42612.html>.

13 Canto VI: 49-53.

14 *Pryor Convictions*, 55-56

15 Ibid., 32-34.

16 Ibid, 71-72.

[17] Ibid., 94-96.

[18] Williams, John A., and Dennis A. Williams, *If I Stop, I'll Die: The Comedy and Tragedy of Richard Pryor*. New York: Thunder's Mouth Press. 1991, 93.

[19] Campbell, Joseph. *The Masks of God: Occidental Mythology*. New York: Viking Press, 1964, 14.

[20]   Canto VII: 30.

[21] *Pryor Convictions*, 217.

[22] Williams and Williams, 62.

[23] Canto XXXIV: 20-21.

[24] Canto XXXIV: 25-26.

[25] Canto XXXIV: 96.

[26] Canto XXXIV: 133.

[27] Gibbs, Nancy. ". . . In Sorrow and Disbelief." *Time*. Orig. pub. May 3, 1999. Accessed April 15, 2007. <http://www.time.com/time/magazine/article/0,9171, 990870-3,00.html>.

[28] "Water Safety." *Beavis and Butt-head*. Season 4, Episode 10. MTV. Original air date April 7, 1994.

[29] "Columbine Report: Dylan Bennet Klebold/Eric David Harris." Salon.com. Accessed April 15, 2007. <http://www.salon.com/news/special/columbine_report/ SUSPECTS_TEXT.HTM>.

[30] Anthony, Ted. "Reconstructing the Columbine Horror." 15 April 2007. *The Daily Camera Online* (Boulder, CO), 54 pars. <http://www.boulderclassifieds.com /shooting/reconstruction.html>.

Conclusion

[1] "Colbert Roasts President Bush—2006 White House Correspondents' Dinner," April 29, 2006. Accessed via Google Video, Dec. 1, 2006. <http://video.google. com/videoplay?docid=-8691839177758574879>.

[2] *Borat: Cultural Learnings of America for Make Benefit Glorious Nation of Kazakhstan*. Perf. Sacha Baron Cohen. Dir. Larry Charles. 20th Century Fox DVD. 2007

[3] Philips, Emo. *Emo Philips Live at the Hasty Pudding Theater*. Perf. Emo Philips. Dir. Cynthia L. Sears. HBO Home Video, 1988.

CPSIA information can be obtained at www.ICGtesting.com
Printed in the USA
BVOW11s0826270814

364444BV00009B/819/P